ATTEN~~T~~

MW01284842

¨THE FIRST LESSON¨ CD
IS OFF THE MARKET
AS OF THE PUBLICATION OF THIS BOOK
AND WILL NO LONGER BE AVAILABLE FOR SALE!

HOWEVER:

You can get it directly from me when you identify all errors deliberately left in this book and send them to me.

It is my fervent desire that you really read every word and do not skip anything, hence the incentive.

I will reward your efforts with a gift of ¨The First Lesson¨ CD if you send me a list of the words and their pages.

Please send your list to: <u>musicvisons@aol.com</u> and you will receive your CD.

You can also watch 18 segments of one of my master classes on <u>u tube</u> or <u>my space</u> and you are always welcome to check out the blog:

<u>http://whateverhappenedtogreatsinging.blogspot.com/</u>

WHAT EVER HAPPENED TO GREAT SINGING?

It's Time For:

A REAL CHANGE!
REAL ANSWERS!
REAL TECHNIQUE!
REAL TRUTH!

by the Author of

The Voice: A Spiritual Approach to Singing, Speaking and Communicating

Edition 1 & 2 and the "Revealed Version".

❦

Miriam Jaskierowicz Arman

ISBN: 1-4392-3042-0
ISBN-13: 9781439230428

Visit www.booksurge..com to order additional copies.

INDEX

PLEASE DO NOT BUY THIS BOOK:

Unless you seriously wish to change your life as a Singer,

Unless you are ready to throw your old ideas and notions out of the window, because you know that they have not served your Instrument to achieve its potential…

Unless you decide to study page by page and not skip anything and give this real serious consideration.
Every page is important in its own way. Nothing in this book can be skipped-if you do, vital and connective information will be lost.

SPEED READING DOES NOT APPLY HERE!!!

*** Absolutely do not buy this book, unless you have a teacher who supports you IN THIS JOURNEY.

It would be counterproductive to work along our guidelines and then to go to someone who is not supportive of you. Your Brain/mind/body would be confused and the exact opposite of what we want would be achieved - that is not what this work is all about. Unfortunately it is going to be very difficult for you to find someone who knows this work – please find someone who is at least ready to explore this with you.

Unfortunately, most teachers are totally unfamiliar with this methodology. If you find one, please let me know.

*This Book **Does Not Create Voices**, Only G-D Can Do That.*

This Work Takes An Existing Instrument And Indicates The Way To Bring It To Its Fullest Potential. If You Are Willing To Do The Work, I Will Teach You.

Please, Do Not Think That You Will Be A Star Because You Are Following These Instructions.

Having A Voice, Even A Great Instrument, Does Not Guarantee Anything. Having A Great Instrument Is Obviously A Plus, But Many Instruments, Which Naturally Are Not

So 'Great', Have Made Wonderful Careers Because Of The Personality, Discipline And The Loyalty Of The Singer.

It Takes Work, Perseverance, Devotion And The Understanding, Commitment And Trust To Follow These Guidelines.

I Hear Voices, I Hear Potential, I Express That…But That And Five Cents Will Get You Nowhere Unless Everything Else Works Together.

I Do Not Make Stars*; But If You Have Star Quality In All Necessary Areas And You Are Willing To Put Your Ego Aside And Learn, Than Go For It.*

Nothing Will Be Achieved Unless You Keep Up Your End Of The Bargain….Ultimately If You do not Make It, You Have Only To Take Yourself To Task…Don't Come Accusing Me – You are Barking Up The Wrong Tree!

Please consider carefully what you are doing. You only have ONE Instrument.

Selling books is NOT the goal here; making a real difference in your life and in your Voice is!

With eternal devotion and gratitude

In loving Memory of my Mother

Mila Jaskierowicz (Z"L)

Being deserving of her love is my life's achievement.
I never gave up and she rewarded me with the greatest blessing.

Mother, you are forever in my heart.

To the Lubavitcher Rebbe

Menachem Mendel Schneerson (OBM)

Whose profound teachings and great humanity
Are a constant source of inspiration in my life.

Dedications

This book is dedicated to the memory of my beloved daughter, Aviva Hope, who was taken from me much too soon on Thanksgiving Day, 1996.

A few days before she left this world, she asked me to promise her that I would write this book. Because her life was dedicated to helping and giving to others, she wanted me to share what I know with generations of singers yet to come.

She loved until the last moment of her young life, and in that love, I found my peace and strength to go on, to teach, to write and to continue my work. Her life enriched so many and it was her wish that mine do the same. I hereby re-dedicate my life to be the best person/teacher I can be and fight for the integrity and principals I believe in.

I love you forever, Vi! Please sing celestial melodies for all of us with Hashem's Malachim (Angels)

Jonas Jaskierowicz (Z"L)

My Father, My Hero

I also dedicate this book to the memory of my beloved father, who gave me courage and strength to fight for what I believe in and whose life and personal integrity illuminates every day of my existence.

And finally, there are the Voices of Six Million, who never had the chance at life, who burned in gas chambers, singing "Ani MAAMIN — I Believe," while being led to their deaths.

May my work be a tribute to their memory and to those beautiful and talented members of my family, my grandparents, aunts and uncles, who perished, just because they were Jews.

To Jim Parker

My Student and My Friend

Jim and I had real plans for his career. He was a beautiful soul, a brilliant man and incredibly committed. He was a great admirer of this work and a great critic. I knew that no matter what, I could always count on him for complete candor. He taught me a great deal. I am incredibly grateful for that and I miss him terribly.

In the great "Academy in the Heavens" he 'IS' singing and making sure that everything we have learned together is being put to great use.

Jim, Wednesday afternoon, 3 pm, will forever be your time in my schedule.

Acknowledgments

I wish to thank my students in all parts of the world who have worked with me, respected me, loved me - and made me very proud of them. To them I am grateful, for without them, I would never have been able to profound all the guidelines and concepts outlined in this work. Their generosity in sharing their thoughts with me, their allowing me into the deepest crevices of their souls, their being open to my constant and endless querying and their permitting me to enter the sanctuary of their Voices, has taught me beyond measure.

I am deeply grateful to all the spiritual guides who have chosen me to be the vessel that imparts their knowledge to the singers/students who enter my life.

Thank you, Muchas Gracias, Grazie, Toda Raba, Spasiba, Kozemem Sepen, Danke, Merci, to the outstanding Maestri with whom I have worked, who have assisted me with my singers. A future "thank you" to all of the extraordinary talents whom I have not yet had the pleasure of meeting and to those who will read and use this book and will understand it and create their destinies with it.

I thank all the Rabbis and Cantors, who have found their way into my studio and have, by sharing their wisdom, guided me into the "Revealed Version (Third Edition)." Their patience with me and my incessant questioning has opened the door to much of the spiritual knowledge, which I hope will offer the key to all those who desire Revealed Truth in finding the true potential of their Instruments.

I thank you all for the encouragement to write this book and I know that even though it may be **ME AGAINST THE WORLD,** you are all behind me. Your continued support has been beyond valuable, beyond compare, and your successes have made *"Whatever Happened to Great Singing? Possible* and **necessary.**

Extra special and heartfelt thanks to Adele Amodeo, a special friend and supporter.

Most of all, I thank G-D for guiding my way into this work.

It has been a very hard, arduous and often tragic road, filled with tears, strife and pain.

I have been terribly disappointed and felt utterly used by some of my students – I always ponder human nature but am too 'small' to really understand its wondrous workings. I have never learned to be like others and do it for "the money"… My unfortunate problem is that I care deeply – always. Even when the hurt seems too much to bear, He always gives me the strength and the power to carry on so that I can spend every possible moment of my life teaching.

I thank Him for my hearing and listening, my feelings and my instincts, for having given me this marvelous gift of being of service to others which I promise to value and cherish all the days of my life.

I invoke His blessings for this new book and pray that my life and work will be a source of Light and inspiration to all who seek the answers.

Setting the
Record Straight

I am a **Vocal Technician, a Vocal Reconstructionist, not a 'musician' per se** and even though I have been blessed with a fantastic musical ear and know an incredible amount of repertoire - classical or otherwise, I consider myself primarily a Voice Specialist. I speak the languages in which I teach virtually fluently: German, Italian, English, Hebrew, and Spanish (which is now fluent enough to teach in). I spoke Russian quite well, but now do not have enough opportunity to practice it, but love the repertoire and music...the repertoire in French is about the same…

I do NOT teach the 'music', but once the Voice is in place, we take the music which you learn with your accompanist and put it into the Voice, one note at a time. Don't expect to get away with anything.

There are those who would call me a 'Quack'… oh well, everyone is entitled to their opinion, the results thank G-d speak for themselves. Bring me a Voice and I WILL show you 'my' quackery!!! The singers who walk through my doors (virtually all of my students ever) are the products of the so called "Vocal Experts".

These people speak with an incredible authority, teach at the most prestigious institutions, yet the results in most cases are disastrous. If they took the time to really listen and go beyond their own limitations and egos, the world of the Vocal Arts would be a much better and safer place. I suppose that after so many years of remaining silent and behind the scene, the time has come to step out of my comfort zone.

Here is the **Real Reason** for writing this book in this way, at this time:

I had a student, an extraordinary talent; a brilliant young woman, with a beautiful Voice and a very special soul, sensitive and incredibly intuitive, a born singer.

When her father brought her to me, she had a much damaged, wobbly Instrument due to her vocal training at the University of Xxxxxxx, but she knew instinctively that there was something else there - and her father knew and believed it too. I think she was 19 when she came the first time. I almost cried when I heard her, an utter disgrace.

We began work and things moved and shifted rapidly. Her real vocal potential emerged physically Sound and grew in height and splendor. While her father accompanied her, my student made incredible progress. He was very supportive and loving and really believed in the work, saw the extraordinary progress and was very vocal and affirmative about it.

Then, her mother who had studied and was a degreed speech therapist/ pathologist, I am not quite sure, decided to attend her lessons. I felt a tension between mother and daughter, but really had no idea as to how deeply rooted the problems were. We continued making progress, but it was obvious to me that after the lesson, her mother would ply her with all the stuff she had learned in college while earning her own degree and discredit our work.

Her interference created doubt and secondary impulses in my student and it became apparent that she was suffering physically and emotionally. Even though she (the mother) witnessed steady progresses in her daughter, she ultimately decided that my "credentials" were not up to her "snuff" and stopped the lessons. In a conversation, which I will never forget, she brought up all the old 'knowledge' she had gathered during her degree studies and told me that according to her; I simply did not know what I was doing. It did not matter to her that her daughter's Voice benefited enormously in every respect. Her jealousy, smallness and utter ignorance closed the door to this young woman.

In reality I was hoping she would sue me and we could have this great Class Action Suit and bring in the hundreds of students of the past 15 years or so who had been damaged to no end by others including Voice teachers, universities, unnecessary Operations etc. and who came to me to be re-constructed – ultimately walking away singing, speaking and at least greatly improved. - I could then prove, in a big public forum, what horror is being perpetrated out there. It would have caused a big PR splash and so many singers would have benefited. But I guess she decided against it and so I decided to finally write this book.

Actually, I have to thank her. Without her insults and pulling away her daughter, whom I cared for greatly, this book would not be written.

Anyone who does not think I am "degreed" or competent enough can certainly go have their Voices ruined by someone else who is. Thank G-d we all have choices we need to make. It's a pity that a person's better judgment is clouded by his/her own small vision, personal limitations and ignorance. *As I said before, I will go anywhere, at any time, to show and prove what incredible results my work accomplishes. I challenge the world, I challenge the institutions…It's time for Change!*

(These lines were written way before they ***became politically correct).***

✲ ✲ ✲

This is not a "religious or specifically spiritual" book, yet I am religious. My approach is clearly technically oriented. The concepts I teach are mine. I did not learn them anywhere-not in a university, not in a conservatory- nor are they out of books I have read. I "teach" them based upon my own learning and experience ONLY!

Yet, let me be very clear - I take no credit for them.

They were literally given to me by the highest spiritual source and I fully acknowledge that. When you read my story you will understand more... please, not now...but when the time comes at the end of the book. By then everything will make perfect sense to you and what now seems presumptuous and perhaps pompous, will by then become totally obvious.

I will make "foreign" concepts clear to you. You may or may not accept their origin - that is up to you. My desire is to be candid with you, not to mislead you, to guide you into what I know to be correct, vocally Sound and completely complementary to the vocal Instrument. I will teach you what is physically healthy, spiritually profound and what has worked for countless singers all around the globe and also why it works.

Only Giro-Vocal-Motion-Technique can be classified as real BEL CANTO – Beautiful Singing – NOTHING ELSE!!!

I am very emotive about my feelings and I ask you to allow me the space to vent my frustrations with the "powers" that be. This is a mission and in this fight, like any other, may the best win... I fight for it to be YOU, the Singer.

In this book I am going to share correspondence and comments, hopes and views of others you might relate to. Thousands have written from every corner of the globe and for this I am grateful – but the powers at be, the ones who run the schools and Operate on voices, the impresarios who choose and ultimately the public at large, know little about you and me.

This has to change – Now.

Read the book and give it to someone who knows someone who can bring it to someone else and then on to the next one who hopefully has a friend at the New York Times. If we combine our forces the world of Voice will be a better place for all concerned.

Notes

Correspondence, Explanations, Accolades, Accusations...

I begin with a letter I received from **the International Voice Foundation** after sending them my first book and asking to be allowed to address their forum. 10 years later and the 4ᵗʰ book, basically nothing has changed..

I had a student in Florida who had seven nodules on his vocal cords and the night before the surgery, the receptionist at the doctor's office told him about me. He called – tell you the truth I thought it was *a cranck call* – he explained his desperate situation and I told him to come immediately. Needless to say he never had the operation. From not being able to work because he had no Voice, he became an actor, a singer, married and has a baby – maybe two by now. His whole existence changed and his doctor literally 'freaked out' and could not believe what was happening and how/why the nodules disappeared without surgery, speech therapy medicines etc.

This story is one of so many – people with serious diseases which involve the Throat, have come to me and have been helped. Our work is a process - it has nothing to do with instant gratification. Much can be done without invasive procedures by re-education and re-positioning the Instrument and re-constructing it in the right place.

Truth be told, why would an institution which makes their money on surgeries, botox injections etc. send someone to me, or even allow me to share my knowledge with their constituency - after all they stand to loose millions.

Speech pathologists have come to me privately to learn what I do. They are taught the exact opposite. They in turn use this knowledge and it's application in their studios with extraordinary results. One very special woman in Palm Beach, Florida, even sent a letter to her alma mater and the appropriate 'Association' - need I tell you the outcome?

I could fill a library of books with the correspondence of singers from all over the world, but am using just a few comments in these pages which I think might be of interest, even before we begin with our work. Later on, in the Chapter

"What People Say" there will be more and you can always visit the blog: http://whateverhappenedtogreatsinging.blogspot.com/ to read annotations and place yours. Amazon.com is a great source of materials and if you put my name into the browser you will find mountains of stuff.

Someone out there, just please DO SOMETHING!

The Voice Foundation

November 8, 1999

Miriam Jaskierowicz Arman
Music Visions International
One SW 58th Avenue
Plantation, FL 33301

Dear Ms. Arman:

Thank you so much for your thoughtful note and your book. I looked through it quickly as soon as it arrived. It looks most interesting, and I am sure that I will enjoy reading it in greater detail. Congratulations on your interesting approach in voice science.

With best regards,

Very truly yours,

Robert Thayer Sataloff, M.D., D.M.A.
Professor of Otolaryngology
Thomas Jefferson University
Chairman, Department of Otolaryngology-Head and Neck Surgery
Graduate Hospital

RTS/em

"I looked through it quickly"…."Congratulantions on your interesting approach to Voice Science"….tell me that this is responsible behavior by a man who heads up one of the most important 'Voice' institutions in the world? Not a phone call or personal conntact.

A year passed without further comment – meaning that the book went into the garbage – Here is my follow up letter…

International Academy of Voice and Stage, Inc.

1 SW 58th Ave. Plantation, Florida 33317

Tel./FAX 954-792-5204, Email: voiceacad1@aol.com

www.nvo.com/greatvoice

November 1. 2000

Dear Dr. Sataloff,

Well, a year has passed since I sent you my book THE VOICE; A SPIRITUAL APPROACH TO SINGING, SPEAKING AND COMMUNICATING. Here now the long awaited CD.

I know that you truly are interested in the voice, in its health and in its 'life' and because of this belief, I am taking this opportunity to contact you again. If my instincts are correct, we are both committed to the same thing . Our approaches may be different, our terminology diverse, mine communicative, yours scientific, but ultimately the end result must justify the means: A healthy voice in singing and speaking.

Much has happened in the past year concerning my book. Endorsements from Julie Andrews, Richard Bonynge, from the National Association of Music Educators (MENC), teachers/coaches of voice from around the globe etc., singers and so many letters of acknowledgment from people who have been greatly helped and whose voices have been reconstructed , even after having been diagnosed with paralyzed vocal cords or vocal cord nodules.

2

Dr. Lewis Arrandt, a very prominent physician in the field of NEURO-Cranial Reconstruction (President of the International Association) , sent you a letter in February of this year, outlining our collaborative work, combining Giro-Vocal Motion Technique with NCR and the successes we have encountered. The only response to his letter was "I enjoyed reading the interesting enclosures". My letter from you (Nov. 8.1999) said much the same..intersting approach; a quick glance....but no communication since then. I think the importance of my work and and the work we have been doing , deserves more than a cursory glance. I am taking this opportunity to bring it to your attention again.

I am aware of the importance of the International Voice Foundation and am certainly impressed and salute you for the work you have done and are doing.

I have the feeling, that you deeply care about the voice having committed your life to it, much as I have committed mine. Your hurried 'response' to my book and to Dr. Arrandt, sounded to me like a *put off*, a *don't bother me, I am not interested* , or perhaps a *nothing you have to say, can possibly be worthwhile to the International Voice Foundation.*

I can certainly accept your opinion about my work, be it as it may, but total indifference to almost 20 years of reseach and hundreds of students helped and reconstructed, is at least worthy of a serious conversation. I am neither asking your approval, nor am I in need of it. My work and results produced, speak for themselves. It would however be wonderful if I could share my work with you and with the Foudation. As it is my mission to help as many people as I can, a large international body, such as yours, would allow me to reach thousands all over the world, that otherwise might never have had a chance at learning about an alternative possibility of restructuring of the voice, without an invasive methodology.

Perhaps the concept in itself is not acceptable and foreign to surgeons since , after all, surgeries make money. Somehow, from what I know of you and what I have read, I believe, that that is not true for you! As Chairman of the Foundation, I believe your constituency has a right to know, that there *is* another way, a non-invasie way and one that is totally natural and harmless to the system.

I went to look at your website and the "credo" of your organization seems very clear to me:

The Voice Foundation is the world's leading organization dedicated to solving voice problems. Its efforts in funding research, promoting public education and raising the professional level of voice care directly benefit you.

Established in 1969, the Foundation seeks to protect and enhance the gift of vocal communication through:

A NON PROFIT ORGANIZATION 501c3

3

- Research to advance the diagnosis and treatment of vocal problems, including improved non-surgical and surgical techniques;

- Sponsoring national and international symposia and seminars;

- Publishing and distributing professional and scientific publications and   video cassettes;

- Awarding research grants and fellowships;

- Disseminating information through the media.

The goal of the The Voice Foundation is to understand the voice and improve its quality and care.

Understanding is achieved by funding research to learn more about the function of the voice, and to spread this knowledge worldwide.

I am therfor respectfully requesting, that you listen to my 'First Lesson' and perhaps even re-read the book, giving it more attention than just a 'quick glance'. It is my fervent hope that our future conversations will be more fruitful than the ones in the past.

In the hope of hearing from you and meeting with you, I remain with the best personal regards.

Miriam Jaskierowicz Arman

cc.   Gary A. Gatza Esq. , Secretary

A NON PROFIT ORGANIZATION 501c3

No response ever…. By anyone!

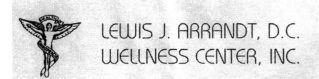

LEWIS J. ARRANDT, D.C.
WELLNESS CENTER, INC.

Phone: (305) 279-0850
Fax: (305) 279-0890

10651 North Kendall Drive, Suite 222, Miami, Florida 33176

February 4, 2000

The Voice Foundation
1721 Pine Street
Philadelphia, PA 19103
ATTN: DR. SATALOFF

Dear Dr. Sataloff:

I believe you are familiar with Miriam Jaskierowicz Arman's book,
The Voice: A Spiritual Approach to Singing, Speaking and Communicating. I read Ms. Arman's book and also attended one of her
seminars.

I was struck with how well her technique of girovocal motion (GVM)
complements a technique, whcih I have been practicing for several
years - Neurocranial Restructuring (NCR), to influence the creation
of a correctly placed vocal instrument. This is accomplished
without any distress on the vocal cords in singing and speaking.
NCR and GVM combine harmoniously, leaving the instrument resonating
in its natural habitat without the use of the laryngeal vibrato.

NCR was derived from a 60 year old technique called bilateral
nasal specific (BNS), papers enclosed. The NCR work invovles
placing small stacked latex cots into the different nasal passages
and then briefly inflating them until they expand into the pharynx.

This has the effect of opening the passageways and enchancing the
motion of the cranial bones via movement of the sphenoid. The
movement improve air flow through the nose and allows the "portal
bones" (sphenoid) to move more easily. This allows for greater
"high breath" capacity (Ms. Arman's terms). This then allows the
voice student to more easily apply the GVM technique.

Page 2 - NCR

Enchanced motion of the skull bones, which occurs due to greater sutural movement, allows for improved resonance of sound within the cranium - all benefiting the voice.

In short, the combination of these two techniques can allow for the development of a healthy, long lasting, properly placed voice.

I would enjoy the opportunity to discuss these techniques further with you, as I believe they can improve the function of the many patients you serve.

I await your reply.

Sincerely,

Dr. Lewis J. Arrandt

February 14, 2000

Lewis J. Arrandt, D.C.
Wellness Center, Inc.
10651 N. Kendall Drive, Suite 222
Miami, FL 33176

Dear Dr. Arrandt:

Thank you so much for your letter of February 4, 2000 and the interesting enclosures. I enjoyed reading them and appreciate your insights.

With best regards,

Very truly yours,

Robert Thayer Sataloff, M.D., D.M.A.
Professor of Otolaryngology
Thomas Jefferson University
Chairman, Department of Otolaryngology-Head and Neck Surgery
Graduate Hospital

RTS/em

This letter, in my opinion is an insult to Dr. Arrandt … Here we are talking about professional peers – colleagues and specialists in their own right –This total indifference is an indication of the kind of ' lip service' I have encountered with the "Associations and Institutions" who are powerful enough to make a difference in disseminating this information and help singers/speakers all over the world. Doing so would of course mean shaking things up quite a bit. That takes courage and perhaps some re-education. It's much easier to write a few nice words to placate rather than do something constructive that might rock the establishment.

From: Stephen Jackson <scyo2@yahoo.com>
Subject: Praise, NCR, and Teaching (two questions and some comments!)
To: musicvisions@aol.com
Date: Tuesday, August 5, 2008, 2:26 AM

Dear Ms. Arman,

First, I must say that I cannot help but think that divine providence brought me to your information! I have been many things in this life, and music has pulled me back over and over again relentlessly until I gave over my will to use the gifts we are given at creation. I am 33 years old, and a baritone (as well as a composer): I was a mediocre (at best) singer for quite a long time. Because I have always felt an intense connection to the text and emotional content of the music I perform, I've been given many performance opportunities that I wouldn't have ever gotten based on the abilities of my Voice alone. I did absolutely everything wrong for a number of years, and finally had the fortune to have a few small pieces start to click into place in 2000 and 2001… I don't want to bore you with a long history as I know that you are very busy and must have time to recharge your own energy and vitality, but your works have touched my life in so many important ways.

I was asked to start teaching Voice in 2003 by a small commercial studio that was familiar with my performance resume and temperament. I have been blessed with great patience and a strong belief that ANYONE who loves music and is willing to put their heart, soul, mind and time into the pursuit will come out the other side with a healthy and facile instrument. I had had at least 7 different Voice teachers who ranged from complete lunatics to mediocre pianists with little to no knowledge of the vocal mechanism. Struggling through my own difficulties with the Voice gave me insight into what many of my students felt (and feel) as they battle the many issues facing singers today. I have read voraciously and sought out as much information on practical and powerful vocal methods as I could with some good success over the years, but NOTHING prepared me for encountering your book! (then a bit later the First Lesson CD)

So many of the pieces clicked FIRMLY into place and the overall picture of what so many people had tried unsuccessfully to lead me to becomes more and more clear as I apply your ideas and technical skills to myself and my students. I am preparing several Opera scenes for a production in a few months that I was dreading until recently, and was recently cast as Olin Blitch in Susanna for spring of 2009. I feel as though you've given me back my own Voice instead of the constructed and manipulated Sound that I had been encouraged to create for so many years. I cannot thank you enough for the beautiful work you have done and continue to do for the world.

The questions I have are as follows -

The ncr.net website is no longer functional, but I found several other resources about NCR on-line. However, none of them speak specifically about the Voice. I am very interested in knowing more about what happens in NCR, and what results your students have achieved. There are no NCR specialists near me, and my current budget will not support visiting those closest to me for some time, but I would still like to know more…

My 2nd question involves something "odd" happening to one of my young sopranos the deeper we go into your technique. She is 18, with what had been seemingly moving toward a light lyric or even soubrette Sound…within the last several months however, the color, size, and intensity of the Voice have grown almost exponentially to the point that I seriously thing she may be on the way to becoming a young full dramatic soprano!!

When she places everything behind the eyes and creates space the way you specify, she gets dizzy, dry eyed, and even slightly faint as the level of resonance increases. The Sound is glorious and free without force or strain, but she is concerned about the physical sensations she is experiencing. I recommended that she accept the new sensations as a "check list" that she is placing the Voice correctly, but I wanted your advice here. I truly believe that she is doing everything "right" so far, and want to encourage her continued progress, but she is frightened by how foreign some of these feelings are.

Respectfully yours,
Stephen Jackson
Desert Moon Academy of the Arts
El Paso, Texas

[I thought you might find this letter interesting from a number of points of view so I decided to share it. As you continue on, the answers to all questions raised here will become perfectly clear].

Subj: **Re: Master Class**
Date: 4/13/00 2:15:48 AM !!!First Boot!!!
From: librado_a@yahoo.com (Librado Anderson)
To: Voiceacad1@aol.com

I'm sorry Miriam but, I don't believe I know enough
English to actually express what I think of your book,
I can say in Spanish that it is "Estupendo".
Now I know how to explain easily to my students
things and facts about the voice that I had never been
able to do before..I hope to have the book translated
into Spanish to have a copy for every one of them. I
can hardly wait to see you on the video explaining
your class...
Congratulations and best regards.
Librado.

— Voiceacad1@aol.com wrote:
> Hi Librado,
>
> Thank you for your request...we do not have the
> video ready yet, but as soon
> as it is, I will keep you on the list to let you
> know. Have you read the book
> yet and if so, tell me your comments please. I am
> very interested to hear
> what you think.
>
> all the best
>
> Miriam
>

=====
    Remember: The Force Will Be With You... Always

JULIE ANDREWS

25th April 2000

Miriam Jaskierowicxz Arman
International Academy of Voice and Stage Inc
1 SW 58th Ave
PLANTATION
Florida 33317

Dear Ms. Arman :

Julie Andrews has asked me to write on her behalf as she is still travelling all around the country and also to Europe — and she wanted you to know that she is very much enjoying your book.

She is thrilled to find clear descriptions of a technique that she endorses and which closely matches that of her early teacher and, happily, that of her present one, and has asked me to order a copy of your cassette, your video and 4 more copies of your book. I have sent the order to Music Visions International.

Ms. Andrews also asked me to pass along her warm regards and thanks you for thinking of her.

Sincerely,

Francine Taylor
Assistant to Julie Andrews

I sent my book (1rst edition '99) to Julie Andrews soon after her vocal cord surgery. Her ordeal began around the time I lost my daughter and I just did not know about it soon enough, otherwise I would have traveled anywhere to see her and make sure that she would not need to have the surgery. Her ordering book of course is very telling and an important vindication of my work.

The principles and precepts of my singing lessons with Miriam are fully accepted and internalized by me. I relinquish and surrender all my misguided and controlling thoughts and fears about singing. The muscles in my tongue release and relax. My tongue rests serenely and does not interfere in any way with my Voice. My larynx is released, and functions naturally. My jaw does not interfere in any way with the perfect production of my Voice. The habitual, residual *fear* in the muscles and structures of my entire body - and most particularly in the physical structures of my Voice - is perfectly released, discharged, neutralized and transformed. I am set free to naturally, easily, confidently, gratefully, radiantly SING. My tuned, true, clear, strong, expressive, artful and compelling VOICE is produced in perfect ease. My music flows in the unaffected and fearless Joy of honest emotional expression. The fear of singing is completely and permanently replaced by the LOVE of singing and performing and communicating.

Jim Parker's credo, written months before he died – this is exactly how he lived with the Voice and inside our work….

RICHARD BONYNGE

Chalet Monet
Route de Sonloup 12
CH-1833 Les Avants
Switzerland

December 22nd, 1999

Mrs. Miriam Jaskierowicz Arman
International Academy of
Voice and Stage, Inc.
1 SW 58th Ave.
Plantation, FL 33317

Dear Miriam,

It was such a good surprise to hear from you in Miami and I am quite ashamed that I did not get back to you before I left. My intentions were good but ....

Thank you so much for sending me your book "The Voice". I think you have stated everything in a natural and clear manner. Singing is often made so complicated but you have said everything in a way that can be easily understood. I have real admiration for you and I think your students are very fortunate. I am just passing the book on to Joan who is looking forward to reading it.

It seems a long time since our meeting in Sicily – so much has happened. I am really sorry not to have seen you in Miami – I am getting old and disorganised.

Joan and I both send you all our best wishes for the coming year 2000 and keep up your good work.

With fond memories

Richard

Richard Bonynge

The National Association for

MUSIC
EDUCATION

1806 Robert Fulton Drive ■ Reston, VA 20191
703-860-4000 ■ Fax 703-860-1531 ■ www.menc.org

October 4, 2000

Music Visions
PO Box 17345
Plantation, FL 33317

Dear Music Visions,

I had the pleasure of looking at Miriam Arman's book *The Voice. A Spiritual Approach to Singing, Speaking and Communicating* in the context of my work with MENC—The National Association for Music Education. It is well-written and informative and deals with a host of performance difficulties. I've seen many singers suffer physically and emotionally devastating vocal problems that required painful and complicated surgery. It's nice to know that in at least some cases, there is an alternative. Arman"s "spiritual approach" to the voice should be require reading for all vocal teachers and their students.

Sincerely,

Ella Wilcox

Ella Wilcox
Book Review Editor, *Teaching Music*

...and then of course there are the extraordinary people who have open minds and souls ...I did a workshop for MENC ... they were hanging off the rafters...

INTERNATIONAL ACADEMY OF VOICE AND STAGE INC.
A non profit organization
1 SW 58TH AVE. PLANTATION FL. 33317
TEL. 954 792 5204

Thomas Cleveland, Ph. D.
The Vanderbilt Voice Center
Director, Singing Arts & Sciences
Associate Professor
The Village at Vanderbilt
1500 21st Avenue South, Suite 2700
Nashville, TN 37212-3102
Phone 615 343 SING
Fax 615 343 0872

Dear Dr. Cleveland,

I have just received a letter for Dr. Ariadna Moreira, asking me to get in touch with you and that you are interested in meeting with me when you are in Miami. I would be delighted.
Dr. Moreira is a student of mine. Unfortunately her Brazilian fire sometimes gets the best of her and she does not do what she should, but I know, that once she is here with me on a regular basis, she will make the necessary changes in her speaking voice.

When she came to me the first time, she had been taught to constantly pull down of the voice down and push forward. She had no height and an under-rasp that indicated placement was much too low.....at any rate, when she sings, her voice is in good position...not nearly as good as it should be or can be...but at least acceptable for the amount of time she has studied with me last summer. I am looking forward to working with her The instrument will be first class, once I can keep a watchful eye on her.

Please allow me to share a bit of my work with you:
I am working with persons who have been diagnosed with spasmodic dysphonia and who have had Botox injections. We immediately cut the injections and in a matter of 10 lessons or so, their speaking is greatly improved and in a few months completely restored. Vocal cord nodules are gone in about 6 months without surgery....this of course besides my singers, whose voices I reconstruct after many years of singing and wobbling into perfectly clear and beautiful, young sounding instruments, no matter what the age (my oldest in 67 and she will debut at 68).....Speech Pathologists come to me to learn what I do , in order to use it on their patients....patients with paralyzed larynx learn to speak normally, better than before and , and , and

I am sending you my book and a copy of my CD via snail mail and look very much forward to meeting you and our connection. I am working on some truly amazing discoveries re. Autism, which I am now in the process of patenting,,,,,Its a very exciting time ! Thank you for being so wonderful with Ariadna.

I am enclosing my websites for your perusal intlacademyofvoiceandstage.com
musicvisionsintl.com
Amazon.com: The Voice: A Spiritual Approach to Singing, Speaking

all the very best

Miriam Jaskierowicz Arman

Thursday, April 26, 2001   America Online. Musicvisions

Just for your information – Dr. Moreira went on to sing beautifully, invited me to do a Master Class at the University of Evansville where she herself taught Voice. She now lives and sings in Italy.

Needless to say, there was no answer to this letter either…

Subj:	**Thank you**
Date:	5/24/2002 7:40:03 AM Central Standard Time
From:	springse@wfu.edu
To:	Musicvisions@aol.com
Sent from the Internet (Details)	

Hi Miriam,

I have a lot going on and very little time. But before too much time passed, I wanted to tell you how much I enjoyed meeting you. You are a very special person.

Once I can sing my high notes again and am living proof of your technique, I'm thinking I may approach the person who oversees the voice therapy. I think he would be open to this. (He personally had some vocal problems years ago and did some pioneering. Apparently they told him he wouldn't get better and he did anyway - using a self taught technique.)

I have leave now. I'll be back in the office Tuesday.

Regards,
Sarah

Monday, May 27, 2002 America Online: Musicvisions

CANTORS ASSOCIATION OF FLORIDA
3040 Lillian Road, Palm Springs, Fl. 33406
561-966-5051

December 24, 2003

PRESIDENT
Cantor Murray B. Yavneh

VICE PRESIDENTS
Cantor Irvin Bell
Cantor David Rosenzweig
Cantor Saul Rubinstein
Cantor Irving Shulkes

MEMBERSHIP
Cantor Zvi Adler

On December 17th, cantors from several areas in South Florida gathered under the auspices of the Cantors Association of Florida for a very special occasion: Miriam Jackierowics Arman, PHD, distinguishewd pedagogue and lecturer in all matters having to do with the production of voice, in speaking and singing, presented a Master Class in Voice, its Production and Physiology.

Dr. Arman's presentation uniquely focused upon a spiritual approach to speaking and singing and communicating.

The audience of cantors, all professional singers in their own rights, was held rapt and hanging on every word. Unquestiuonably, Dr Arman captured the rapt attention of her audience. She began with an overview, including the use of visual aids, of the process of voice production in the human being. She continued on to clearly identify the techniques of singing by the proper intake of air and the controlled placement of sound which insures a clear tone, large sound and effortless singing (or speaking) in a manner which communicates and captivates the listener. And captivate is precisely the word to describe the reaction to her lesson from the assembled cantors. Several voiced the desire to arrange for private lessons to continue learning and improving what are already professional vocal instruments.

Dr. Arman has lectured throughout Europe, the United States and Israel, so her expertise in vocal production is well known and documented. But she is now the "buzz" among the cantorate. To say she connected with her audience would be an understatement, to say the least.

Smll groups usually gather after a lecture of this kind, and this was no exception. Clearly, several cantors who had personal knowledge of singers who had called upon Dr. Arman for help in overcoming serious vocal problems were animatedly relating to others how their own serious vocal difficulties had been rather quickly overcome with her help in the past.

The Master Class was held in the main sanctuary of Temple Beth Israel on Military Trail in Deerfield Beach, Florida.

Dr. Arman's extraordinary expertise was clearly on display and her audience of South Florida cantors were spellbound and most willing, figuratively sitting at her feet, hanging eagerly on every word, every demonstration.

Dr. Arman actually had the courage and confidence to demonstrate her techniques with a volunteer, Cantor Sheldon Chandler, who , also in a display of courage, was led by Dr. Arman into the production of a strong, beautiful and youthful voice in front of all the assembled. A good teacher needs a willing, intelligent pupil. Cantor Chandler proved to be an excellent subject as the demonstration of his live voice, in front of an eager, live audience, was most successful.

Respectfully Submitted by

Cantor Murray B. Yavneh, President

November 5, 2000

Dear Miriam Arman:

This letter is to say: "Thank You Miriam Arman" for writing "The Voice".
Please allow me to tell you my story.

In November of 1999, I had surgery on my right caradid artery. The
thorastic surgeon informed me that I would have to be speech free for 2
weeks. He also said that he had cleaned out the artery, and did not need to
close the incision with staples!. I followed his advice and spent the next 2
weeks banging on tables to get attention, not to mention the writers cramp I
was afflicted with as I jotted anything I wanted to say onto a large yellow
tablet, which, by the way was pretty difficult, as Thanksgiving, with a house
full of guests happened during that period of time.

The two weeks passed and I tried to talk, but the sounds that came out,
might just as well have been made by Alvin and the Chipmunks. The
holidays came and went as did my voice. Also, since the day I awoke in the
recovery room, I found it difficult to breath. I saw the surgeon again and he
did not seem to think there was anything to worry about, that it would all
clear up very soon.. During this time I practiced Reiki on myself and did a lot
of praying. By January my voice was a little stronger but only for the first
few words of a sentence with the remainder of the sentence fading out to
emptiness.

January 3rd, 2000 I had an appointment with an E.N.T. I told him that I
felt there was a problem with my voice, that it was a strain to speak, and it
was not as deep as usual. Also, after speaking for a few minutes my voice
would fade away. The doctor, not knowing my true voice, did not understand
how there could be a problem, because the few words he heard sounded
okay to him. I truly think, that he was simply pacifying me when he said;
"Okay, lets take a look down there. The doctor sprayed a numbing agent into
my nasal passages and inserted a long metal object into my nose and down
into my throat. His diagnosis (I really think he surprised) was that the right
side of my larynx was paralyzed and he said, that it could possibly heal itself
within the next 3 or more months.

The doctor informed me that if it did not heal itself, there was a surgical procedure that could mend it, but in the meantime he suggested that I should not force my voice, that I should take it easy. I followed his advice.

It was during that time period that one of your students, Bambi Liss (my co-worker), gifted me with a copy of your book, "The Voice: A Spiritual Approach to Singing, Speaking and Communicating," Bambi insisted, that if I practiced the exercises in the book it would give me back my true voice.

First I read the book, then I practiced the exercises. I continued to practice the exercises for the next 3 months and found that the quality of my voice had dramatically improved. Additionally, not only did the quality improve, but I no longer needed to strain, it was so much easier to speak. I did not think that the improvement would be so dramatic. I am now able to speak clearly.

The E.N.T. doctor rechecked my larynx 5 months later and found that, although I was able to speak so well, the right side of my larynx was still paralyzed.

I would like to end this letter by saying, although the right side of my larynx is still paralyzed, my voice has improved greatly, I speak without struggle, and without pain. If anyone were to ask me to express my feelings in two words, those words would be, "pure ambrosia."

To date, I continue to follow the exercises outlined in your book.

And so I say, "Thank you Miriam Arman for writing ", "The Voice".

Very truly,

Estelle Joseph
902 NW 130 Terrace
Sunrise, Florida 33325

e-mail Stelly89@aol.com

David N. Haron
16 Weaver's Hill
Greenwich, Connecticut 06831

September 26, 2000   fax   203 532-4510

Dear Miriam:

I have just finished listening to the instruction CD
and am in profound awe at the light you shed on what is
least understood. I am of the opinion that I have more luck than
brains in seeking you out, and sensing a depth of connection with
your message. I have so much to learn, and I really want to find
the freedom which is the goal you point to in your suggested
directions.

Your sincerity comes through, without embellishment, to lead the
fortunate listener to a fresh level of understanding and revelation.
Lady ! You have absolutely galvanized the essence, in myself for sure,
of what impels me to deepen self-understanding. I know that somehow
I must createthe means and opportunity get the full measure of your
teaching. To sum up, you have scored a bull's eye with the CD. I know
the costs involved of CD production. You might consider also putting
it on tape. CD or Tape, there is a hungry market for serious students
of Voice.

Thank you so very much for your trust and friendship. I cannot wait
for the time we must surely meet.

Meanwhile, I shall read your words, and listen to your gripping
words on the subject that has brought us together.

PS: I shall visit BORDERS in White Plains, close to my abode, to check
out possibilities.

Most Sincerely,

David Haron

Greenwich Senior Academy

BOARD OF EDUCATION OF THE CITY OF NEW YORK
TALENT UNLIMITED HIGH SCHOOL
Sal Mazzola, Assistant Principal
Performing Arts I.A.
300 East 68th Street
New York, New York 10021
(212) 737-1530 ext. 431
Fax: (212) 737-2863

International Academy of Voice & Stage, Inc.
Miriam J. Arman, Ph. D
1 SW 58th Avenue
Plantation, FL 33317

May 17, 2002

Dear Dr. Arman,

I would like to take this opportunity to thank you on behalf of the students and staff of Talent Unlimited High School. The master class that you provided for our students on April 9, 2002 was most memorable. The students appreciated your expertise and experienced and innovated approach to vocal technique.

Thank you for your offer to return and work with the students in the fall.

Sincerely yours,

Sal Mazzola,
Assistant Principal

Frank Sinatra

SCHOOL OF THE ARTS

Elliot Salow
Principal

February 25, 2002

Dr. Miriam Armond
1 Southwest 58th Avenue
Plantation, FL 33317

Dear Dr. Armond

I would like to take this opportunity to thank you for your wonderful vocal workshop given to the students of the Frank Sinatra School of the Arts. Our students were thrilled to be in the presence of such a respected artist and were highly appreciative of your professionalism and most of all your warmth. Ms. Best, our music teacher keeps commenting on the wealth of information you imparted to our students and how they were able to synthesize and utilize your vocal methods. It was a highly informative and entertaining session.

Our doors are always open to you and we would welcome a return visit at any time. I am sure the students in our school could continually benefit from your excellent techniques and your passion for the art of singing.

Once again sincerest thanks for your interest in the Frank Sinatra School of the Arts.

Very truly yours,

Elliot Salow
Principal

ES:is

At La Guardia Community College 29-10 Thomson Avenue, Room C404
Long Island City, New York 11101
Tel: (718) 361-9920 Fax: (718) 361-9995

53 Covered Bridge Drive
Flat Rock, NC 28731
09 January, 2002

Julie Andrews
Greengage Productions
10520 Wilshire Boulevard
#1002
Los Angeles, CA 90024

Dear Ms. Andrews:

It is almost a year now that I have wanted to write you about
a woman I had heard speak, who I feel confident could help
you with whatever voice/vocal difficulties you may be
experiencing, but circumstances have always interceded,
preventing me from getting to it . . . until now, when I have
actually had a personal successful experience with her
services and ability.

Enclosed is a copy of Miriam Jaskierowicz Arman's business
card from the International Academy of Voice & Stage. I
heard her speak almost a year ago, and immediately thought of
you after hearing the live testimonials from singers and
vocalists she had helped quickly and completely.

Although I took her card for you, I had occasion to call her
just yesterday. She was gracious enough to immediately help
my son, who is a singer and was suffering from a severe vocal
disruption in the middle of a major musical project. The
improvement I heard in his voice after speaking with her for
just a half hour on the phone was phenomenal, and I knew I
had to write you immediately.

I write you about this purely in the belief that this woman's
expertise can be of great benefit to you. She and I do not
know each other; I was just another face in the audience to
her. But as soon as I heard her speak, I just knew she was
capable of doing what she said she could . . . and wished
that you knew about her.

It is my hope that this letter will prompt at least an
inquiry on your part, and I am even more hopeful that Ms.
Arman will help . . . not, not help . . . that she will solve
and completely eliminate whatever vocal difficulty/problem
you may be experiencing.

My very best wishes to you and hopes for your success.

Sincerely,

Madeleine Kay Bar-Sadeh

Enclosure

Bcc to Miriam Jaskierovicz Arman

Voice Teacher's Comments

Subj: **Master Class order**
Date: 3/15/00 3:51:59 PM !!!First Boot!!!
From: marty180@juno.com (Martin L GREEN)
To: voiceacad1@aol.com

Dear Ms. Arman,
I have been using some of the mental imagery I read about in your book
"The Voice" with my voice students at the community college level and it
has been very effective. I would like to order the video, "The Master
Class"

My Mastercard number is
I don't know if it's possible to answer a question just by email, but I
have always been taught that tightening the stomach in any way tightens
the throat.   Do some students do this when they are trying to involve
the pelvic muscles? Is it a matter of keeping the tightening low enough?

Thank you for your work and for sending the video.
            Sincerely,
            Martin Green
Martin Green
1151 Veramar Court #104
Corona, CA 92882-6423

Home phone 909 736-7453

Subj: **Thank You**
Date: 3/20/2002 1:43:09 PM Eastern Standard Time
From: rdcw@rcn.com
To: Musicvisions@aol.com
Sent from the Internet (Details)

2 November 2001

Dear Miriam,
I want to thank you again for the private voice lesson & group Master Class I took with you in NYC in October. I have been a voice teacher for 18 years, in NYC and the South Jersey/Philadelphia area, and have worked with many, many hundreds of rock & pop singers, from beginners to major label recording artists. I am also a professional jingle singer and a singer/songwriter, currently completing the recording of my own CD project. I have experienced incredible results with the technique I teach and practice. I am very cautious about other techniques, after suffering and struggling with vocal issues and various teachers many years ago. After reading your book. I was open to trying a lesson with you.

Since our work together. I have been practicing your concepts and bringing them into my body & voice, and I am seeing much benefit. I am freeing up my voice even more. and find that I practice my own technique in a more productive and focused context. resulting in more depth of sound. with still less effort or strain. I am working the concepts into the training with my own students, and am seeing positive results with them as well. Their sound is more open, less forced, and more 'on-the-breath.

I think your book is helpful, and I am glad I had the opportunity to work with you in person, to more fully grasp the concepts and apply them hands-on with your guidance. I know I will be seeing you again.

Best wishes,
DEB CHAMBERLIN,
Gloucester Township, NJ

Roman Kofman, Chief Conductor of the Kiev Chamber Orchestra Professor of the P. Tchaikovsky Kiev Conservatory, Kiev Ukraine (original text)

"I am very well aware of Ms. Miriam Arman as an excellent expert in the sphere of vocal. In Ukraine she carried out numerous master classes both for students and for well-developed artists/soloists of the Philharmonic Societies and Opera Theatres.

The master classes of Ms. Miriam. Arman were great successes because she demonstrated the perfect knowledge of vocal mastery, deep experience in the ways of Voice training, delicate style, feeling.

Ms. Arman easily comes into contact with her students; her lessons take place in the atmosphere of absolute confidence and enthusiasm.

She has perfect results in her teaching. The artists singing on the best scenes of the world are among her students. I hope her experience, skill and energy will be of great use for those who wish to acquire the secrets of the vocal art."

Advanced Fertility,
Gynecology & Laser Surgery

Care you can feel confident about

January 03, 2001

Re: Miriam Arman
        Planation, Florida 33317

To Whom It May Concern:

Miriam is the unusually gifted and talented teacher who comes along only once in a lifetime. She have a rare and uncanny, intuitive ability to ascertain the student's problem, as difficult as it may be at times, and to determine precisely what solution should be applied.

I had the great pleasure of meeting Miriam several months ago and during this time, she has substantially improved my speaking voice and has given me the confidence and skills which were so elusive before with numerous other teachers. In short, she has performed nothing short of a miracle on voice.

I have the greatest regard for her as both a teacher and a very caring person. I wish her the very best in all her endeavors.

Sincerely,

Ronald J. Patterson, M.D.

KOUT VOCAL STUDIOS
1435 DENTWOOD DRIVE
SAN JOSE, CA 95118
SDKOUT@AOL.COM
408 265-9691

JANUARY 24, 2006

Dr. Miriam Arman
840 Montgomery Street, Apt. 2A
Brooklyn, NY 11213

Dear Dr. Arman,

Hello my dear friend. What success I am having with the new techniques you kindly taught me. I have been in Florida as you know giving Master Classes and some vocal sessions.

The responses are fabulous. The sounds these women are producing are better than ever—clear, bell-like, resonant, in-tune and beautiful. I cannot thank you enough for sharing with me.

I also taught a class this past weekend at our California regional education weekend and the students were blown away. It has been a challenge to convert all of my teaching material of 40 years, but I have almost finished all of my teaching classes.

Enclosed is a check for $928.55 for 49 books (25 to my home in San Jose and 24 to Annie Gooch in Florida).

I will be ordering more books before I depart for New Zealand in May.

I hope you are feeling well and your work is as rewarding as mine is these days.

In harmony and love,

[signature]

Shirley Kout is one of the most extraordinary persons I have met in my life. As you go on in this book, you will see who she is - she organized a master class for me with her students and her choir members and went so far as to inform the heads of 'The Sweet Adelines' to have my book reviewed by their staff (3rd edition - The Revealed Version). This attests to a "real teacher", a responsible & caring teacher – ego is only secondary to the success of her students – G-d Bless you Shirley

Notes

The Greatest Changes

In 1999, I began teaching Orthodox Jewish Cantors and Rabbis.

My first such student was Rabbi Chay Amar. He came tone deaf (or so he thought), desperate, yet full of hope and desire to learn how to sing and speak, in order to start his own Chabad Community in Golden Beach, Florida.

He was Lubavitch and unbeknownst to him, he would be Instrumental in changing my life, setting me firmly on the road to becoming involved in the study of Chassidus and a follower of the Lubavitcher Rebbe Menachem Mendel Schneerson (OBM). With Chay, and because of his perseverance and dedication, the word got out, that there is a "woman" who teaches Voice to religious Jewish men, without singing even one note herself (according to Jewish law it is not allowed for religious Jewish men to hear the singing Voice of a woman).

More "Black Hats" began arriving. Rabbi Amar began singing, becoming himself known as an eloquent and powerful teacher and lecturer. He recorded a CD in France and today leads a thriving and growing community and Jewish Learning Center in Golden Beach, Florida. He sings for both his Ashkenazi and Sephardic community with joy and gusto.

The spiritual aspect of the Voice has always been extremely important to me. I understood from the beginning, that without Spirituality, the real potential of the Voice could never be accessed to its fullest - hence the original title "The Voice: A Spiritual Approach to Singing, Speaking and Communicating." Because of my own personal studies and the incredible work with all of my students, as well as the extraordinary experiences with my Rabbis and Cantors, so much more has been revealed to me. Over the years this has lead me to a much deeper level of understanding and has made a tremendous impact on my teaching and therefore, upon all of my students.

✿ ✿ ✿

Before its publication, I struggled much about whether to share "The Revealed Version"(3rd edition) with the world. Ultimately I decided that this information must be made available to all, because this knowledge is universal. No doubt, some concepts might seem "different" at first glance and some of the terminology might be very diverse from what you are used to, but the effort of learning this new vocabulary is well worth the final result.

Viva la difference! I have tried to make the words and concepts easy to understand by using common terms, so everyone can easily relate and benefit.

The Chapter, "Hashem (G-d), the Voice and You", is very special and filled with some powerful innovations. I am sure you will find it very helpful, insightful and extremely supportive of your efforts.

PLEASE DO NOT READ IT NOW... WAIT UNTIL YOU ACTUALLY GET THERE. ONLY THEN WILL YOU 'GET IT'.

Over the years, I have worked with countless students from all over the world: vocalists, children, teachers, speakers, speech pathologists, doctors, ordinary people with serious medical problems related to the Voice. If they arrived pre-surgery, in almost all cases, surgical intervention became unnecessary and their problems were resolved in just a few months.

In all these years I really have not met anyone I could not teach. I do however believe, that *not* everybody in teachable - not because of how or what I teach, but because of their own individual personalities and character. Each Voice has a special magic button.

It is up to the teacher to find it, it's up to the student to allow and follow it!

What and how I teach has had a major impact in all instances, even if a student, for whatever reason has walked away. Seemingly destroyed, wobbly Voices return to glory - better than ever (at any age) - and with diligent work and care, the Instrument can be re-built and re-positioned. The willingness to learn new concepts, change old notions and ideas, along with the unwavering commitment of the student and the teacher return the necessary results.

By the way: ***Age is NEVER a factor***. Contrary to public belief, the Voice never needs to wobble because of age; it (the Voice) never gets old, etc. and those who perpetrate this misinformation, which is total nonsense, use it as an excuse for bad singing. The Voice is meant to last a lifetime. We are conditioned by the so called "expert opinions" to believe, that vocal deterioration is to be expected after, let's be conservative and say 55, or 20 (more or less) years of a singing career. I have proven repeatedly that with the proper work, there is limitless potential at any age. It takes profound dedication to the work, patience and endless faith, but it can definitely be accomplished.

The listening, hearing, and the total nullification of **SELF** on the part of the teacher are paramount. This is **not** about his/her Voice, **not** about demonstrating how it is done or what it should Sound like – **this is about the student's Voice ONLY!!**

Many would-be teachers have arrived in my studio to observe my teaching. I beg for more **committed persons** to actually take on the teaching end of this work, but almost everyone who came to learn how to teach, has left singing.

In MY thinking, **A SINGER IS NEVER A TEACHER**. The great need for teachers, who are dedicated to the learning of HOW to teach and how to really listen, is vital and of the greatest importance to me. I have to duplicate myself, many, many times over. Unfortunately, what we have teaching today are many "would-be singers" who could not make it in the business, who then become teachers, but whose real passion is "their own Voice" not yours.

In this book, you will find much new material. Go slowly, Chapter by Chapter . . . build with and add on each piece of knowledge gathered. Only when you have mastered one, go on to the next. **DO NOT** read the book all at once and expect to understand it - you won't. Take your time. Each Chapter contains important information that the Brain needs to absorb, before it can actually produce the Voice.

I want to take this opportunity to thank you for all of your very special personal and honest letters/ emails in which you share your stories, your successes as well as tales of woe. I am so grateful to hear how much "The Voice" and this work has changed your lives. A graduate of a very prestigious New York Music School recently wrote to me lamenting about 'being a "damaged musician"… My heart goes out to her and to all those who unfortunately feel like she does – I cannot help in other musical disciplines, but when it comes to the Voice, the answers and the results can be found right here!

PLEASE JUST ONE THING:

 DO NOT, UNDER ANY CIRCUMSTANCES TAKE ANY OF THESE CONCEPTS OUT OF CONTEXT.
 ONE CHAPTER FOLLOWS THE OTHER AND DEPENDS ON THE OTHER – IF YOU SKIP ANYTHING, NOTHING WILL MAKE SENSE. AS I HAVE MEN-TIONED IN THE BEGINNING, AT THE RISK OF REPEATING MYSLEF – SPEED READING DOES NOT WORK HERE!!! DO NOT SKIP!!!

There is not a place in the world today where the book or the CD "The First Lesson" is not being sold. I have received letters from the Far East, from Russia, the Middle East, Europe . . . small villages, big cities . . . and the response to this work has been overwhelmingly positive. The book is now being used by universities and colleges as a textbook in their Vocal Pedagogy departments, teaching teachers this technique . . . full choirs are using the book—speech pathologists have come privately to learn.

With **this** book, new breakthroughs will be achieved, and what has already been accomplished, will flourish and continue to grow.

With G-d's help, you who read these lines will soon be introduced to a new way of thinking, perceiving, and relating to your Voice and your life.

May you be blessed with a Voice that communicates the best of who you are, in all phases of your life.

Notes

WHAT EVER HAPPENED TO GREAT SINGING?

Whatever happened to the longevity of the Voice?

Whatever happened to the career that lasted a lifetime?

I could tell you many stories that have unfolded since I began writing and re-writing these 4 books - stories that would capture your sensibilities, imagination, indignation, stories that would surprise you and infuriate you. You cannot even imagine the variety of personalities, some of the deviousness, the disloyalty and downright meanness and lack of integrity of some singers who have come through my studio, who have taken my time, energy and knowledge and then turned around and said "I am the one who did it all by myself – now I do not need you anymore and I certainly would not give you the credit for MY accomplishments".

On the other side of the coin, of course, there is fierce loyalty, endless devotion, love and total dedication to our work – and that is what is keeping me going and plugging away at making a real difference.

Thank G-d, the good always outweighs the bad…but boy, when it hurts, it hurts a lot. All of my experiences, from the very beginning, led to only one conclusion: This book, just like "THE VOICE" had to be written.

In the first edition, I was cautious not to "offend"; in the second edition and the third, much was revealed and I became bolder. In this one, **I pull out all the stops**.

Here I address everything that bothers me, everything that upsets me, day in and day out. I confront the incompetence of the mainstream institutions teaching Voice, teachers who do not have the slightest idea of what they are doing and are therefore (UN) intentionally ruining Voices, destroying precious potential. I speak about egomaniacs who hound their students day and night, practice malicious mind control, and virtual psychological warfare to keep their students coming to them, telling them the most outlandish things about what kind of lifestyle, foods, and drugs, etc., that will make the Voice right. **This time, I accuse!**

So many Voices that were once beautiful walk through my door, lustrous Instruments to start with, that were "beaten" into submission by utter incompetence.

I am tired of hearing the same stories over and over again and I am miserable at the end of the day thinking that I need to clean up that which others have left for "vocal garbage". Singers who study at well-known universities, with 'illustrious' teachers and the most prestigious music schools around the country and the world, come to me with wrecked Voices – it is outrageous. Thank G-d, in 95% of all cases I have ever taught, we were able to turn over a new leaf….the other 5% walked away to do their own thing…whatever…

I listen, day after day, to the stories of so many and if I told you the letters I receive, you would not believe what is going on in the world of singing… well, perhaps you will and perhaps you are one of those to whom it has happened…one of the ones who, for years learn with someone and wind up with vocal cord nodules, have surgery, go to speech therapists/pathologists, get endless prescriptions, spray stuff into their throats and at the end of the day, give up their dreams because there just is no help and healing to be found. Well, look again.

Enough of all the negativity! I decided to go out on a limb for you, to take on the system and to hopefully make the "Idol" worshippers sit up and listen...really listen. After years and years of teaching and sitting in my studio, hour after hour, the time has come to let go of all the pain that I experience when I meet a student who has been to nine teachers or six or three , who walks in with his/her Throat in a "sling," thinking his/her vocal life is over.

Why come to me? Well, in all desperate cases, hope springs eternal and the Voice wants to be heard…."I've got to try again – A Singer's Credo!" After a few months of re-constructive work, they realize that, thank G-d, "it's really only the beginning" and not the end.

"Listen all of you out there" to the great Voices of the past and ask yourselves: "What ever happened to great Singing??" I mean real singing and real top- notch singers not digital sounding boards? I am talking about singers to whom you could listen and feel something, who made you happy inside and whose Voices elicited deep emotions.

There is another Frank Sinatra out there, there are Perry Comos and Johnny Mathises and Nat King Coles; and there are Carusos and Giglis and Pavarottis and Domingos; and there are Scipas and Galli-Curcis, Tebaldis and Sutherlands and Lilli Ponses – there is another Barbara Streisand, another Aretha Franklin…there is a Bing Crosby and an Ella Fitzgerald, a Richard Kiley; there are and always will be beautiful Voices.

Today, most of them are hidden beneath the belting, screeching, shouting and rasping - and because they really cannot sing, they 'Rap'…. Is it just about a style? I cannot answer that, but in my mind nothing substitutes Real Singing.

Notice how the "old" stuff is always "in"…how great music remains through the ages and the "soul" of a song never dies, nor does the Voice that sang it. The "great singer" of the past is always emulated, his music always revered and his talent always appreciated.

Some careers start out in a promising and splendid fashion, but after too few years, it is over and gone - the Voice begins to wobble, crack. What happened? WHY? It is so sad.

The country watches auditions of people who actually think they can sing - their teachers tell them so and delude them into the idea that they have a chance at "popular greatness." When ultimately, they are put in their real place and terribly disappointed, they have to deal with insulting dialogue by individuals who have not the foggiest idea of what real Voices are all about.

Some time ago an "Opera singer" won *American Idol*. Tears were shed…what a sight, "real emotions". I was appalled to think that someone would actually call this "real singing". Truth is that there is a beautiful Voice in there that needs lots of serious training, but please, give me a break. If they really cared about these singers and the whole thing was no more than a publicity/money ploy, they would make sure that he and others get proper analyzing without being bashed and are shown the way to some masterful Voice work.

Don't think for a minute I am only talking about what might be considered pure classical singing and training here – no way. I am talking about Jazz and R&B and Soul, about Broadway and Pop and Reggae and, of course, Opera; I am talking about the state of the Art as a whole.

Some Opera Voices, who are being paid top dollar today, would not even be allowed into the chorus in Toscanini's (legendary Italian composer) time. This is a malady that affects and has spread through the Art of Singing as a whole. It has become a money game like everything else. Look at some of the most popular "fallen" young stars – a few years of mega-stardom, then mega scandals - what a pity… what a waste… Let us begin to really sing again!

Today, the idea is to "Create Theater", spectacle, Paparazzi material, that sells magazines and CD's and mostly covers up for bad singing – who cares, its news.

Get as much as you can out of a Voice now – who cares about tomorrow – there certainly is another one (Voice) where that came from to fill the stage, the hunger of the public and the pockets of the powers at be.

The real respect and reverence of the Instrument does not exist anymore – classical and popular alike. Everything has become what I call 'Fazzoletti Singing' – (like a Kleenex – use it and throw it away). Sorry, but for me that kind of mentality does not work.

It all really begins with Maria Callas and the following Chapter is dedicated to what in modern times and perhaps for all time, will be considered the greatest Diva ever. Unrivaled in life, career, scandals, hoopla, in her voracity for public accolades… in short, everything about her, changed the face of the musical/vocal word forever. There have been greater singers than Maria Callas, but considering all circumstances surrounding her existence, there is no one like LA DIVINA!

Notes

_____

_____

_____

_____

_____

_____

_____

_____

_____

_____

_____

_____

HOW AND WHY I HOLD MARIA CALLAS RESPONSIBLE FOR RUINING GENERATIONS OF SINGERS!

(No one would ever dare say that, but I dare!)

I consider Maria Callas to be the ruination of generations of Operatic Voices - Sopranos for certain. Her antics, her persona, her hunger for fame and publicity all destroyed her own Voice and, of course, generations of singers to follow who wanted and want to be just like her.

Having said that, I also consider her a most extraordinary vocal talent; a truly stupendous actress, a phenomenal musical and stage performer and a master of vocal interpretation - I regard her Voice loss and subsequent death, as a crime. To think that such talent would be lost to the world because of **Ignorance**. (And that was then, in the times of the 'Golden Age' – just think about what is going on today).

The ONLY reason she lost her Voice was because she <u>was not taught properly to begin with</u> and when the Voice began to show unmistakable signs of wear and deterioration, NO ONE was there to re-construct and save this noble Instrument. IGNORANCE my friends, IS NOT BLISS!!! And Maria Callas' life, career and Voice are a testament to that.

I sit listening for hours to the young Maria…what incredible potential, what a divine, awesome talent, the pure drama in the Voice, the expression – but by no stretch of the imagination anything of what she should or could have been. With what she achieved in her career, she barely touched what could have been the greatest female Voice ever. Her musicianship was astonishing, her devotion to the score, her demands on herself…all superlative.

What then ruined her?

The great turning point in Callas' career occurred in <u>Venice</u> in 1949. She was engaged to sing the role of Brünnhilde in <u>Die Walküre</u> at the <u>Teatro la Fenice (Italy)</u>, when <u>Margherita Carosio</u>, who was engaged to sing Elvira in <u>I Puritani</u> in the same theater, fell ill. Unable to find a replacement for Carosio, Maestro Serafin told Callas that she would be singing Elvira in six days; when Callas protested that she not only did not know the role, but also had three more Brünnhildes to sing, he told her "I guarantee that you can."

In Michael Scott's (founder of the London Opera Society) words, "The notion of any one singer embracing music as divergent in its vocal demands as Wagner's Brünnhilde and Bellini's Elvira in the same career would have been cause enough for surprise; but to attempt to essay them both in the same season seemed like folie de grandeur". After the performance, critics would write, "Even the most skeptical had to acknowledge the miracle that Maria Callas accomplished" …

Well, when you've done it once, you can do it again and so on, and pretty soon, you think yourself infallible and that is the beginning of the end.

The Diva was created not only by her singing, which no doubt thrilled audiences beyond their wildest imaginations and of course thrust open the doors to all the hoopla in the beginning years - but later by the scandals of her "life performances" which dominated and captured the imagination of the public - ultimately, without a doubt, causing her vocal and physical demise.

The spectators destroyed her just the way they created her. When she toured with Giuseppe Di Stefano (that's another story which perhaps, someday, I will reveal), it was a musical fiasco for both - the public, however thronged to see the caricature of what were two of the greatest singers of the time. The public is cruel.

Callas took with her generations of would-be Sopranos who marvel at her life, her career, and the spectacle of her Voice – the adoration of the public, money, and fame. Ignorance is the ultimate culprit.

Where were her friends, her teachers, her doctors and the "real" people who cared? Who advised her about the Voice in her later career? Why is it that people are there on your climb up and surround you with "love and concern," but when you are losing it, when you are down, there is no one who will have the "guts" to say, STOP- you are on the wrong track. People made millions off her, where were they when she needed someone truthful to guide her back to vocal health?

Her singing career was over by the time she was 40…for an Opera Singer, usually the prime vocal years. She was used and abused as an Artist in the same way she used and abused her Instrument and I, for one, cry for it. When you read her repertoire from the beginning of her career and what she did vocally to achieve her fame, it is obvious, (I am certain not only to me) that though she was a consummate musician she totally disrespected the needs of the Instrument. I don't want to go into the details of all of my thoughts on Callas; suffice it to say that her public 'figura' was the beginning and the end. She died at 53.

The Voice did not kill her- *not having the Voice,* **killed her.**

Somewhere in the depth of her Artistry she understood finally what others did not. I am sure you remember the phrase "It's not over until the fat lady sings." It is a well-known "fact" that Opera singers used to be overweight. No good reason for that at all, as you will learn, but the statement reflects that in previous eras, the external "look" was secondary only to the Voice. Callas took the "weight" thing to a whole new level and again set the standard.

Today, looks are primary - the quality and excellence of the Instrument is secondary. Today, beautiful faces and bodies are singing and sadly that is the criteria. I would never say that having both is not ideal, but if a choice has to be made, it should most definitely be based upon vocal merit and not on waistline.

So many attribute Callas' vocal downfall to weight loss…I do not!
I attribute it to ***Voice loss.***

Her body issues became the criterion for the future of other singers, just like her Voice did. Shortly before her death, Callas confided her own thoughts on her vocal problems to Peter Dragadze:

"I never lost my Voice, but I lost strength in my Diaphragm … Because of those organic complaints, I lost my courage and boldness. My vocal cords were and still are in excellent condition, but my 'Sound boxes' have not been working well even though I have been to all the doctors. The result was that I overstrained my Voice, and that caused it to wobble." (Gente, October 1, 1977)

She speaks about *overstraining* being the *cause* of the wobble, **but she does not speak about WHY she overstrained**. I firmly believe that she did not know technically how to prevent it. She was never taught any other way. If she had, her history would have been shaped in a different way and so would the history of the singing world (classical for sure). The effect of her vocal demise was certainly evident to all and **no one was able to help her** –sad state of affairs, don't you agree.

The greatest Soprano of our time, who could afford the finest, the most prestigious doctors/teachers/therapists, could obviously not find a competent professional to help her save her Voice/career/life from self-destructing...

By the time you will finish reading this book you will know and understand the reason and how to prevent your own vocal ruination.

Callas herself stated that in Opera, acting must be based on the music: She said: ***"When one wants to find a gesture, when you want to find how to act onstage, all you have to do is listen to the music. The composer has already seen to that. If you take the trouble to really listen with your soul and with your ears - and I say soul and ears because the mind must work, but not too much also—you will find every gesture there."***

Oh, how right she was! If only she ***understood*** her own knowledge.

Once, while living in Italy, I had a student who came to me and said "I want to Sound just like Callas, I will do anything"...I tried to talk her out of it. I could not, and stopped teaching her. She got quite a ways and today sings in many international Opera Houses, but she never discovered the real beauty and capability of her ***own*** Voice. She was obsessed with what I call the "Callas Syndrome".

Emulating someone, even the greatest, will only lead to destruction of the true potential of your *own* Voice and that - in my opinion, is always the beginning of the end. ***TO THINE OWN SELF BE TRUE***...first rule of the house!

✲ ✲ ✲

Publicity is great, but real SINGING is greater.

No one has done more to make Opera public than the late Luciano Pavarotti - he was a great singer, at least until the mid-seventies, early eighties. When it came to HOOPLAH, he was the master. Vocally though, I always still considered him "old school'.

With Pavarotti, there was a real Voice, there was a great personality and persona, - and He was a beautiful, natural talent who was not ruined by a bunch of egocentric teachers. Arrigo Pola did not teach him very much of anything and his second teacher, Ettore Campogalliani was considered one of the last great masters of vocal technique and teacher of greats. Pavarotti was a singers singer...like all, he had is personal "stick", but until the mid to late seventies, he was worth listening to. Domingo constantly got better as the years went by and remains the consummate musician but never achieved the public adoration that accompanied Pavarotti's career.

Carreras had a most beautiful Voice but technically could never quite 'support' his Instrument, even before his illness…what a pity.

The "Three Tenor Concerts" (Pavarotti, Domingo and Carreras) of course took the whole thing to another level which I personally do not appreciate, but even I have to admit that the 'spectacle' of it all brought Opera close to millions. Pavarotti's popularity is unparalleled in the history of singing. He was, much like Enrico Caruso and Mario Lanza adored by the media and to his great credit inspired and stimulated the multitude with his vocal/personal 'grandness' . No one has taken his place and perhaps no one ever will!

The price he paid for his lifestyle took him from us much too soon but his vocal legacy will remain forever.

Notes

MUSINGS

One day I was on the phone with some big company and "Muzak" (easy listening station mainly oldies, R&B and vocal goodies) was playing - what a joy to hear, what beauty in Sound, in word, in content. I realized where I had to go with this and that just writing a 4th edition of "The Voice" simply would not do.

I became aware, as so many times before, that the "average singer" would not look for Spirituality in the Voice and therefore would never find my book, find my work, and find the truth. So I decided to be daring and get your attention. I even stopped charging for my Master Class DVD's and put them on **You Tube and My Space** for free to make my work available to anyone.

There are those who will be angry with me, those who will condemn my work, those who will call me a 'quack' and who will say that I am *lacking their* kind of "knowledge"… the fancy terms, the medical expressions and experience of a doctor or musician, the degree which impresses them - they will say that the way I do things is too simplified. Well, that's the way things should be – natural, simple and easy to understand and achieve.

There are those who ask, "Who are the great singers you have produced?" My answer to them will be – Great is relative. To me, all of my students have great potential, besides it's none of your business! When singers come to me (not all, but many) they are usually in deep vocal trouble and do not want their problems revealed to the public. Confidentiality on my part, if the student wishes it, is assured. As for the rest: It is my job to put it out there, to offer it - what a singer does with it, is his decision, not mine. Whom you trust and whom you decide to study with and why, depends on your own judgment. Do your homework seriously. To study with someone just because John Doe goes there or the fact they taught 'so and so', is not a good reason. You must choose based upon what works for your Instrument and resonates in your soul.

Voice lessons are the lifeline of a singer, always. You need the information how to understand and play your Instrument…you need to learn and dedicate and work. The Voice is not to be taken for granted under any circumstances. You need to respect and have faith in your Instrument. You need to know that this is a lifetime commitment, not a whim…the work is constant. Since you actually cannot hear yourself (as you will learn), your Maestro is the guide to the Voice. His/her knowledge of your Instrument is paramount. If he/she knows what they are doing you will keep the Voice for a lifetime.

The production of the Voice, the way the Instrument is built, is the same for all Voices. How far each Instrument is brought into its potential and the desire of the singer to achieve his/her goal, is what finally determines the genre he or she chooses and whether or not they will be successful.

Please understand that it takes much more than "just a Voice" to be victorious. Who you are as a person has a great deal to do with whether or not you will be successful. Do not blame anyone for your own shortcomings....accept responsibility for your life, your choices and for your Voice. Study!

I want this book to open your eyes to what is going on around you and I want you to strive for excellence and not accept less. I want you to hear and listen to what I have to say, to try it and feel it and achieve the highest level of your own potential no matter what genre you sing. I am tired of singers who stay around a couple of years and then turn to drugs and alcohol because their Voices "are shot" (never happens, just misplaced). When a singer loses the use of his Instrument, it is like cutting off his legs...he is lost. A singer must sing, and the great ones sang until the day they died. Instruments are built for a lifetime, not a couple of years...age is myth...vocal incompetence is the killer.

A Singer is born, not MADE.

Many times, when I was apprehensive and wanted to turn back, because I thought of what others would say and how they would react. My Inner Voice always strongly objected and said: "What are you afraid of? You know what you have done is good and the ones, whom you have sent on their way, have given you the right to share the knowledge. It does not matter how others will feel or how they will judge, take your stand and open yourself up to the world."

In 1999, when the first edition of the "The Voice" was released, I could not imagine how the world of Singing would react . . . it has been simply incredible. One thing is for certain: All comes in its own time. It is my mission to work each day, give my best, be there for whomever needs me and do the work, which G-d has given specifically to me. If you ask me why, I cannot answer; all I can tell you is that this is the way it is.

I have said many times and want to do so again, here at the beginning:

There are many teachers in the world, with many ideas and theories.

Until now, I have not refuted their ideas, nor stood up "against them", but you know what? It is time that I call out for the truth and I make myself heard.

When I listen to what is considered great singing today, I am appalled …The "really" Greats would turn over in their graves.

Am I competing with what is being taught out there? You bet I am!

I am disillusioned with the results of what is taught as 'teaching methodology' today and, if you are truthful in your heart of hearts, so are you. Here in this book, as before in "The Voice", I have outlined WHAT I teach, HOW I teach it and what has been so incredibly helpful and successful with so many students all over the world. I share my work with all those who *wish* to partake of it and without reservation; *I challenge those who will not. Bring it on – I am ready!*

My teaching spans over more than 25 years. The students I have taught, by the beauty of their Voices and their beings have enriched my life tremendously. They are my extended family. I have "lost" some, but have helped hundreds and hundreds more. *It is all about choices.* Those who walked away decided to do so **not** because what I taught them was not valuable or that it hurt them in any way, (G-d forbid), but because they simply did not have the stamina and discipline it takes to achieve what I ask of all of my students.

I do not allow the easy way out. I do not teach for the dollar - I teach for passion of Voice…I go for the "one note" always! If you do not have what it takes, go on your way, do your thing, and don't bother me. If you should wind up in the heap of mediocrity, blame those who put you there and yourself for not going for the gusto. I am out for excellence – that is who I am as a teacher and a person and that is what I expect of my students.

Lately, I choose very carefully to whom I wish to impart this information. I have been deeply hurt and that hurt has caused me irrevocable physical and emotional damage. I do understand though, that this too is part of the "game" and considering all, **I am powerfully challenging all opponents**.

I have the great privilege of touching many lives—my students, in turn, have blessed me, in the most extraordinary ways and they have shaped my very existence to the core. Through much personal pain and heartache, it is the Voice, the divine beauty of the Instrument, the perfection of its creation and the devotion of my students that brings me to this point. It is because of their/our suffering that I venture out to reach YOU!!

I care so much about you, the singers, the professional speakers and the children who are already struggling vocally at early ages, being taught wrongly in schools and being encouraged to project Voices beyond their vocal means by parents who think they are doing the right thing. I reach out to the communicator in all of us and hope that this work serves as enlightenment to each and every one who comes in contact with these pages.

I have added much new information, I have revised and revisited my own work a thousand times – I have been guided to find answers that will make a huge difference in your life. I share with you – please share with me.

"We create our tomorrows by what we dream today."

"You are the sum of your thoughts and feelings, plus or minus ... positive or negative."

"If you can dream it, you can achieve it; and if you can wish it, it can and will be yours."

"A singer is only as great as his last performance."

These are some of the phrases I use in the very beginning lessons to establish the relationship between my student and myself. Teaching is not only about the vast technical knowledge of the Voice, but also the proper application of a great deal of humanity. The more positive your attitude, the easier you will be able to assimilate this information.

As a teacher, I build a bridge between my students and myself; and that bridge enables us to communicate in such a way that our experience is one of love, sharing, lots of work and ultimately great accomplishment.

THE WORK WE ARE DOING HAS SOME UNDERLYING DEFINITIONS WHICH MUST BE LEARNED AND OBSERVED:

"YOU ARE WHAT YOU THINK."

"WHAT IS IN YOUR THOUGHTS WILL DETERMINE WHAT WILL EVENTUALLY BECOME THE VOICE."

"YOU ARE THE SPEAKER OF SOUND, NOT ITS CREATOR."

"THE VOICE WORKS WITH YOU, FOR YOU, AND IN SPITE OF YOU."

When you internalize these concepts, everything that I will put forth here will become very clear. The actual physical effort, once the knowledge is thoroughly absorbed, is minimal. The whole idea that singing is difficult to achieve is totally blown out of proportion. Ultimately, *singing is as easy as speaking and if you can do one, you can do the other.*

I am certainly not saying that every Instrument is great, but what I am saying is that some potential exists in everyone and that attaching yourself to that spark, is worthwhile.

The Brain does not care which notes you want to sing, the Brain will interpret the knowledge of the music and the words according to the "information" it has from the onset. You will hear me mention this many times.

It is vitally important to understand that singing and speaking are one... that the same Instrument is a responsible for producing both, so switching into a "singing mode" absolutely makes no sense at all, does it?

The Voice is ONE continuous LINE which moves like a pulley system. (Intrigued? Read on!) How to achieve this continuous, seemingly endless line of Sound is what we will conceptualize and accomplish.

What we will learn here is how to apply information that will ultimately change your **thinking** according to "new knowledge" and when that happens, the whole "difficult thing" will be broken down to simply "**Thinking and Speaking Sound**."

Believe me, I am not saying that achieving this level is easy, but what you will hear me say repeatedly is the following:

"The knowledge of the body determines how it will react."

In other words, if you teach the body the right thoughts, if you teach the vessels (you will understand this later) how to receive and how to give, they will do so at "WILL". Your thinking appropriately WILL ultimately produce the desired responses. The most important thing is for the Brain to unlearn past bad habits that were damaging to the Instrument, and learn new ones that will protect and re-teach it to function without inhibition, force, pushing, etc.

Vocal health and beauty are not accomplished by anything other than re-training your thinking and knowledge. How to realize that is what this book is all about.

I ask you to read and learn without judgment…open yourself up as you were when you were born and knew it all from the start. I ask that you be PATIENT and allow your personal patterns to emerge and that you celebrate a new Voice, one that may be a stranger to you, yet represents truth. I also ask you to allow yourself to feel, to be sensitive to your Instrument and "auto-critique" honestly. Following the old patterns will not accomplish change.

Conquering new knowledge and incorporating that into your daily routine will make a huge difference in the way your Instrument responds. If you have problems, do not hide behind them…doing this work will give you a precise and cohesive structure and patterns which will define your **'newly found Sound'. If you expect to retain the Sound you have at the onset of this work, forget it! You have no idea what your real Instrument Sounds like – but you will!**

Please read everything, many times over….there is so much information to comprehend and import into your consciousness. Every detail counts, nothing is superfluous here! To succeed, you need TRUST, FAITH and GUIDANCE….avail yourself of it all!

I have said so before, say it again now, and will say it a thousand times more:

"You are no more than a Speaker of Sound;

You are your Thoughts and your Perceptions;

You are a combination of Thought, Speech, and Action;

Your Will and Your Desire are the essence of your Voice;

Speak and Sing out of your Brain and let the body be the vessel that responds to your desires;-

Follow your **Internal Hearing and Listening**: worry about what goes **IN** and **NOT** what comes OUT; if it goes in correctly, the outcome is assured;

Thinking correctly becomes speaking and singing correctly."

All this will become clear as we learn concepts that will achieve this re-training. You will be utterly amazed that everything you have heard or thought you knew about the Voice will change and so will your life as a whole.

"YOU CAN ONLY FLY IF AND WHEN YOU ACCEPT WINGS!!".

A few days before the final edit of this work, my dear student YDS from Brooklyn came here to study. This statement 'arrived' while we were working together and I share it here and now because to me it is the basis and the sum total of everything I teach. Nothing will/can make any difference unless you accept the wings and unless you WANT to fly.

SOAR LIKE AN EAGLE - SPREAD YOUR WINGS AND FLY!!!

Notes

THE SECRET OF THE GREATEST SINGER EVER – FINALLY REVEALED

For those familiar with Opera, the Tenor Enrico Caruso, was and will always be the greatest singer of all time…bar none!

For those of you who do not know him, read up and listen to some recordings on the Internet. It's worth the trouble. [His recordings are basically done with a megaphone – Imagine if he had had a digital soundboard.]

CARUSO – "THE MOUTH THAT COULD CRADLE AN EGG"…This is possibly one of the most guarded secrets of the Voice.

Perhaps 13 years ago, I purchased a complete set of Caruso's recordings on 78 records. The magazine which accompanied the recordings was published by the Metropolitan Opera in 1975 and in it I found the article *"Caruso, The Mouth that Could Cradle and Egg."*

I had listened to the recordings hundreds of times – there is no Voice that compares to Caruso's in brilliance, in technique in color, in beauty…NONE. His Voice and what he achieved with his Voice was and remains amazingly unique and enrapturing. He is unequaled.

The magazine part which accompanied the recording was obviously always there - I just never took the time to read it until one day, I thumbed through it, and all that I have ever taught about the Voice over the past thirty years was validated, vindicated and cleared.

WHY no one knows this, teaches this, examines this, I have no idea, but to me and to my students this is the one of the greatest **SECRETS of all time to unlocking the "Voice".**

In the **Chapter on the Egg**, I will explain everything to you in great detail. Please **DO NOT SKIP** any part of the book, otherwise you miss important steps…no rush, all in good time.

The above-mentioned magazine has various articles about Caruso, his drawings, photographs, etc.,-interesting tidbits about the greatest singing icon of our time, the Voice which set the standard for excellence and production.

On the last page of the magazine there is this obscure article titled **"The Mouth That Could Cradle an Egg".**

When I began using and teaching with the Egg in 1996 or 1997, I do not quite remember the auspicious day, but for certain, I had no idea that Caruso used the Egg.

The reason I "conceived the Egg" was because one of my student had a serious problem with a retractile Tongue. I desperately tried to help her (with the Spoon), but the moment she tried to put the Spoon into her mouth the Tongue pulled back. Suddenly I had the most powerful inspiration, jumped up and ran to the fridge to get an Egg. "You are not going to put a raw Egg into my mouth" she pleaded. "Yes I will!"

That was the day it all began with the Egg and from the first day it has been a revelation and enormously important to all of my students, whether they loved it or hated it, the EGG always wins! And When the Egg wins, my students Win!

The "Egg" is not mentioned in any of Caruso's publications on vocal technique. I do not think that the Author, Quaintance Eaton, who wrote the article in reference, was aware of the incredible significance her words would have on the world of singing when she wrote the following account:

"Evidence exists in Boston of one aspect of Caruso's vocal apparatus. A dentist who practiced there in the early part of the century took plaster casts of the mouth cavities of many Opera singers to prove that the size and shape of the mouth chamber has a great influence on the size and the quality of the Voice.

The inside of Galli-Curci's mouth, for example, proved to be narrow and high, rather like a gothic arched roof. **Caruso's, on the other hand, was a great, round sphere, as big as an orange. Dorothy Benjamin, Caruso's wife and no relation to Dr. Harry said once that he (Caruso) could put a large Egg in his mouth and close his Lips over it without cracking the shell...."**

By the time you get to the Chapter on the Egg you will understand how and why he used the Egg and the extraordinary "coincidence" of the work we are doing here. Only when you have gone through all the work will this make sense…but SENSE it will make!

Notes

In the Beginning ... Once upon a time

....there was a little boy playing with old and dusty things in the family attic. In a far corner, he detected an oddly shaped black box and went immediately to check it out. To his great surprise, he found the box in pretty good shape on the outside—other than the mildew and the dust, of course. But the big amazement came when he opened up the case. Underneath the beautiful, red velvet lining, he found a lovely looking violin, which seemed to have been polished only yesterday—a bow, strings and other strange looking things... he had no idea what some of them were. "Wow, what a find! I wonder how much it's worth?" he thought to himself. Immediately he decided to pay a visit to the old bearded man who owned the music store down the street.

None knew exactly from where the old man had come, or how long he had been there, but the little boy remembered that sometime long ago, he had seen a violin hanging in the man's window, and he had admired it. So, with the black case in hand and dreams of riches, he headed off to the shop. When he entered the music store, he heard wonderful Sound. The old Victrola in the back was playing, and the small store seemed filled with the delicious tunes of piano and Voices, violins and flutes. The little boy just stood there for a moment, taking it all in. What a strange and enchanting place.

The old man smiled at the boy with his wise, blue eyes and beckoned him to the counter. "Well, well, what do we have here?" he asked. "Oh," said the little boy, "it's a violin I found in the attic . . . so I thought I'd bring it to you and see if it's worth anything and if it's still okay."

The old man opened the case, removed the velvet covering that lay neatly over the violin, lifted the Instrument out of its case and gently placed it under his chin. Then he took the bow, tightened it and began fingering the strings and adjusting the neck of the Instrument. He knew exactly what he was doing; and he did so with love, smiling all the while, enjoying himself and this adventure. The little boy watched in wonder. "Perhaps one day I, too, will play the violin," he thought to himself.

The first Sounds the Instrument made were kind of squeaky, harsh and non-melodic . . . somewhat hard on the ears. However, all at once, as though something magical had happened, the violin started to sing. Beautiful tones began on the top and continued to the bottom, creating a haunting melody . . . resonating throughout the store. The old man's eyes lit up like two light bulbs, and a great smile played across his Lips. "This is a fine Instrument," he said. "Yes, a very fine Instrument." "Is it valuable?" asked the little boy. "I mean—if I sold it—how much money can I get for it. The old man smiled knowingly and said, ***"My dear young friend, the value of the Instrument is not as important as who is playing it. In the hands of someone who does not know how to play it, the Instrument is worthless - In the hands of a master, a very plain 'Woolworth' (old-fashioned five and ten cent store) model turns into a Stradivarius."***

So it is with the Voice, the greatest Instrument of all. As we begin on our path together, it may seem arduous and a bit difficult at first—because it is unfamiliar—but I promise you that very shortly, you will understand everything about the Voice and will be glad you chose to become a "master."

The violin cannot be played in its case. It has to be taken out and put in the proper place for playing. Only then can the master create beautiful tones and melodies. The same thing applies to the Voice.

✲ ✲ ✲

I am probably one of the most fortunate people in this world, who wakes up every morning excited about the day—about the discoveries I will be making and the joy I will experience . . . the sharing . . . the love that is in my life. I give myself completely to my passion and, as my students will tell you, I live my life to its fullest when I am teaching.

I am a purist . . . I abhor spectacle for the sake of spectacle. I love the performance, but I am not a lover of mega-concerts, nor do I believe in the Sound systems used to make them possible. I want to hear the Voice, the pure Sound, the beauty, every note, every magnificent nuance of a beautifully played Instrument. I want to be transported by music, the Artistry, the quality of the singer, not the hoopla that goes along with mega-productions. I am old-fashioned. Perhaps I do not understand or care about the money angle of the whole thing. I certainly don't believe that it should be the motivating factor for a performer. For me, the focus is the Voice, and that is what it will always be.

Each Voice is so different. Each student is so special, so individual in his or her needs, and I treat all of them that way. Each one has a magic button—a word, an action—something that will make him finally click and find the Voice. Finding and understanding that magic button is the key. Discovering it usually takes time, but that is what makes the whole process so wonderful and exciting. I live for the moment in which both the student and I capture and achieve total transformation, because when it is right—you and I will feel splendid, elated, joyous, and easy. You will be flying, and I will fly along with you.

Specifically, when all is said and done and everything is in place, **you will not feel the Voice at all anymore**; it will have disappeared into the head. You will hear echoes of Sound that are perfectly placed, **yet out of your control**. You will make them in comfort and without effort—this is where we are heading with these lessons, and this is the place to which I will lead you: total and complete comfort without strain, force, or trepidation.

To ultimately play the Instrument perfectly, absolutely no physical manipulation of any kind is necessary! You must be completely free to give yourself to the music, the drama, the Art of singing and the interpretation, without ever worrying where the Sound will be coming from, or what it Sound like on the outside. *Thinking will become the key to 'speaking the Sounds'* and the Voice will be perfect in its own world.

I have come up with specific guidelines that will apply to everyone. There are hundreds of variables in the Voice, and after reading and digesting this book, each of you will begin to understand your own Instrument and will be able to make evaluations that will be good for you. Read each Chapter many, many times over. If you keep in mind the most basic things we are discussing here, you will do wonderfully well. I will make it very easy for you, so follow along and most of all—enjoy.

This is not a "scientific book." There are no fancy terms or drawings. The few drawings I chose to include are those I draw for my students every day. They are easy to understand, because they go along with the ideas I am presenting here. I want to teach you just as I teach my students. I have broken down the concepts in such a way to make it easy for you. Expect to see different terminology than you are used to and learn to integrate this terminology into your own vocal vocabulary.

The individuality of Voices always fascinates and amazes me. The Artistry of singers and their tenacity and dedication to making their Instruments work, really intrigues me. The countless ways the ardent student tries to produce the Voice, when in reality it is already there and so little has to be done to reach utter perfection in vocal emission, utterly baffles me.

In all the years I have been teaching, I have never quite understood, why we think of Voice production as something so extraordinarily difficult. Perhaps the fact that it really is so simple is more than we can allow ourselves to hope for, much less accept as truth. How can something, that is thought to be so terribly difficult, really be so easy and accessible?

The mystique placed on singing does not help our thoughts, either. After all, our *famous* singers are bigger than life and, to most of us it seems hardly possible to achieve such a goal.

Does this line of thinking reflect your sentiments? Well, let me burst your bubble. It is easy. It can be done, and after you have it, feel it and achieve it, you too will agree that singing is such a natural thing - a child can do it….

When you cannot feel the Voice anymore because it seems totally out of your head … When it does everything on its own, and the only thing you have to do is hear the music in your head and allow the Brain the freedom to do all the work… when you allow your Lips to simply speak it… that is when you will KNOW the Voice.

You will hear Sound such as you have never heard before. You will experience feelings that seem surreal. You will find yourself floating in space and making music at the same time. You will be at one with the universe!

This is not going to be a terribly complicated and long book. It does not need to be. Nevertheless, if you, the singer, really read these lines and take them to heart, everything that has been unclear regarding the Voice until now will be unveiled before your eyes. I will explain it all to you in these pages; and for the first time since you have begun trying to sing or speak properly, you will fully understand how to do it right. All will make perfect sense to you.

The Brain must accept, conceptualize and understand all thoughts; and since the Brain is the major contributor to the proper working of the Voice, logic and intellect will tell you that this, and only this, is the right way…

Think before you speak – think before you SING!

I will repeat myself many times in various contexts, because one concept will congeal with another at different steps of our discovery. That is, because these concepts must be reinforced again and again, so the Brain can compute, analyze and finally comprehend and incorporate the necessary actions into its reflexive motor system. Each Chapter can stand by itself and bring you right back to the beginning concepts.

What begins as a learning experience will become an entirely natural thought process. I call the whole process *"Brain imaging"* because once the Brain can form the image of what we are talking about here, you are home free. All of this requires trust above all and that is what I ask of you. The choice is always yours; but I know that if you let me guide you through this process, you will be successful at understanding and producing the Voice.

✧ ✧ ✧

Singers have this very special instinct of survival. I have noticed it in so many of my students. Some of the comments I have heard a thousand times are:

"Something doesn't feel right… I leave my lesson, and my Throat feels like it belongs in a sling."

"I'm always hoarse after I leave my teacher."

"I have studied for two years, and nothing is happening; but I know, I just know that I have a Voice."

"When I sing for a little while, my Throat becomes tight: and I feel like I can't go on."

"There has got to be something else, something really natural…I hear the Voice clearly on the inside, I know I hear all the right Sounds and I do hear them perfectly, but when I sing my friends tell me I am tone deaf and should not even sing in the shower…." …and you listen, you accept their judgment and are intimidated and embarrassed, but deep inside you KNOW THAT THERE IS SOMETHING ELSE!

Perhaps you can relate to some of these comments and perhaps you have others – please write and share them with me. This profound knowing is that same instinct which also confirms that you have finally encountered the right thing.

Let your logic guide you and know this: **if you feel anything while you are singing, other than the things we will discuss, you are doing it incorrectly.** If it hurts, stop immediately. Re-read the sentence of instruction and then try again.

Please, let me say one more thing to you before we get too far into this:
I know there are hundreds of Voice teachers and just as many theories on the proper way to sing. I am not interested in arguing but if I have to in order to save a Voice; I will challenge any of them. "Live and let live", that is my motto, but the Voice reigns…don't mess with it.

I am writing this book to prove that this is the ONLY way to have a healthy and well-homogenized vocal line and an Instrument that is TUNED PROPERLY and plays beautifully. I am here to share my knowledge and experience with you… and I am here to protect your interests! The most important thing is that you wind up with a beautifully healthy and finely tuned Instrument.

I envision singers who are vocally proficient and confident and communicators who can do so easily and without feeling pain. ***What I teach I will prove at anytime, anywhere, to anyone, in any forum, bar none. I stand exclusively on my own.***

One last bit of advice: If you are studying with a singer, please beware that you do not try to emulate him or her. His Voice is his own; his interpretation of how he constructs the Voice for himself is also his own. Make sure you always stay true to *your* Instrument. Work within your capabilities and allow your Voice to shine through, without taking on the vocal characteristics of your teacher. This is very difficult, particularly if you are studying with someone who has made a brilliant career or is famous, or perhaps has taught someone who is very well-known on the music scene. It is quite natural to become enamored with the Sound of someone else's Instrument for the right or the wrong reasons - but please, try as best as you can to develop your own.

The ego of a "singing" teacher wants you to Sound like him (mostly without his being aware). He will judge your Instrument by his vocal standard, by the way he produces his own Voice - your Voice can only be secondary in his own mind, not because of anything other than nature itself. I am unequivocally opposed to a teacher singing during a lesson to demonstrate what needs to be done. ***A teacher must be able to communicate to and with your Instrument, not <u>be</u> your Instrument!***

Here I offer you my way of teaching. Ultimately, you will know if it is good for your Instrument. Let your feelings and intellect guide you. Your body will tell you by its responses to what you are doing, whether it accepts or declines. Trust your innate perceptions; they are rarely wrong.

Singing is as natural as speaking, and it should be effortless. Permit yourself to experience what I put forth to you. Do not immediately judge by your previous experiences; do not be negative, please. Give this a chance. Only then can you make an informed decision.

There is no mystery to the Voice. There is, however, the miracle of the Voice - accepting this is the very first step.

Let us begin our discussion by trying to understand what our individual responsibility to the Voice really is. I know that by the time you reach the last page of this book, you will sing, be happy, feel wonderful and have the stamina to continue singing for hours on end. You will be able to reach the heights within the Voice that you have always dreamed of but never believed you could achieve - and it will be easy and effortless.

It is vital that we understand from the onset that the Voice is a gift, part of all the other wonderful attributes that were given to us when we came into this world. The Voice is the combination of all our emotions and feelings, as well as our physical, psychological and mental abilities. It combines all our capabilities and asks us to bring them to life in the most natural and uninhibited manner, so as not to hurt or damage the Instrument in any way. To really tune the Instrument, you must be fully cognizant of it. You must know its workings and needs in detail understand its idiosyncrasies. You must understand all the elements involved, the way it functions and what you can expect from it. You cannot fix a car without knowing all of its parts and understanding where one fits into the other. Most of all, you must be willing to spiritually dedicate your Voice, everyday a-new to the ONE who gave it to you in the first place.

I truly believe that if these prerequisites are not met from the start, there is no possibility of understanding or "mastering" the Voice. You will be able to sing, but to really make a career for many years to come is almost impossible. To be in tune with your Instrument means making the decision to truly love it, care for it, respect it, understand it and above all, to dedicate it.

We must understand that the Voice does not belong to us. Since it is a gift, it must be cherished as one. I *thought* I "lost" my singing Voice at a very early age, and the realization that I could not sing made me sad beyond belief. It was only later in my life that I discovered, that destiny had chosen a different path for me. Teaching others brings me the greatest satisfaction. I was really meant to be a teacher from the onset. I am grateful to have been chosen as a vessel to grasp and perceive the Voice and thus, to be able to help others in attaining self-expression, their destiny, passion and Artistry.

It took quite some time to get here, but here we are; and we're both ready - me, to make sense of everything you need to know to begin becoming proficient at using your Voice, and you to experience and partake of it.

People are always amazed at how I can teach without being able to sing. Well, my dears that is the miracle of who I am and in the last Chapter, I will share my story with you.

I simply communicate the knowledge I was given.

The knowledge you will need to use the Voice properly consists of the intricacies of the Voice, the way it works, how the body reacts, how each note Sound when it is perfect and what is imperfect. My students comprehend our *language* without a problem (it usually takes three hour-long lessons to comprehend the vocabulary and to conceptualize the theory) and so will you.

I am a TEACHER, not a SINGER! I am hard and difficult, unrelenting and loving, kind and supporting, incredibly demanding, a perfectionist and downright driven to achieving the perfection of your Voice. I am the same with every one of my students and I do not care who they are or where they come from. To me, each one is a Voice that needs to communicate, with extraordinary potential for good. I am a Teacher, a vessel, a giver, I am here for YOU!

If you plan to challenge yourself, you are my kind of student. If you are lazy or disloyal, go away, I do not want you. If you want me to teach you and then give the credit to someone else, you will lose my respect, support and my friendship…you are here to do the work and together we will achieve your goals.

Many of the ideas I put forth may seem abstract in design, but trust me; they are entirely *" bio-available."* This method requires that your thinking process actually change. In the beginning, it demands a real leap of faith; you are walking blindly—at least until this begins to make a little bit of sense. However, at the end you will ask yourself, "How come no one else has ever explained this to me before?" Well, perhaps someone has; most likely they did not, so do not worry about it. Work with what you have today. Everyone knows what it should Sound like, what is beautiful and right… but how to get there and how to make YOU get there, well, that is quite another story. With the explanations I give to you here, you will understand this incredible natural puzzle inside your own body.

Let begin taking the Instrument *"out of the box."*

Notes

Spirituality & the Voice . . . Why?

What does that have to do with the Voice anyway?

Well, just imagine for a moment the real power of music, any kind of music. Think of its therapeutic value: the way it can make people feel when they listen; the communication gaps it can bridge between nations and cultures; the way it can overcome you, when you are in a bad mood; how it makes you feel when you are happy; the way it can send chills down your spine. Music, music, everywhere. In offices, on answering machines, in the home, while riding a bike or sitting on the beach, while at your place of worship or while you're working out.

The power of Sound: remember it. Music moves your spirit and your soul and your mind it moves your body . . . your very essence. It can bring you to tears - happy or sad. Whether you sit in a church or a synagogue, a Buddhist temple or a Muslim mosque, you will hear music. Music, celestial Sound we associate with G-d, with angels, with heaven itself. Music grabs you, enfolds you, heals you, brings you profound joy and lightens your sadness. Music is, in itself, Spirituality. Through music, you can achieve a heightened sense of being and become sensitized to feelings and emotions.

In the last five decades, there has been an incredible upsurge in Spirituality. Everywhere you turn, people are talking about angels and communication with the "beyond." Their interest in the world's environment and other life forms has taken on an entirely different scope. There seems to be a yearning within us to know more, to answer age-old questions, to find the common thread in our lives, to attach ourselves to something that is beyond ourselves. Practices like Reiki, Kinesiology, Reflexology, Hands-on Healing, Acupuncture, etc., all indicate resurgence of interest in the natural law of things. Look at the incredible impact "The Secret" has had on our society. I have been teaching the principles of "The Secret" to my students for years….someone much smarter than me packaged it and brought it to the world, which was ready and embraced it.

The "material" realm has also taken on a different meaning in many cases. Of course, we have to earn money to survive economically in this world; but the incredible thrust of the fifties to achieve more than our parents did, this exhausting competition that the baby boomers felt, has, to a large extent, been replaced by values that go beyond the house in the suburbs, the two cars in the driveway and the "keeping up with the Joneses." There is a new kind of opening within us, a need to comprehend the metaphysical and to make it part of our everyday living.

Self-help, New Age, Homeopathy, Herbology, Natural Foods, Alternative Medicine – the incredible growth of all these disciplines, point to only one direction: our need and desire to feel better - physically, mentally, emotionally and, above all, spiritually.

The statistics of how many people take self-help courses, read New Age books and shop at health food stores is astounding. This shows us clearly that our lives are changing. Our personal needs are more directed toward introspection and self-realization. Our communication skills have to change to accommodate our internal changes, and this is precisely the subject on which I want to focus. Let your inner Voice guide you and you will come to see the Light.

Did you know that singing and speaking are the same?

The way you speak is also the way you sing. Essentially, you are using the same system, only less of it when you are speaking and more of its potential when you are singing. It is as simple as that. Your speaking Voice therefore is also your singing Voice.

Most of us speak incorrectly. We use our Throats; and even though we may Sound and feel scratchy and complain of discomfort, we do not do anything about it. Some of us have a very nasal Sound, taking the entire ring and point out of the Voice. Some singers may sing correctly, but speak incorrectly or the other way around. The results are difficult to deal with and can cause quite a bit of trouble.

Most of it is not **our** fault. We have been instructed to "keep it down," to speak quietly, to drop the volume in our Voices to adapt it to the needs in our daily lives. Our environment, our peers, our parents have made demands and we have complied. No one ever thought that those demands might have a negative effect on the Voice.

When a baby is born, it does not know how to modulate the Voice, how to make it quiet. It screams "at the top of its lungs," and if you watch, its belly pumps all the while. A baby never gets hoarse. Response is instinctive. No one needs to teach a baby to cry or coo. Very soon though, all that changes.

"Shhh! Keep it down. Daddy is sleeping." Slowly the Voice drops lower and lower from its *'natural position'* and finds itself another *'logical'* home - the Throat. We learn to speak with and from the Throat. We learn how to manipulate the Throat and everything around us references the Throat as the appropriate place where the Sound is produced - and so we use and abuse our Instrument all of our lives. We also take the Voice for granted. We simply do not think about it. It is here to serve us, and serve us it does - relentlessly, day after day; the means by which we communicate… no one worries about it.

No one unless they know, or unless they have serious problems, gets up in the morning and thinks: What must I do for the Voice. It is there, always - unless of course something is WRONG, at which point it becomes tragic.

Have you ever thought what life would be like without the Voice, without the ability to say the things you need to say in daily life? Have you given thought to what your life would be if you could not tell your child, "I love you" or speak words of solace to the friend who just lost his mother? What would your life be without language? Imagine yourself in silence for just one day. Take a moment and think of how incredibly important your Voice is to you every moment of every day and how lucky you are to have it for every conceivable situation of your life. Think of the pain you would never be able to express, the joy you would have to hold inside, the songs you could never sing, the tunes you would never hum.

From this day forward, you who are reading these lines will no longer think of the Voice the way you did up until now. From today on, you will change your whole perception of the Voice, for speaking and, of course, for singing. All you have to do is follow me on this path and the Voice will open like the blossom of the most precious flower on earth…believe me ***Miracles Are Possible and Achievable NOW !!***

Whether you will sing or speak professionally is not important here. It is paramount that your Instrument is tuned properly and that your wonderful gift is preserved for a lifetime. That is my mission and that is ultimately, what I am here to share with you.

Notes

How to Begin?
"The AIR – "Lifeline of the Voice"

I used to call the "Air" breath, or high breath. I sometimes still do, so please don't get confused. Over the years I have changed the language, because whenever I would say "breath (e)," my students **inhaled** the Air deeply into their Throats and chests and then exhaled as they began singing. Obviously, they did this because of how they had been taught in the past - the concept being, that if you do not do this, you won't have enough Air to complete your phrases: **This is absolute, total nonsense. STRIKE THE WORD 'INHALE AND EXHALE' FROM YOUR VOCAL DICTIONARY!**

If you *inhale* the Air and then try to get it back up, you are automatically empowering the use of the Throat. The Air must then be pushed out and forward, straining muscles and forcing the Air out of the mouth. The Jaw naturally must become involved. Interestingly enough, most singers are taught to rip open their mouths….no wonder lyrics are so hard to understand.

Speaking position must be maintained, always. Therefore, when we speak about Air or Air Movement, we speak about only the natural Movement/flow of Air. We are looking for is a ***passive*** Movement instead of an ***active*** one.

You physically DO nothing; you *only* mentally guide and feel everything.

As an aside, just for your information:

You *cannot* possibly' inhale' enough Air to do what is needed, but there is *the potential* to **connect** yourself to the Air, which already exists in the body in the appropriate place. This is part of what you will learn. **The entire body, whether you actively breathe or not, avails itself of the Air which already exists in your body.**

Every part of your physiology is involved because obviously, a continual flow of oxygen exists. The bloodstream carries this oxygen to all the organs and nourishes the Master Computer, the Brain. Since warm (hot) Air rises and the normal body temperature is 98.6 degrees, the Air is forever rising and the Brain is oxygenated on a continuous basis. I do not want to take this any further at this time, but please keep this logic in mind before you think of taking the next deep breath through your mouth and into your chest.

The Air is the lifeline of the Voice. How you 'intake', distribute, and support the Air will ultimately determine where the Sound goes and how the Sound is moved. The Air is the motor and the support system of the Voice. To master it is the most important task we must set for ourselves.

The kind of intake of Air I am talking about is totally natural – nothing exaggerated and certainly nothing that the audience should hear or be aware of while you are singing.

I absolutely abhor hearing a recording where the singer's breath is audible. It absolutely destroys the flow of Sound. If a breath is taken after just a few notes, the vocal line is irrevocably broken. In my explanations, I will be very specific and give you step-by- step guidelines so you can easily follow.

Just to tell you, right off the bat: Each Air Movement - and there will be three different areas – will lead to the next. Each builds on the next until the *final* entrance is reached which puts us into the *final position* for the beginning of Sound and Vowel. **Only there does everything come together**. Learn each phase thoroughly and get comfortable with it. When you master one *only then* go on to the next.

Open your mouth slightly, **not more than the natural drop of your Jaw.** Allow the Air to enter. **Do not inhale** under any circumstances. Begin guiding (mentally) the Air inward from the top of your Front Teeth and feel it travel along the roof of your mouth (Hard Palate), all the way to the back. You will experience a cool sensation along the Hard Palate (roof of your mouth), all the way into the back of the Throat.

When it seems that you cannot go any further with the breath, you will have arrived at the Soft Palate and The Hole, which is the exact place where you need to be. The spot where you feel the coolness is the Soft Palate. The reason you feel coolness in the back is that the Soft Palate rises and an important opening is created.

Every note and I mean every note, that you will ever speak or sing must **be initiated above** this place. When you can conceptualize this Movement of the Soft Palate moving upward and backward, all the other pieces of the puzzle will fall in place quite easily. The most important place inside your mouth is right there. It is because of the rising of the Soft Palate that the Throat opens – nothing is more important than that. **A completely Open Throat is the basis of a liberated Instrument.** Please remember, this is only the beginning, the first step. As we become more familiar with the whole system, we will be referring back to this cool spot quite often.

You do not have to worry about taking Sound up or down any more. No changing of positions is necessary. It all begins right there **above the Soft Palate**. Not quite yet, but a bit later on, you will understand why and how.

It is important that the Air be consistent, the same way every time. This is one of the very important technical aspects that you really have to learn and on which you must concentrate.

I want you to practice allowing mouth Air to move in that way *only*. Later on, I will add other elements so you can fortify your position. Once the Soft Palate is in place, it should not move . . . at least, you do not move it physically. Later on, the Air from Diaphragm will gently move the Soft Palate when necessary.

While on the subject of "high Air" and Soft Palate, I must introduce you to one of your new terms: **The Portal Bones**. Do not look this term up in any medical dictionary, because you will not find it there. My students are very familiar with the Portal Bones, because I made up this name to help explain the pathway of the breath. It is easy to find them by following these directions:

Take a drop of tea tree oil on both thumbs. (Do not ever be without this stuff! You can get it in any health food store—it is a fantastic antiseptic (100% Australian is the best). Use it sparingly, just a drop. It sensitizes the area and your sensations in the area will be heightened; Do not swallow it, please use just a dab). With your thumbs pointing upward, trace your top teeth until you reach two round little bones just behind your wisdom teeth. (If you do not have wisdom teeth, don't worry, the portals are always easily found.) You must allow your Lips to spread slightly to get your thumbs that far back - your Tongue will automatically drop down. By *guiding - allowing the Movement* the Air upward, which is a mental rather than a physical action, past the Hard Palate, the uvula and into the Soft Palate, you will feel the pulling backward and upward of the Portal Bones, guiding the tissue of the Soft Palate naturally into the right direction - up and back.

Perhaps at this point you might say: "Now, don't tell me that bones move... bones cannot pull up and back." You will encounter some concepts here that you may never have perceived before; if you open yourself to the possibilities, you will notice how easily you will change your perceptions and habits once you know what is expected. We are able to achieve anything with our minds. If you fathom the Movement of the Portal Bones upward and backward, it will help you to accommodate the Movement of the Soft Palate.

This Movement is extraordinarily important in our process. By just allowing the Soft Palate to pull back, you will understand the Movement of high Air and will have made a very important discovery. Do it often to remain very familiar with this process, and make sure you allow yourself to be aware of this Movement at all times. Do it in front of a mirror and see what happens.

The Portal Bones not only serve as guides for **up and back which is essential in our process**, but also serve as sentinels, to make sure the Voice never falls below this point. As long as the Voice is above the Portal Bones, (the Soft Palate is attached by tissue - now it makes more sense) you are in a safe zone. You are *only* SAFE when Sounds move above the Soft Palate inside the 'Chamber', always and forever up and back. Please consider that if Sound is not moving above the Soft Palate it moves below it - that immediately involves the mouth and the Throat which is precisely what we do not want.

Most of us speak from inside the mouth. If you check yourself, you will see that you make the words right around the area of the portals. Well, from now on be mindful NOT to create your words inside the mouth. Please remember that for later. It is a little too early in our discovery to go into more detail, but please understand that the Portal Bones are very important.

The minute the Vowel Sound falls below the portals, you will crash into the Throat, the Tongue will rise and the Throat will close. The Air will then have to push forward in order to get anything (Sound and words) out. That is a "no-no!" Please cultivate this Movement of Air and you will notice that the further you are able to stretch the portals backward and upward, the further back the Soft Palate will rise. That ultimately means more height, width, vibration and size of Sound.

This is Movement of Air and the lifting of the Soft Palate is NEVER, EVER to be confused with making Sound inside mouth, or vibrating and manipulating the vocal cords and Larynx to achieve Sound or vocal quality.

Now, let us recap "high Air" and what will happen when the Movement is correct. Three things will automatically occur:

1. Your Soft Palate will lift upward and backward because it moves with the Air and with the help of the stretching of the Portal Bones backwards. You can also watch the uvula rise toward the roof of your mouth. It will almost disappear in the process. Once it (the Soft Palate and the uvula) is in the up position, no more Movement of Air forward or downward, ever.

2. As your Soft Palate and uvula rise, your Tongue and Larynx will drop, completely opening your Throat. If you have a highly developed Adam's apple, you will see it drop with this process; if you have a smaller one, you will still feel the Movement of the Larynx downward.

3. The Air will automatically move down the column of Air and your Diaphragm will inflate like a balloon, using your natural energy to expand it (the Diaphragm) outward. It instantly fills up with Air. Allow this to happen effortlessly.

These three things must be accomplished with the high Air from the mouth- - every time, no exceptions. This discipline is the beginning. You will be ready to take the next step once you: 1) get used to the idea of ***allowing*** Air flow into your mouth without inhaling into the Throat, feeling the coolness on the Soft Palate and its Movement backward and upward, and, 2) know that that Air Movement "moves" your Portal Bones and 3) experience the drop of the Larynx and the Tongue, which opens the Throat and the expansion of the Diaphragm.

A note of caution here: Do not breathe through the nose for the moment. ***Forget that the nose exists***. Concentrate only on developing the sensation of allowing the Air to flow upward in your mouth and remember: Guide the breath upward mentally past the Hard Palate onto the Soft Palate. Never lead the Air downward into the Throat. If you lead down into the Throat, that's where everything will begin and end – exactly what you are trying to avoid. So be very conscious of always feeling for the sensation of Air on the top.

Now feel the connection of the Air to the Diaphragm. What goes down must also come up again. By slowly pulling inward on the pelvic muscles, which are located all the way on the bottom of your belly and sort of hold up the Diaphragm, the Air will slowly rise. In women we call these the 'baby muscles'; in men they are located just above the groin. With the help of these muscles, the Air is once again gently moved upwards, in exactly the same way it came down. The Throat must remain open, the Larynx and Tongue must remain down and the Soft Palate must be in up position. The Movement is always gentle as to not disturb the open Throat. If you pull inward too hard, the Soft Palate will rise too high and Sound will wind up sharp; if you do not pull enough, the Soft Palate will eventually lose its height and the Sounds will be flat.

It is extremely important when using the Diaphragm to understand that it is used ***only*** as a support system for the Soft Palate and Open Throat, it is ***not*** the system *of moving Sound*. ***It must also be clear that the Soft Palate is the support system for*** *the entire system. Without a raised soft plate and uvula, pulled back Portal Bones and an Open Throat nothing will work!*

The Diaphragm has nothing to do with the actual "size" of the Sound, but has everything to do with the support of the Sound. **Anyone who tells you that the Voice starts in or with the Diaphragm simply has no clue!** The Diaphragm is necessary as a support system for the Soft Palate and Open Throat - that is it. There are Voices that are in such perfect position and so well trained that the use of the Diaphragm is relied on very little. When everything is really set up correctly, the Diaphragm works on its own without your having to do much of anything. Its action and re-action is natural.

Essentially, what you must understand is that the 'Voice' is Air; and the more Air it receives, the more beautiful the Sound will be. The Diaphragm has a function, an important one and has to be understood and utilized properly.

Taking this premise into consideration, the building up of Air, the strengthening of the pelvic muscles and the flexibility of the muscular Movement of the Diaphragm will be important when the time comes. The more Air you naturally get into the Diaphragm, the more you will have available for Movement later. Having said that, I will reiterate that there are Voices that will never need to worry about that, but really, they are few. Please, cultivating the expansion and Movement of the Diaphragm is important to most singers.

Please remember that the Air must move through an Open Throat without constriction or interference of any kind. The Movement of Air through the Throat must be smooth and not be felt by the Instrument in any way. This is vital. The Instrument has to be free to use the Air in the way it needs to, without manipulation of any kind by you….none. (I do not consider the use of the Diaphragm manipulating the Voice, only supporting it).

The deeper the Air in the Diaphragm, the more powerful the muscular function of the pelvic muscles, the more the Soft Palate can rise and remain in a raised position. Remember, depth is height.

I recap: Do **NOT** take your mouth Air by inhaling it, but by allowing and feeling the Movement of the Air entering your mouth. Keep the natural drop of the Jaw – no greater opening is necessary. Speaking position is your guide. The more relaxed the jaw, the facial muscles and the Throat, the easier it is for the Air the move where it needs to go without pressure or force. Any Movement that causes tension to the system is wrong! This allowing of the Air to enter must be deliberate by thinking and envisioning it. You have to "do" nothing physically.

Your knowledge, that the Air enters an open vessel (the mouth), what it has to accomplish and how it must be used, is all you need. The mind does the rest. That knowledge accomplishes a high Soft Palate, a dropped Tongue, which is majorly important for an Open Throat. All these elements are the key to a relaxed and healthy Instrument, which, in turn, connects to the Diaphragm, establishes firm support for the Soft Palate and provides enough Air for the ultimate speaking of the **consonants "outside"** the mouth. **Consonants *only* are 'dictioned' at the outer part of the Lips with the help of the Front Teeth and the tiny Movement of the Tongue.**

I will just give you a couple of examples to help you understand better.

Visualize of a fountain that is thrusting its water up into the Air. Picture a ball on top of the water and imagine the ball being lifted by the water pressure and kept in place. Then think of the fountain suddenly being turned off. What happens? The ball immediately drops hard. The same holds true with the Sound. Drop the pressure of the Air from the Diaphragm, and the Soft Palate will fall instantly. When that happens, the Sound position falls, and you are right back where you started from — in the Throat. It is therefore crucial to make sure that the Soft Palate always remains raised. That in turn automatically keeps the Tongue down low in its bed, and allows the Throat to remains totally relaxed and open.

Another analogy: Think of an oil drill digging deep into the ground. Suddenly it hits oil - the black substance shoots up into the Air. If there is nothing to catch it, the oil will simply return to the ground and diffuse once again into the earth. Well, for our purposes, the Air is the oil, and the Soft Palate is the receptacle. You get the picture.

Now let's talk about the Larynx and Open Throat for a minute. If there is deliberate Movement of Air in the Throat, you will have to push the Sound forward. The Larynx will come up and try to help you make the Sound and therefore close the Throat. The Sound will be much lower than it should be (you may experience phlegm and scratchiness). That is unacceptable.

In my opinion, the *laryngeal vibrato* (vibration created by the Movement of the Larynx) is a <u>serious defect</u> in the Voice and is the beginning of the end of beautiful singing, causing the dreaded wobble in the Sound.

Statement: The Air and Air Movement create Sound vibration naturally if and when the Voice is in the correct final position. Anything and everything else is wrong and harmful to the Instrument.

Pushing Air forward closes and constricts the Throat and the Air can no longer move freely to keep the Soft Palate raised. You can then pull in on the Diaphragm all you want, but the Air will not pass through a closed Throat. You will push and force. NO!

The Larynx must remain in a down and relaxed position at all times; the Throat must be open in order to let the Air pass freely and reach its ultimate target—the Soft Palate and The Hole.

You must always be aware that as you are reaching the heights of the Soft Palate you might feel a head rush and become slightly dizzy. Do not worry. This is the Air moving into/through spaces where it has not been before. Continue to strive for the height and the depth of the Air. It is an indication that you are on the right road. As the body becomes used to it, this heady sensation will go away. At this point, you are learning to open higher spaces. The closer you get the Air to the Brain, the dizzier you will feel but with constant use, the Brain will get used to the extra oxygen, and the dizziness will stop. Please remember this for later on.

Did you know that the greatest enemy of the Voice is your Tongue?

Well, think of it. Most of us move the Tongue backward when we sing. It's one of those reflexes which definitely are not in our best interest. The Tongue must be flat and limp at all times. It must lie relaxed in its bed and be used only for the purpose of excellent diction. It must never - I repeat **NEVER**- move to the back or rise up in the back. If it does, it closes the Throat immediately. Try it, and you will see what I mean. Make a real effort to keep the Tongue flat. Rest its tip against the roots of your lower Front Teeth and keep it there until you need it for making your words, just like in speaking. You might find it difficult at first, but it is essential.

Most of my students consider this a big problem, because they never before paid attention to the Tongue or to Open Throat for that matter. Keeping the Tongue still is an absolute necessity in our progress. You might say, "But aren't there some singers who lift the front of the Tongue up - famous ones at that?" True, but besides being wrong, it is downright unsightly and uncomfortable. Since Open Throat must be accomplished and most singers don't know how to do this, they use the lifting up of the tip of the Tongue as a crutch. Notice that when you do this the Throat opens. Keeping the Tongue still and relaxed is essential. Keep it limp, flat and down.

To recap our first steps again:

Guide high Air from the Front Teeth past the Portal Bones and the uvula all the way into the back, toward the Soft Palate/Hole.

Lift the Soft Palate with high Air and the help of the Portal Bones. (The Soft Palate is the soft place all the way in the back on the top, where you feel the coolness of the Air.)

The Tongue and the Larynx drop naturally.

The Throat opens automatically.

Allow the Air to move down through the column of Air to reach into the Diaphragm. The Diaphragm expands naturally. The pelvic muscles immediately lock up and begin pulling the Air in and up, thus keeping the Soft Palate in a lifted and high position.

The Larynx and Tongue remain down, and the Throat is open as the Air passes through.

Always think of leading the Air far back and high up toward the Soft Palate. That will cause a pulling back sensation of the Throat and a greater opening. As we continue, you will experience the opening of the Throat by various other means. Please keep in mind, the further the Throat opens the freer the Instrument will be to play, as it should.

One thing that may help you conceptualize the Larynx more easily is the fact that the vocal cords are in a box (Voice box, in common terms). There should be no voluntary Movement inside that box. Remember the violin? In order to tune and play the Instrument properly, it had to be removed from its case and placed into its rightful place under the chin.

The Larynx will try (since those muscles have been used for this Movement for a long time) to come up and help you, but they must be kept down under all circumstances. NO MOVEMENT PLEASE. The steadier you can keep the Larynx, the easier everything I am explaining here will be for you. Please make a most serious effort. (If you are singing from the right place and the Larynx comes up, you will hear the most awful gargling Sound and feel real discomfort.)

When a box is closed, nothing or little can come out of it. There is no exit from the bottom of the Throat. In order for the Air to do its thing, it must rise to the top. That is where we want it, above the Soft Palate. For now, please try it that way. Later we will add other features that will enhance and grow the space we need for the Voice.

Keep the Tongue flat and limp at all times and use it only for pronunciation and articulation (diction/consonants) of the words, just as you would in speaking. The most important thing high Air does is to lift the Soft Palate, drop the Larynx, open the Throat, and attach this Air to the Diaphragm. Once the Soft Palate is lifted, it is imperative that it remain in the high position and not move. If there is Movement on the Soft Palate, it can be heard in the final Sound and that is unacceptable.

Notes

How to Move the Air

We talked about high Air from the mouth. Now let us become more precise. What exactly does that mean?

Think about it. If you move the Air down toward the Throat, you are empowering the Throat. The Air is stuck in there and the only way out is to push it out of the mouth. So, as we learned, allow the Air to move up to the Soft Palate and feel the coolness and the lift and the opening (Hole, Open Throat, and lowered Tongue) each and every time.

Open the mouth just slightly, as we did before. Concentrate on the Air just beneath your upper Front Teeth, passing the roof of your mouth. Feel the Air moving backward and upward, past the Hard Palate, the uvula and the Portal Bones, lifting the Soft Palate. This is the natural passage of Air; everything else is unnecessary and will not achieve the desired results. Only when the coolness of the Air hits the back of your Soft Palate, you are in the right place.

Now visualize (being able to do this is very important) the Air hitting the back of the Throat, lifting the Soft Palate, opening the Throat, dropping the Tongue and the Larynx and moving (Air) downward into the Diaphragm. Then picture the pelvic muscles locking up, pulling the Air back up through the Air column toward the Soft Palate. All this takes just a second. Now you have two Air sources on top of the Soft Palate: Air from high "breath" and Air from the Diaphragm. Both sources converge on the Soft Palate lifting it up to maximum height, opening the Throat and exposing The Hole, all the way in the back of your Throat.

When you look at yourself in the mirror and watch yourself allowing the Air to enter as we discussed, you can see the space where The Hole is located. With some people, you can actually see the indentation; with others, it is covered; but in all cases, the space, which is located in the very back part of the Soft Palate, seems to be pulling further back as you pull on the Portal Bones. Try always to have this picture in your mind. It is quite important that you see what is happening there in your mind's eye (the Third Eye).

Put tea tree oil on your thumb and stick it straight back into The Hole until you feel bone. "Disgusting," you may say. "It makes me gag…"

True. Watch a moment and notice that if the Tongue is down, you won't gag. It is the reflex of the Tongue that makes you gag (we will discuss this in great detail later). Pull the Air slightly upward, and your thumb will enter into The Hole, just beyond the Soft Palate; lift gently. You will feel the upper end of The Hole, and now you will easily understand into how the Air moves through the tissue into The Chamber and the final position of the Sound. This is a large space filled with great possibilities. This space is imperative in the understanding of Air Movement.

It is from the "Hole" that the Air passes into the Giro - *"the turn of the Air/Sound"*. The important thing is that you find The Hole and are mentally able to lead the Air to it. This entryway is ultimately responsible for creating the bottom of the Giro. I refer to this as the "back door."

At his point we have the Air in The Hole all the way in the back. What now? How do we move it? What happens next?

High Air has moved the Soft Palate upwards, has opened the Throat and The Hole and created the low end of the Giro. Air now enters the Giro (the actual bottom of the turn of the Sound), and floats above the Soft Palate into the cranium, then turns above the Brain in an empty space and exits (See drawing, *Air Movement*).

The reason for the upward Movement of Air is simple. It is warm (98.6 degrees) and warm Air rises. For us, this Movement is crucial, because on the **up-swing** of that Air, we allow the Air to "pick up" the Sound and the Vowel. The "Vowel-Sound" will then be produced inside the "source space," (we will define this later), turn over, and angle toward the Third Eye.

Speaking, and only the Intention of Speaking, will then complete the Movement by pulling the Sound and Vowel toward the intention of word which is at the top part of your Lips, directly at the Front Teeth. ***It is there, and only there, that Sound and word come together***. If this is not achieved, Sound and Vowel will be in the mouth, in the Throat and must be pushed forward – no choice. ***All of your vocal problems stem from here***. PLEASE REVIEW THIS CONCEPT MANY TIMES UNTIL YOU FULLY COMPREHEND IT.

There is only a split second between the raising of the Soft Palate, the turning of the Sound and the actual exit of Sound and word.

We will call this moment **"Lag Time. "**

You must understand that it is the ***Intention of the Word*** that moves the Sound when it is in final position. Nothing else! Once the rising Air has produced Vowel

Sound (literally picked it out of your Brain), the Intention of the Word will take just as much Air as it needs in order for Sound and word to couple and exit together.

This is a very important thing for you to remember: The more forward (at the Front Teeth, at the Lips) the Intention of the Word is, the higher the Sound will move inside the Giro. The word **intention** is crucial here. Intention is mental, not physical, so all you will ultimately have to do is intend the word to be forward, and it will be. (The exact space we are talking about is right at the tip of your nose and the space above your upper lip.)

YOUR THOUGHTS PROPEL THE ENTIRE SYSTEM. YOUR KNOWLEDGE COMMANDS...YOUR BRAIN HAS TO BE IN CHARGE.

Never push the Sound! Never push the Air forward. Think only of keeping the Air moving upward and backwards. The Air, which moves up from the Diaphragm, keeps the flow of the Air to the Soft Palate, making sure it is lifted at all times. The Soft Palate keeps the Giro and the Sound Movement in position. The more flexibility of the Soft Palate you develop (Movement with Air); the higher the Sound can rise. Speak the words as forward as you possibly can. Feel the vibration of the word at your Front Teeth and the top of your Lips.

Do not make the word (Vowel Sound) in the back or anywhere inside the mouth.

The back (Soft Palate, Hole, the opening of the Throat, etc.,) always remains till and non-moving; the word (consonant and Vowel Sound combination) is always made in the front at the Lips—the combination of Vowel Sound and consonant (word) occurs only on the outside, never on the inside of the mouth.

Only when there is this distinction between Vowel Sound and consonant - and they both have their own "distinctive" position/production - will the Voice be in place, remain in place and circulate in a rotary motion above the Soft Palate, without ever touching the Throat. In other words, the Soft Palate is the dividing point for what is happening: the Sound moves above the Soft Palate inside the Giro, and, 2) the mouth cavity, the opening of the Throat, Soft Palate etc., simply provide the support system for that Movement and allow the Instrument to 'play' as it was designed.

Please, be very clear:

You do not know/or will ever know, how to 'move' the vocal cords to make them do exactly what you want - only your Brain and your Birth-Knowledge know that. You can try, and many do. You may think that by physically vibrating the cords you are achieving the true vibration of Sound – wrong. You can push, force, and think that you are in control of their functions – but you are not. It is the Brain, which knows how to play the Instrument; it is the Brain, which moves the Instrument, and **it is the Brain which determines** where and from where the Sound will be taken, to be properly produced by the **Instrument.**

Therefore, what I am saying here boils down to this:

"You are in total control mentally. The physical expression, Sound and word, is a mental process. Your 'mental' self controls the physical; the Sounds produce themselves inside the Instrument naturally without YOUR physical involvement (pushing, forcing, straining etc.). You're thinking correctly and knowing the process is what ultimately produces the results inside your Instrument naturally. The more you think this way, the easier it will become – the more you fight it, the more resistance you will experience. **Allowing this** to actually happen is majorly difficult – but that is what it's ultimately all about – Being in total control without physically controlling and manipulating the Instrument. **YOU ARE THE SPEAKER OF SOUND, NOT THE CREATOR**.

If you move the **word** backward, you will **collide** with the flow of Air, which will raise the Tongue immediately, close the Throat and make you push forward in order to produce the "word" combination (Vowel Sound and Consonants). If Vowel Sounds are made in the mouth (as most singers/speakers do), the pressure created inside the mouth and on the Soft Palate will cause the Sound to be stuck and eventually cause a wobble.

Result: Low Sound in the Throat, pressure and forcing, inability to continue singing for a long period of time, difficulty in speaking clearly, will ultimately result in "Potato Sound". The Sound will simply close the Throat, thereby closing off the Air supply and you have no choice but to push forward to release the Sound through the mouth; you are then forced to engage the Jaw. You will notice most singers today use the Jaw. Sometimes, there is so much tension that it actually wobbles and then, of course, so does the Voice. The Jaw must **never** be held, never be tight and must open only as it would in speaking - the natural drop of the Jaw! No more.

Very important to remember: If you lead the breath into the Throat, you are empowering the Throat. The Air has no other exit than to push out against the vocal cords, using the Jaw and the Throat muscles to achieve this. If, however, you keep the breath high and up above the Soft Palate, the body reacts naturally and the Air can move freely and support the Soft Palate without ever engaging the musculature of the Throat. The Instrument can "play" without pressure.

✫ ✫ ✫

Let us stop here and talk about some other important concepts.

I know most of you think there is some magic formula to the Voice. I hate to disappoint you, but there is not.

There are, however, a number of rules that must be observed at all times. This part is not creative. This is machinery, detail, nuts and bolts. This is technical execution. It must be the same way, every time, consistently, no matter how high or how low the Sound. The more mechanical the intake and distribution of Air, the more freedom you will have for the interpretation of music and the lyrics, and the less you will have to worry about running out of Air or having the Voice fall. It is just like starting a car. You turn the key in the ignition - go; you shift the gear - it moves - you give it gas, and you are on your way.

Allow the Voice to be natural. Get out of its way. Let it do its own thing. The Voice knows instinctively where it has to go; it really needs only limited help to move the Sound from where they originate. What it does need is for you to know how to guide and distribute it correctly; the right mechanism will automatically be engaged to produce proper action.

The Sound ultimately needs to be spoken and properly supported. You **cannot make** the/a Voice. The less you do as far as actually manipulating the Sound, the better. Count on the knowledge you are providing to the Brain and its innate knowledge of the Instrument. Be in complete control of all the important functions we are talking about, but *give up your control of Sound production by laryngeal manipulation*. If you are physically involved in Sound production, you will manipulate the Sound. Allow the Brain to "produce the Sound" it hears and perceives. Only it (the Brain) knows where and how to find the right Sound and word combinations and where to create them. Only in this way will you be free to speak, interpret, and allow the Instrument to achieve its maximum potential.

Your job ultimately is to think the Sound and word combination and then speak it!

By the way, have I mentioned to you that you already know everything I'm teaching you here? The information I am providing you with, is not new to you; consciously it is, but subconsciously the Instrument already knows everything we are discussing here and identifies with it. The Instrument was given to you in perfect working order along with the original package of your talents and attributes. I call this Birth-Knowledge. All you and I are doing here is rediscovering the original blueprint. I am bringing it back to your conscious mind by re-familiarizing you with the original set of instructions, which along the way, seem to have been misplaced or forgotten.

If you feel the Voice **IN ANY WAY** (other than what we will determine in the end of our work), you are definitely doing something wrong. The natural Voice is free and easy, relaxed and uninhibited. There is no need to force it, ever. Pull the Diaphragm a little harder for very high notes, but make sure that the Air never, ever pushes the Voice forward! Allow it to flow from you. Guide it, but do not force it.

When you are in the final position of the Voice, you will not feel anything. It will seem that it is floating on Air – and of course it is. You will feel vocally out of control. You will think the Voice is somewhere above you, outside of you—and it is. The feeling is totally liberating. Wait until you discover how utterly fantastic singing can be.

See the Voice. Visualize the spaces, the places, and the system. The more in tune you are with your body and mind, the more successful you will be in arriving at your final destination: a beautiful, trouble-free Instrument which is tuned to perfection. The Sounds are visible if you open yourself up to it. Close your eyes and allow the Air to be your guide. We will discuss more about visualization as we go along.

Until now I have not mentioned a very important part in our quest for the Voice: *The Third Eye*. It sits in the middle of your forehead between your eyebrows, above the bridge of your nose. It is extremely important, not only when you are actually visualizing Sound, but for over-viewing the entire system. If you close your eyes and concentrate, you will find that you can actually see through the Third Eye. Sounds dance before you. You can see the Air carrying and 'spinning' the Sound; you can see the pelvic muscles flexing; you can see the opening of the Throat and the dropping of the Tongue and Larynx resting in their down position, you can see the Sound floating over the top of your Brain and exit through the Third Eye.

The Third Eye opens up another dimension to the Voice. By cultivating its opening, you are not only privy to the secret of the Voice, but also to the secrets of the universe. The more you see the Sound through the Third Eye, the more you are concentrating on the top portion of your head, the better your chances of reaching the highest possible position. Try it. I am sure you will open yourself to a whole new way of *touching* the Voice. (The Third Eye, by the way, is a physical opening. If you look at an x-ray of the skull, you will readily see it…the fact that it conceals a vital spiritual connection and how it does so, will be discussed later).

Do not make the Voice. **The Voice cannot be constructed, it must be instructed**. The Instrument is already there. All you need to do is tune it. Don't try to be something you are not or make the Voice into something it is not.

If you are a light Voice, don't try to be a dramatic Voice. Accept your gift and do the best with it that you can. Use it wisely, because if you don't - the ONE who gave it will take it back, and you will lose it. Allow the Brain to take over; neither force nor push is needed; common sense and natural instinct will go a long way. If it feels right, chances are that it is and if you do not feel it at all and it virtually moves on its own, it is perfect. That does not mean that you should work haphazardly, or without using all the tools you have been given so far. All I am saying is that any kind of strain, feeling cramped or need for pushing is unnatural and should never be part of your vocal training.

I do not know how many singers I have met who have told me that throughout their studies, they knew something was wrong with the way they sang. They felt it … the sixth sense of the singer. Go with it—always!

Listen to your inner Voice in truth without deluding yourself into thinking that you know the answers. You will know the real TRUTH.

I have taught countless student and not one has ever complained to me about experiencing discomfort of any kind, when using this method. On the contrary, they were amazed at the comfort they felt. I constantly ask. The kind of relationship I have with my students is one of total frankness. We talk about the Voice, their feelings and exactly what they are experiencing, mentally and physically. I feel very strongly that excellent communication between teacher and student is necessary in order to produce the results we are looking for. I know what I know from experience with my students and from… well, we'll talk about that later.

[Truthfully, I have actually stopped teaching students because I felt that the level of communication necessary to achieve positive results was not possible. Believe me; I have taken on much abuse because I really believed in someone before finally cutting the strings. As I said before – It is all a process and I too have to learn, sometimes at tremendous personal expense].

Do not stretch the Voice beyond its limits. Everyone has his/her own Instrument, and each Instrument is as individual as the person in whose body it is housed. How many wonderful Voices have been ruined because of straining beyond capacity? Why and for whom are you doing that? If you were blessed with a certain Sound, why make it into something that it is not meant for?

Patience is a virtue. In time the Voice will grow; it is a natural, physical (muscular) and mental process; but that growth should never be motivated by the needs of the career, the manager or money. Think of what you are doing. Singing repertoire that is inappropriate today means the loss of the Instrument tomorrow.

Oh, I know about pressure, the jet-age singer, the demands of the career; but I also know that Voices used to last for a lifetime and that the great singers of the past sang until the day they died - and they sang a great variety of repertoire. Their secret was that they never sang "out of their Voice." No matter what role or composer they approached (I am talking about classical and Opera singing here), they always sang in the same way, using the Instrument in the same manner. No changes, no bellowing or dropping the Voice to achieve a darker Sound, no fake 'chest'. Natural and free always! Listen to Gigli singing *Nessun Dorma* or to Caruso singing *Una furtiva*.

Darker and deeper, higher and more "vibratious" Sound is NEVER accomplished by pushing down on Voice, but by pulling it upwards and backwards. The larger the Giro (turn of the Sound), the more height and depth there will be to the Sound.

Many singers of the past would sing beautifully until the day they died. Very few singers today last that long - too few. Careers are short-lived, all because the Voices are overtaxed and technically used improperly. If you sing the way we are discussing here (and we are only at the beginning), your Voice will grow naturally and will serve you a very long time. So please, take care and do not overstep your vocal limits.

Trust in the Air. It is the lifeline for the Voice. It is always there when you need it. After all, it is Air that allows you to live. Most of the time you do not even think about breathing- it just happens. Take an example from that. Learn how to use this Air to your best advantage and make it work for you. Sounds too simple? Forgive me, but I cannot make it more difficult. That is all there is. Actually, as I said before, you already know everything that I am telling you. When you received the gift, it came with a set of instructions that you, unfortunately, did not follow from the beginning. Perhaps you think all this too simplistic. It just could not be right. It Sounds too easy. Yes it is, but please remember:

"The Voice is simple in its complexity and complex in its simplicity". If you get this, we are making progress. Don't be upset; today is the beginning of the rest of your life as a singer. If you really listen to your body, your internal Voices and instincts, you will see that they will not lead you astray.

I cannot tell you where specific notes are made. No one can and if they say they can…Oh well - It's up to you to believe or not.

Only the Master Computer, "THE BRAIN," knows where to put and how to create each individual Sound. I can only teach you where the places for the Sound are and how technically to get there. The rest of it is birth-knowledge.

These things which we are learning now, have nothing to do with Artistry. This is something that simply has to be learned, abided by and secured. **The technical aspects of Voice production can be applied to any Voice, male or female, high or low. It is simply the way the Voice is constructed.**

The idea that there is a different technique for a Tenor Voice than for a bass is absolutely wrong. G-d did not create different body constructions for different Voices. Larger, smaller, thicker or thinner, longer or shorter vocal cords indeed, but the *parts* are all the same; and the place where the Voice lives is also always the same. The cavity size of the mouth may be different, the head, the cheek bone construction, all that has to do with timbre and size and color – but it certainly has nothing to do with HOW to play the Instrument.

The consistency of technical execution is what makes it or breaks it. If you listen to Caruso or Chaliapin, you will hear the production of the Voice in the same place – the Sound, the pitches, the color, the size is different, but the technical aspects of their Voice production are the same. The extraordinary ring to the Voice, the wonderful height, the depth of Sound, the brilliance of tone that is what creates "mastery" of the Instrument.

If you master your body, your perceptions and inclinations, you can "master" the Voice – since we are humans and innately imperfect, we will always have to do the work in order to remain at top level. A runner never stops training…his muscles would not respond if he did not work on it every day; Well, for the Voice, it's exactly the same. You are in constant training. The Artistry comes with interpretation, phrasing, musicality, etc.

Great technique facilitates great Artistry; great singing simply does not exist without great technique. A synergy must be accomplished in order to achieve perfection in the Voice. Trust your Instrument and inner senses to know what feels right. **Guide** your Instrument to find its natural habitat. Accept it and allow it to happen.

Your internal listening and hearing are paramount, of course. Their message to the Brain is translated into action, and your body will do the rest. Focus on these three little words: **Listen, Interpret, and Execute!**

Listen internally to the Sound. Hear and see the Sound in your mind (Third Eye). Allow the Brain to interpret the music and find the exact position of each Sound and word (note). Execute by using what we have learned so far: high Air, Open Throat, pulling slightly in on your Diaphragm, allowing the Sound to move effortlessly. Then intend your speaking the words at the Lips and the Front Teeth. Pronounce properly. The Intention of the Word is extremely important and pronunciation is crucial. I cannot emphasize this enough. The more *forward (Lips, Front Teeth) you are in the positioning of the final words, the greater the potential for keeping Vowel Sounds in line.*

Remember: It is the **Intention of the Word** that moves the Vowel Sound; Vowels are created on the up-swing of the Air in The Chamber above the Soft Palate, not pushing and forcing. Sounds are always moving in one direction only: **upwards and backwards**—no matter what. *The lowest Sound, therefore, is the highest one up and the furthest one back - the highest Sound therefore, is also the highest one up and the highest one back.* **Since Sounds move only in one direction, there is absolutely no need to worry about changing positions for high or low Sounds or for high pitches or low ones. Once you are in the highest position, all Sounds only move further up and further back** *with the natural, internal flow of the Air. Sounds are never deliberately moved either forward or down***wards. All Sounds must stay in one line on the top and remain there always.**

Why? We are in an ***endless loop*** of Sound, inside the Giro. There is no beginning and no end. If you close the Air on the top of the Giro and at the Lips, you will have flawless Sound/word combination in your speaking and gorgeous vibrations and overtones – a homogenized Sound.

If however you close by lifting the Tongue or by closing the Throat, Vowel Sound will fall straight into the Throat. You can be sure that the next breath and therefore the next Sound will begin right there and you are right back where you started from. **Vowel Sound always begins on the top and ends on the top. This is a RULE!**

There is only one position for all notes. High notes, low notes, all in the same place. No dropping into the Throat for low notes ever, no pushing forward into the chest…awful and so bad for the Voice. In the Chest Voice Chapter we will profound this subject.

Everything is done in one place, ONLY. That is what gives you the coveted vocal line and a homogenized and even Sound –no matter how high or how low you need to go. Only there are the brilliant and gorgeous natural vibrations, overtones and harmonics, only in this place will the Voice feel natural, comfortable and effortless.

Stay in line, always following the Air upward and backward, toward the tips of your ears on the slightest angle.

Get away from the idea that Sounds have to be pushed forward and out of the mouth to be powerful and big. The word is always in the front at the Lips, comfortable speaking position. Understand that Sounds are always moving over the top of each other. The Giro moves up, never down, so ALL Sounds are always carried upward in a spiral-like motion, attached to one another (legato), never dropping.

If you can assimilate this concept, the battle is almost won.

Notes

Placing the Air

Now the Air is circulating in the correct place and your Soft Palate is up, your Tongue and Larynx are down and the Throat is open we can take the next step. The Diaphragm is extended, the pelvic muscles have locked up and you are slowly pulling in on the pelvic muscles to pull the Air from the Diaphragm back up - all the while keeping the Throat open and the Tongue and Larynx down. The Movement is very natural to the system – you simply are re-learning it. You almost do not have to think about it once you know it, because the body will initiate it, if the "Movement of Sound" is in the right position and if the Vowels are NOT formulated in the mouth.

Now please put some tea tree oil on your thumb and follow these steps exactly:

Start at the Front Teeth (on the inside of the mouth) and move the thumb back along the Hard Palate. You will feel a hard ridge between the hard part (roof of your mouth) and the soft part (Soft Palate). Pass the ridge and move your thumb all the way to the back. Feel your uvula (the little thing hanging from the roof of your mouth that has no apparent purpose), go past it, and when you get all the way to the back, where it is soft, push your thumb up gently. You will feel The Hole. Keep pushing up to familiarize yourself with it.

It is terribly important that you know precisely where it (The Hole) is. **Then move the Air, the way I explained before** and you will immediately feel that the Soft Palate moves up. Keep your thumb there and do it again and again and again until you get this.

In the beginning, this might cause a slight gagging effect in some of you, but in time, as you get more familiar with the feeling, this reflex will stop. For now, suffice it to say, that The Hole plays an incredibly important role in our work. The more you can get "into it," the better it will be for you. The most important thing you must remember is that the Soft Palate moves, but **that it really needs the Air to do so**. As long as you keep a steady flow of Air and you keep the Diaphragm pulling in gently to support it, your Soft Palate will move effortlessly as needed.

It is vital that you remember that the Soft Palate must move up toward the "top" of your head. Let me rephrase that. **Imagine - visualize** your Soft Palate moving up towards your Third Eye, while simultaneously pulling toward the back of your head. The higher the Air moves the Soft Palate in the up direction, the more space you will have inside the mouth. The further it moves toward the back of your Throat, the wider and rounder the Sound will ultimately be.

Let us call anything below the Soft Palate "bottom resonance chamber". The Voice moves from the ***top*** (of the Soft Palate) to the **top** (into the Third Eye), and the further the Soft Palate moves backward (with the help of the portals) toward the back of your Throat, the larger a space you create. ***THERE IS NO DOWN POSITION OR DOWN MOVEMENT*** (of the Soft Palate) ***EVER***!!

Everything depends on your understanding that the Voice/Vowel Sound, **move from the top** (Soft Palate) **to the top** (Third Eye) inside The Chamber – not inside the mouth.

If you move Sound or Vowel down, your Voice will fall into the abyss of the Throat and you have no choice but to push forward. If you start in the Throat and try to move up, you will have a break/crack in the Voice—and that's ugly. Stay up there and feel what happens. All of a sudden, you'll have an incredible height in the Voice—no more falling and no sudden register changes that make the Voice Sound different. The dreaded "registers": top, middle, and bottom are a thing of the past – the Voice is homogenized and even, no matter what changes there are in the pitch.

We are looking to accomplish total ease - no strain, no tension - and all because of this one little place. What a revelation! Try. Remember always to take into consideration the rules we talked about. Here are some more to add to the list:

Never pull on the Voice. Allow the Air to do the job. *The Air will not hurt you, forcing the Air will.* In other words, don't look to make the big Sound from the Throat—no manipulation of any kind, please. There is no need for pushing and forcing, the size of the Voice will increase naturally once it is in "final position" and moving properly. Get out of the way, mentally and physically. Allow the Movement to happen naturally. The power comes from the Air, not by pushing, pulling, or straining.

Try to keep your mouth as small as possible. Pulling the Jaw down will pull down the Soft Palate. All the work you are doing to keep it up will be in vain if you rip your mouth open. Remember that singing is speaking. How far does your mouth open when you speak? Please keep this in mind. It is vital. If you open too much, the precious Air will escape much too quickly, and you will not have enough to finish the phrase. Besides – try speaking clearly with your mouth ripped open – not very pretty or comfortable is it? The internal space will close as well and once that happens, it is the beginning of the end.

I know this is contrary to what most students of the Voice have previously been taught. It is my suggestion that you use your logic and try it yourself. You will immediately notice the difference. The actual vibrating/vibrations of the Sound come from a completely different place, about which you will learn later, (final position). Of course, there are times when you will have to open the mouth a bit wider…the body will tell you…but always be moderate and remember: not too much. Keep your speaking position as much as possible. Think of a reversed megaphone, large in the back (Open Throat) and small in the front (mouth opening).

All Sounds are produced in the same place. High notes, low notes, all notes - and all Voices. There is no need to switch your position. The top is your comfort zone, always and without exception. In order to achieve a homogenized Sound—top to bottom, even and harmonious- you must remain in one position. Only this will give you the coveted vocal line which, in today's singing is oh so elusive. You may color the Voice any way you want by just thinking and perceiving it, but always in the same place and never with the use of the Throat. You will never Sound like you have two, or even three different Voices; Registers never break into chest, middle, and head Voices. What nonsense! **What you need is just one beautiful Sound throughout the whole "range" of your Voice.**

Think of a violin. From the lowest notes to the highest, its Sound is even, beautiful, and in line. If you listen to the greatest classical singers of the past, such as Caruso, Gigli, Bjorling, Wunderlich, Pons, Chaliapin, Curci, Pinza, Flagstadt, Sutherland, Del Monaco, Ponsel, Tebaldi, Bastianini, Melba, Scipa (and even those who were not considered the greatest, but had only medium-sized careers until about 1965), you will hear that their Voices were all "placed" in one position. They stayed in that place and did everything seemingly effortlessly. No straining, no scratching, no flat or sharp notes - just gorgeous, floating Sound, all in one place.

That is the way the Voice was taught at that time. The natural placement of the Instrument is there. What has happened along the way is disastrous to the Instrument and those who are teaching methods of manipulating the Throat, falsetto, vibrato and all the "speech-level stuff", are responsible for the destruction of the Vocal Arts as a whole.

Float all Sound on the Air. Think of every note as needing its own Air in order to exist. Without Air, it fails; with Air, it lives. Our bodies need Air to survive; so do the Sounds we make. Always keep the Air high and as far back as possible. Do not drop it (Air) by pushing forward. If you do, you will disturb the natural Movement of the vocal cords and the Larynx—and you know what that means. Air moves all by itself, naturally guided by the process we are learning. Speech will take as much Air as it needs. Rely on the Lips, the teeth, and Tongue to **know** what they need to do.

Emphasize your words. If you do not place the words all the way in the front at your upper lip, at the outside of your mouth just by **intending**, you will obstruct the flow of Air and you will ultimately have to make the "words" inside the mouth. The Intention of Speaking is exactly that – an intention. The Brain alone knows how the whole thing works perfectly and how to move thoughts and Sound according to 'your desires'. Trust and Allow!

I cannot stress enough that the Sound and the words are made in two separate places: Sound and Vowels are above the Soft Palate and the words (consonants) are spoken with the help of the Front Teeth, Lips, and Tongue. You should feel a slight vibration of the words right under your nose on your Lips. The more to the front you are in your diction, the more you will free up the back and the top to do the work for you. If you concentrate on the word, the high Air will find its natural place and will do what it has to. So concentrate on your speech; that is imperative. Think of almost spitting the words out —not screaming, but really pronouncing and "dictioning" them.

Let your two Front Teeth be your guide. Use the tip of your Tongue and use your Lips, but keep all Movement to a minimum (just as in speaking normally). The less you move the mouth, the more stable the position. The "impostation" (positioning) of the word in the front is directly responsible for freeing up the opening on the top. Very soon, when we add the final elements to this puzzle, you will understand this point even more.

Imagine smiling in the back by lifting the Portal Bones. Put that smile also into your eyes and see what happens. Stand in front of a mirror and watch yourself. Imagine that you can only communicate with your eyes and that you wish to tell someone you love them, but only with your eyes. Feel your Soft Palate rise almost automatically. Feel your cheekbones raise effortlessly. Keep that smile in your eyes forever. If you do that, you will not fall nearly as easily because the Air is in a high position and in a much safer space. Believe it, it works like a charm. **Do not smile with your mouth until *after* you have finished singing.**

Always keep the Front Teeth delicately covered with your upper lip. Do not pull it (the lip) down, but simply *intend* to cover it. Pulling the Lips apart spreads the Sound; it squares off the back, and that is counterproductive. Our intention is to always keep the entire mouth cavity as round as possible. A square peg does not fit into a round Hole; and if you think of the entire system, everything is round: The Hole, the Soft Palate, the opening to the Throat, the Giro—all round.

Your facial muscles and your Jaw should be fully relaxed....as should be your chin and mouth. **All the Vowel Sounds are made behind your eyes**. Actually accustom yourself to speaking behind your eyes; that is, form your Vowel Sound behind the eyes.

You've never thought about the fact that the eyes speak, have you? Amazing! Well, it's high time you think exactly this way because with our work, you'll find that this concept will make the whole conversation come together and will keep you "high" at all times. Remember, THE EYES ARE THE MIRRORS/WINDOWS OF THE SOUL" and if you speak from the soul, you will speak truth and in the art of communication, singing and speaking, that is the key.

Have patience please! The 'final position' of the Sound is based upon everything we have discussed until now. Unless you are very familiar with this information, have internalized it, are able to visualize and conceptualize it, have made it a part of your total though process, you will not be able to accomplish it, it will not work. So please, as I mentioned before, one-step at a time, only then, move on.

Notes

The Giro - What is it?

The **Giro**, (also called the turn of the Sound or the endless loop of Sound) is the most important feature of the Voice. When you can feel it and conceptualize it, you will understand why the Voice stays in one position and how it is possible to make all Sound without switching to different places. All the notes that you ever want to make are made inside the Giro – the turn of the Voice. Round and round, forever turning and circulating in the *empty* space **above your Brain**. I hinted at it, when I told you, that the Voice moves up toward the Third Eye, and when I mentioned about pulling the Air back, thereby creating a larger space that will allow the Voice to widen and grow larger. This up-and back Movement of the Soft Palate facilitates the creation of the Giro.

When you listen to great singers, you will hear that they make Sound transitions with great ease; pitch changes from high to low are virtually indistinguishable, totally in line. The Voice just went to where it had to go… even and beautiful, a round and in-line Sound, without effort or stress on the Voice. *These singers were turning the Voice.* They were using the Giro. No register changes! NO PASSAGIO… NO STRANGE-SOUNDING HEADVOICE AND FALSETTO, certainly **NO *Laryngeal Vibrato***….Mezza Di Voce, piano, pianissimo yes, but nothing that was produced inside the Throat. We want to achieve that same, even Sound throughout the entire vocal line. That kind of Sound, vocal line and "control" is only possible when using the Giro, because *no position changes are needed*.

Of course you remember the Portal Bones and The Hole that we talked about before. You also know by now to smile in the back into the Soft Palate, which will heighten the sensation of cool Air, lift the portals and open the Throat wider.(Do not pull on the Lips, please; that will only pull the Air out of line and square the Sound.) Put your smile into your eyes.

You are also aware that by taking high Air, the Soft Palate and the uvula will rise and create the space needed to expand the Giro. And you know that the Throat has to be open and the Tongue and Larynx have to be down. So basically, all is set for the Giro to turn the Voice.

Now we are going to get a little more abstract in our thinking and feeling.

All the way in the back where the Throat ends, where your thumb could not go further because you felt a bone, there lays the" secret of the Giro... the secret of the Voice, the secret of life itself: *"The Bone of Life!"*

The Bone of Life is the beginning of the Giro, the springboard, the lowest part of the Giro, the depth of each individual note. Don't look for this term in the medical dictionary- you will not find it. Like the Portal Bones, it is an expression and image I use to help you understand where we are going.

Kabbalah, the ancient Jewish mysticism of the Torah (the Five Books of Moses), explains that the Bone of Life, which lies exactly between the bottom of your cranium and your first vertebra (Atlas), contains all of the DNA necessary to re-create a human being. It is said, that on the day the Messiah comes, all of those bones -the only remains of the human body which through the ages will not turn to dust - will once again be the basis for human forms and be able to once again receive souls.

I formulated my thinking many years ago, and understood why the secret of the Voice lies exactly in the same place. Find the place in the back of your head (it's almost like a little indentation) just in between the cranium and the first vertebra and familiarize yourself with it. Find the same spot internally by thinking and allowing the Air to move to the furthest point in the back of your Throat and you will have unlocked a great part of the mystery of the Voice.

If you allow the Air flow all the way toward the Bone of Life and keep the Air there as much as you can without pushing it forward, you will achieve the perfect lift-off for the Sound. From there, the Air moves up into the Giro and because of the free Movement of Air, you are assured of *homogenized Sounds that do not break "registers."*

I object to the terminology of 'registers' because when the Voice is in line the way we have just learned there are no "registers".   However for the sake of making you understand something that you in some way are familiar with I will use the term. **KNOW THAT ALL VOWEL SOUND (REGISTERS) ARE CONTAINED INSIDE THE GIRO.** All Sound, all colors, aperto/coperto (open/closed), chiaro/scuro (light and dark) —all of these depend upon the Movement of the Giro. All, I repeat **ALL**; Sound are inside the same endless loop of Air, that circulates inside and above your cranium. No switches of position are necessary to achieve an incredible diversity of Sound-*all are positioned in the same place.*

Sounds too easy to do? Is it too hard for you to believe? Is it too far out? Perhaps at the moment, but in my studies with my students, I have found time and time again that this concept has opened the door for them to understand the Giro perfectly. So I suggest that you give this a chance without prejudging. Let yourself experience the power of the Bone of Life and with it, the full opening of the Giro.

So, here we are:

High breath pulled back by the Portal Bones toward the Bone of Life, the"Hole"is opening naturally and the Air moving up and back into the Giro towards the Third Eye. This is your point of entrance. You will notice that in this position, you will have maximum capability of Movement, and the Sound will feel easy, round, and high. This is partially the way to get you into the final position.

Perfect this Movement and very soon, we will add the last fragment of our puzzle. Again, you might feel a little dizzy, and that's a good thing. *Please remember this place for further reference as we go along.*

The light-headedness comes from the Air. You are now able to move very high and can continue climbing. Think of your whole head opening up, better yet, imagine yourself without your scull covering your Brain…imagine everything opening to the top to accommodate the Air. Are you surprised at the height you can achieve? Well, don't be. Everything is possible with the Giro. It turns the Sound literally over the top of your Brain, in open space, exiting Vowel Sound through the Third Eye. The "Vowel Sound waves" then are sent to the Front Teeth and Lips in order to couple with the word (consonants) and exit together.

What you will begin to feel now is wonderful resonance in the entire mask and head (not to be confused with a nasal Sound which occurs when you squeeze the Air through the nose by pushing forward). The Voice will ring high, round, and be perfectly in position. The vibrations of the Voice will be perfect, so will the harmonics and the overtones. By the way, if you feel the Sound ringing in your ears, or if you feel a tickle in the ears, you are a little too low. Pull the Air further back and higher up and the Sound will move upwards, causing the ring and tickle in your ears to go away immediately.

Think of the Giro as a Ferris wheel. Round and round it goes. All the cars are attached to it and they, too, are going around. Imagine car #5. Get in it. The motor begins to move, and your car is climbing higher and higher through various positions. But car #5 always remains car #5. Well, that is the Giro. It takes the notes, on the Air, into the stratosphere—effortlessly. All Sounds are made inside the Giro. One great turn is capable of creating every Sound you will ever need.

If you drop Vowel Sound outside the Giro, you'll put pressure on the Soft Palate which will automatically drop or flutter. That puts the Jaw to work and initiates the drop of Sound into the mouth. Once the Vowel Sound is in the mouth, pushing forward is the only way-obviously the wrong way-to move the Sound out. Keep the Air high at all times in order to move the Giro and make sure that the Air from Diaphragm supports the Soft Palate, which in turn supports the flow of the Air inside the Giro.

Remember that the motor (Diaphragm) must never stop until a phrase is done. Keep the smile in your eyes always. In everything we have just described, YOU DO NOTHING other **than think the process**.

Physicality is replaced by mentality.

Because you know the process, it happens; because you understand the needs of the Sound, namely the correct entrances and movements of Air, the outcome will be extraordinary. The less you interfere with the knowledge we are putting into your thinking, the better, easier, rounder the Sound will become, the grander the expression of the word and the less control you will exercise.

This is your safety zone. Nothing can happen to you there. Stay and bask in glorious Sound. Perfect this position and you will never have problems. Only there can you be truly comfortable. Only there lies the real beauty and total freedom of the Voice . . . its roundness, depth, and height. Technically, this Movement must be achieved every time. This begins to open the door to the Voice; this combined with all the things we have yet to talk about, will allow you to become vocally liberated.

Now you know about the Movement of mouth Air, the Diaphragm, the Soft Palate, the Giro, and the way to move the Air from the top of the Giro to make the word. You see how easy it really is. This analogy might make it easier to visualize:

Think about a bow and an arrow. Think of pulling the bow string all the way back, tightly, until you cannot stretch anymore. Now release. The bow will fly in the direction into which you pointed it and hit its mark, depending, of course, upon how good your aim is. If you guided the arrow low, it will hit low. If you aimed high, that is where it will go. The expert shooter hits the center every time, because he is exact in his technique. That is what is required of you, and the way you aim the breath will determine whether you reach The Hole and the Bone of Life and go into the Giro, or not. Make this your top priority.

If you allow the Air to move high, the Air will move deeply into the Soft Palate, the Bone of Life, and The Hole and create a powerful Giro. The deeper the penetration of the Air, the higher the Soft Palate will be; consequently, the lower the Tongue will go and the more open the Throat will become. The further back you pull the Soft Palate on the top, the larger and rounder the Sound will be. If you concentrate on that, you will notice that the Air will go into the right place every time without your even thinking about it.

The whole procedure becomes instinctive and, after all, that is what we want. You do not have time to think about these things when you are singing. You have to worry about music, lyrics, the orchestra, a band, stage directions, your partners, a conductor, etc. The last thing you will want to think about is where to put the Voice and how to do it. You will be too involved with other things. It will take a little time for the Brain to understand this, but believe the freedom to do all the other things will far outweigh the momentary hurdle.

Think of a baby. When it is born, it can hardly do anything; but as it grows, it learns all kinds of responses. First turning, then crawling, then sitting, then standing and walking. Everything takes time. The Brain has to adjust the body to all the new information. The same holds true with what we are doing. For so many years, you have done it in one way. Now it is time to change. New information must be assimilated, and the Brain will do so; your job is to train the body, (the Brain, your muscles, your thoughts etc.) to think that way –

You must develop this thinking process. Always think, "up and back". and envision that the full and total Sound of the Voice **begins on the top of the Giro, in the Third Eye and ends on the top, in the Third Eye**. That is essential. Begin with the smile in the back. This Movement of the Air, as we are learning it, must become automatic and reflexive.

I think at this point you are sophisticated enough to understand the Giro. Now it's time to put all the parts of the Giro together.

Here is the final Movement which has to be achieved in order to produce a complete 360 degree turn of the Sound which begins at the Soft Palate, The Hole, the Bone of Life and ends at the Front Teeth and Lips, with the coupling and the exiting of Sound and word. Each Sound is made that way. Each Sound has its own individual Mini-Giro. (Coloraturas have Micro-Giros that turn extremely fast). No matter what you wish to do, and no matter what your Voices' color or size, whether you are male or female, young or old, have a large Instrument or a small one, the Giro lives and thrives and grows only in that place.

✿ ✿ ✿

The final step in creating the totally integrated Giro is the **NOSE**!

Remember in the beginning, I asked you to NOT breathe with or through your nose? I even asked you to forget it. I wanted you to learn how to move the Soft Palate and to understand the Bone of Life, the Portal Bones, their Movement, The Hole and, of course the beginning of the Giro.

Now, however, it is time that you allow the ***Air from the nose*** to ***simultaneously*** rise with the Air from the mouth.

Do not, under any circumstances pull the Air through the nose - do **NOT** "inhale" the Air. Do not try to move the Air up…DO NOT do anything other than allowing the thinking process to produce the natural result. If you physically move the Air, it will go down into the Throat and empower it. Simply think - allow the Air will be carried and raised through your nostrils to where it has to go in order to open ***The Chamber***… upwards and backwards, naturally, without any physical effort at all. Thinking that way will make it happen.

Think of smelling a rose; it's no more than that. Make believe you are in a meadow and dew fills the Air. **Flare your nostrils slightly** and allow the Air to move through the nasal passage, upward. There are six Air canals, which will immediately open wide and fill up: canals five and six are at the top, at the bridge of the nose, on either side of your nose - they mark the highest entrance of nose Air.

If you are having trouble doing that, take two Q-tips, and slide them up your nostrils very, very gently. Then pull both of them outward and allow the breath to flow through the open space. You will feel a real coolness from the Air, and it is that kind of feeling that you want to re-create every time. The bridge of the nose (canals five and six) becomes immensely important in achieving the highest opening to which we can lead the Air.

This is the front door of the Voice; the back door, as we already know, is made up of the Portal Bones, The Hole, the Soft Palate and the Bone of Life. When you are allowing the Air to lift up, through the nose to the bridge, imagine two big flaps opening outward and allowing a flow through of the Air. The Air then *diffuses under the eye sockets*, moves back past the temples, automatically lifts the Soft Palate to its highest position and allows for the full opening of The Chamber into the cranium.

Now the entire space for the complete Movement of the Giro is available.

Feel that - do it over and over. Those flaps and canals of the nose must remain open at all times. That is essential. By keeping this passageway free at all time, you are getting a constant and continual supply of Air. This Air supports the top of the Giro (the Third Eye), where you need to be. Please make sure never to push the Air into the nose or into the mask; always, as you have learned to do with mouth Air, allow the Air to enter the nose vessel naturally and always allow it to move toward the up and back position—toward the tips of your ears, past the temples, naturally creating an *expansion in the cranium* which you can easily feel. As the entire internal Chamber opens, you will feel the top of the Soft Palate rising to its maximum position. When you feel this opening and are dizzier than you have ever been, you know you are in the highest position of the Voice and the Air can now pick up Vowel Sound combinations and float them over the top of your brain in the empty space.

Just a quick aside here: There is no roadmap which physically tells you how to move Sounds. There are no signposts which give you an indication where inside the brain any one thought or any particular Sound is. No one knows – only the brain knows - your thought processes are lightning speed. There is no time to figure it all out – nothing would ever come out of your mouth if you had to 'go and find it" - even IF you (anyone)knew how to do that. Only the brain knows precisely where each and every thought is and how to create the Vowel/word/Sound combinations you need for speaking and of course for singing. Therefore it only makes logical sense that since it is all there already, it needs to stay and move only there.

You do not hear Sounds in your Throat – but you do hear Sounds and words and thoughts in your head – in your brain specifically – and if you hear them there, the only thing that needs to be done is connect to there and decide to 'share your thoughts by speaking them. Whether that is in speaking or singing is always your decision. Taking the thought/Sound/Vowel out of its natural habitat (the brain) is unnatural and can only lead you into trouble. **Caution – This kind of thinking has absolutely nothing whatsoever to do with 'Head Voice' – all Voice is in the head and there is no distinction except in your desire of how you want to color a particular Sound.** *It is in there that the final Movement of the Sound actually takes place.* This is where the Giro lives.

You will feel a lifting sensation. The Portal Bones are pulling up and stretching back, a further rising of the Soft Palate inside the mouth will occur naturally - you will experience the total drop of the Tongue into its bed, the drop of the Larynx, the opening of the Throat and the Movement of Air down the column into the Diaphragm.

Everything—the entire system—now functions as a whole. That lift of the Air through the nose completes the space for the entire position for the Voice.

`Again, when Air flows properly through the nose, you will feel the Soft Palate rising, the Tongue and Larynx dropping and the Throat opening, exactly the same reactions as mouth/high Air.

Both systems now work together, do the same thing and combine to create the entire structure of the Voice.

If you look at a skull, you will find that you can easily identify the openings. You can easily identify that the Soft Palate and the nose are connected and create sort of suction, a vacuum of Air, *lifting the combined Air upward and backward*. It is easy to understand why the system can only work properly going in the "up" direction, further and further, continuously pumping the Air into your head.

Perfect this motion slowly and smoothly at first, then more swiftly as you become more proficient. Notice that the Air moves up and back behind your eyes. Feel the actual Movement of the Air, the pull on the ocular muscles backward, propelled by the Air. Become very familiar with this place. This is the final number in the equation.

If you do this very naturally, you will feel the complete opening on the top, almost like a secret room opening up to accommodate the Air –that is The Chamber. There, and only there, is the true final place for moving the *Vowel Sound*. This location is the culmination point of all Sound. It is here that the 360 degree turn occurs – not 180, but 360; this is the home of the Giro. This is where it all comes together—where it all happens.

Only by allowing the Air to enter through the nose and mouth simultaneously (in the way with which we are now quite familiar) can you achieve absolute control of the Sound. Every time!

This consistency of Air Movement is really what this is all about. Doing it the same way every time; not thinking about it at all, just allowing it to be completely instinctive; trusting that the Brain, the knowledge which recognizes this spot as the true home of the Sound and the Vowel, will know precisely where every note goes—without your interfering. In either case, you can really do nothing physical in this place. *Here the thought and the Air rule*. The more freedom you give your thoughts to actually process the Sound, the better and more precise the Sound will be.

The Giro is by far, and without any doubt, the great secret of the Voice. Please read this Chapter repeatedly and train your Brain to think of the Voice in that way. I promise you incredible results.

Thoughts are what conceive and perceive Sound and words in the first place. Leaving things as they are meant to be is really the only way to achieve total freedom. Remember what I said before: ***You are the speaker of Sound, not their Creator***. Now this phrase should make perfect sense. In a way, you are actually doing both, you are in control without controlling – and you are totally controlling by thinking, and not by manipulation of the Instrument.

Let us talk about ***LAG TIME***, that magical moment in time that takes everything we have learned and in a matter of a nana second puts it all together for you.

LAG TIME combines simultaneous breath.

LAG TIME: allows the Air to rise to the top of the Giro and turn the Air.

LAG TIME: Allows the Soft Palate to lift to its maximum height – dropping Tongue, Larynx and thus opening Throat.

LAG TIME: allows The Chamber to accommodate the whole Movement of the Giro.

LAG TIME: Creates with your internal hearing and thinking all the Sound inside the Giro (the endless loop).

LAG TIME: allows the Vowel and Sound to couple all the way in the back, on the top, behind the eyeballs, at the tips of the ears, rise inside The Chamber and turn the whole Vowel Sound structure toward the word (consonant, Lips);

LAG TIME: Turns the Vowel Sound 360 degrees by the Intention of Speaking at the Lips, exiting Vowel Sound at/through the Third Eye.

LAG TIME: Moves the Vowel Sound to the Front Teeth to couple with the word (diction); combines Vowels and consonants at the Lips, with the help of the teeth and the Tongue and exit them together as Sound and word combination.

The Vowel Sounds, which always remain in the back, on the top, at the tips of the ears, can never turn over the top if you push them forward. They are instead moved by the circulatory Movement of Air and by intending to speak the word. Only in this way can Vowel Sound and consonants exit together.

This union occurs outside the mouth, never inside. The Sound and Vowel waves couple with the word and thus create the real projection outward.

This instantaneous action, which we have just literally taken apart, is in reality a split-second interval from its inception to its finish. Without Lag Time, without the turn, without this Movement, the Sound will not stay on the top. Instead, Sound and words will mingle inside the mouth and fall into the open pit of the Throat. With Lag Time, however, the Sounds are free to be turned by the Giro and brought toward the word. The entire system depends on it. This is how it moves together and this is how the freedom of speaking/singing is achieved.

Always speak the words, never try to sing them. The less you try to sing, the freer the Voice will become. You have no idea where the Sounds are. I cannot teach you, no one can – you have no idea where inside the Instrument (vocal cords) the Brain plays them.

What you now know, however, is how to attach yourself to the place where it all begins and ends. You also know how to support this Movement in every phase.

Let the rest be done by what has always known how to do it in the first place: The Brain.

Remember, you are the Speaker of Sound!!!

When you move the Air/breath simultaneously from the mouth and the nose, the Air from both areas comes together, turns over the top and moves toward the Third Eye. It is there you must think of beginning and ending the Voice. It is your highest point of reference and the perfect angle for Sound and word to couple and exit. Please, practice this constantly. The mille-second it takes for the Giro to turn and for the word to bring the Sound to the front in order to exit (Lag Time) is of the utmost importance. The more you concentrate on speaking the words in the front (Lips, teeth), the easier this will come to you. Remember that without observing Lag Time, word and Sound will begin in the back, and the Voice will fall into the mouth and the Throat.

In that split-second, all the Sound are constructed by the Brain, the sequence of thought, Sound, word is established - your Instrument is freed up to produce what is needed. Your only job at this point is to do the following:

- Allow the Sound to move upward and backward into the open space (you are always moving into the open space behind your eyes, toward the temples, toward the tips of your ears).

- Intend speech, the more frontal the word, the better (at the Lips, Front Teeth).

- Support the Soft Palate with your Diaphragm, which in turn supports the Giro.

Let this happen naturally. Your *"thinking"* the correct thoughts, is more important than your "doing". Allow Airflow toward the top, and you will feel the kind of freedom of which I spoke previously.

<u>Logical thought</u>: Warm Air rises, that is a fact. We allow the Air to rise through the nose; the Air warms, the flaps open, and the Air lifts. ***Sounds are made on the Air, by the Air and with the Air- another fact.***

Therefore, logically speaking, all Sounds must move upward and backward ONLY because Sounds move on Air, and the Air naturally is moving upward and backward – inward. Never forward.

Any intentional Air Movement forward therefore will push the Sound out of line and move it into the nose and the Throat. **Understanding that is the secret of the Movement of Sound!!**

Notes

Spinging:
The Primal Scream of the Voice

Another new term I'd like to introduce you to is **"Spinging"**.

Like some of the others coined concepts and words of mine, you won't find this in any dictionary either. It is a methodology that I have developed for and with my students. I have found spinging to be vital in training the Brain to understand the Giro.

Spinging is the combination of **speaking and singing in the same place**. Since they are, as I mentioned before, the same, you should have absolutely no problem doing this.

Imagine speaking in one place and singing in another. The switch is at best difficult and mind consuming, so why change at all? If you recognize that the singing and speaking Voice are in the same place, you have solved your major problem. We know that the Voice has to be on the top, behind the eyes, in open space, on top of the Giro.

Let us review how to get there and then learn how to **sping**.

Allow the simultaneous Air (mouth and nose) to flow upward. (The key here is 'allow'.) Make believe that you are smelling a rose. Feel the coolness of the Air lift your cheek bones and cranium, the Portal Bones, the Soft Palate. The Air is on the top of the Giro moving into the Third Eye. Always keep the smile in the eyes. This entire motion opens The Chamber behind your eyes to accommodate the turning of the Sound (Giro).

Follow the Air as far back and high up as it will go, and then, using Lag Time make a Sound—turning the Air, the Sound and saying the Vowel Sound "ee." You will find that you can almost feel the Air moving inside the spheres/orbits and behind your eyes. When you are aware of this, you will find the Voice very easily, because it is there that the Giro is made and the Voice can achieve true freedom.

Always allow the Air to move further up and further back **toward the tips of your ears**, while the natural up-swing of the Air (because of warming of the Air) creates the "endless loop" which turns the Sound and the Vowel round and round behind your eye sockets. **Vowel Sound must only move toward the top of the head on the up-swing of the Air.**

At this point, speak "ee, ee, ee, ee, ee, ee" at the front at your Lips, allowing the Air to pull up and back continuously. **Your ocular muscles behind your eyeballs will help you. There are four muscles behind each eye which I am sure you have not thought about and no one has ever told you about. I suppose if you have gone to an eye doctor for vision they might have been mentioned, but certainly not in conjunction with the Movement of the Voice/Vowel Sound etc. These muscles are vital, very powerful and work with the Air and constitute an extraordinary pulley system for the Air/Vowel Sound combination. There are actually six muscles – we only use four because those are in a 'pull back' position which is perfect for our needs.**

One of my students, came to visit me in Uruguay to study a couple of weeks ago and brought me a book about building eye muscle power for better vision. He was all excited because the specialists reported that 'the (6) muscles that encircle each eye are '150 to 200 times stronger than they need to be for normal use". (Cambridge Institute for BETTER VISION, Martin Sussman - Executive Director, ISBN 1-888534-12-5, 1998) Of course that goes along with what I had been teaching him all along. It is always interesting to me how information which is from another source other than me, makes my teaching that much more plausible to my students. We all need outside sources to confirm what really we already know.

So here are our most powerful allies for our Air Movement and here is the source to which you never knew to connect to before this work. No one ever mentioned it, no one ever thought about it. I have been teaching this information for many, many years and finally 10 years ago published the details of this information in my first book "The Voice".

Another thing on that subject. A few years ago 'contact lenses that breathe" hit the market and I got letters from all over the world telling me that they are now advertising that eyes 'breathe' and that now they (my students) totally understand what I have teaching them. Today is the beginning of the rest of your life – CONNECT!

Now that you know that this connection exists, that it is readily available to you in our work and that you have a complete guideline of how the work

is done, you can overcome any obstacle. Later on I will give the final mantra which will forever change your life.

Remember always that the intention of the word pulls the tension of the Air and Vowel Sound upward and backward and that the word (consonant) pulls the combination to the spoken word at the Lips to combine outside. This connection moves in two opposite directions continuously: Vowel Sounds upward and backward and the spoken Vowel Sounds over the top through the Third Eye combining with the Consonants at the Lips. This connection can never be broken – if you brake it for whatever reason, the Air will fall and Vowel Sounds will wind up inside the mouth.

Moving Air and Vowel Sound without any interference on your part, etc., until you think you have no more Air, becomes easy once you connect yourself to this thinking and knowledge. The fact is - there is always Air available - the Brain cannot live without it. The 'feeling' of not having enough Air is 'mental' if everything is in the right place. A forward Movement cuts the Air, which means that you have to 'inhale' over and over again – hence short phrases – it also means the Sound fell to the bottom where there is really very little Air available. When that happens, you begin to push forward. If you think that there is always more where that came from, your Air 'extension' will increase dramatically – Remember: If Sounds are moving upward and backward they are moving on Air, with Air and into open space. Long phrases and extended depth and height become therefore available without any effort.

Always end the Sound and the Vowel on the top the Giro, never on the bottom. In this way, in the beginning, you will achieve a small, vibrant Sound that you can then make very large by pulling further up and back, deeper and higher. The more you get into the head with the Vowel Sound, the better. Remember to always stop the Air /Sound/Vowel on the top of the Giro, at the Third Eye… which means, always end the Sound on the top of the breath, never on the bottom – never in the mouth and never in the/or with the Throat. When you feel a pulling sensation toward the back and the top of your head, it is correct.

This tension must never be lost - if you lose it, the Giro will drop the Vowel Sound. This tension we are talking about is created and maintained by the ***Intention of the Word,*** coupled with the upward and backward pull of Vowel Sound and Air. Please read this phrase repeatedly until you understand it and can totally relate to it. It is basic to our work.

The word (Consonant and spoken Vowel Sound) is always pulling toward the Lips and the Front Teeth -Obviously – if that were not the case, you would

not be speaking. That forward Intention of Speaking ensures that the tension of the Air and therefore the Vowel Sound, continues moving upward and backward.

Now start the whole process all over again, and you will notice that the Soft Palate naturally pulls higher, the Throat opens wider, the Tongue drops lower and the Diaphragm almost initiates automatically and naturally, while the muscles behind your eyes are pulling Vowel Sound further back and higher up. You will feel incredible vibrations resonating throughout your head, behind your eyes and in your mask. Your ears might ring. The feeling is almost indescribable; but once you have it, you will never let it go because you know it is right for the Instrument. Those are the vibrations of a healthy Voice—not the manipulated vibrato of the Larynx. Imagine that you are actually pulling Vowel Sound through the Air, turning them over the Brain all the way in the back of The Chamber, turning them over the top of the Giro into the Third Eye, round and round.

The eye sockets/orbits and Nose Canals five and six are your guides. Everything in your thinking and speaking begins there. Never must the Air or Vowel Sound drop lower than the Portal Bones.

The "spinging motion" fits the exact shape of the eye sockets. In the beginning, sping softly, and as you become more familiar with the process, add 'even' Diaphragm support to the sping and the sping will increase the size of the Sound considerably - not because you are using the Diaphragm to increase the Sound but because the Diaphragm keeps the Soft Palate up and the Throat open. The greater/wider the opening of the Throat, the more potential in the size of the opening in the Giro. **WHAT IS SET UP CORRECTLY BELOW WILL RESONATE APPROPRIATELY ON THE TOP!!!**

You will notice that the more you sping, the larger and wider the Vowels and Sound will become. More space is opening in the cranium; the joints (in the scull) are actually moving to accommodate the Air, and the Vowel Sound. Essentially, you are spiraling backward and upward toward the tips of your ears and past them toward the Bone of Life. The entire motion (Movement) completes the total ring (vibration) of the Voice. The further back you go, the larger the Voice gets. The deeper into the Giro you move the 'sping', the greater its potential for coloring the Voice, for achieving height and for Mezza di Voce - not ever to be confused with what is commonly called 'falsetto'. The name says it all – false!!!

On one breath you can achieve all your colors - piano, forte, pianissimo…in short, anything you want. By being able to control your thinking and your new knowledge, you are controlling the Air. By moving inside the Giro, you are free to do whatever you choose… All that is left is to SPEAK the SOUND.

Spinging is essential to the growth of the Sound, to creating the necessary space and for the vibrations. You may Sound like a fire engine… Please do not worry about it, just do it! In the end, those who understand what you are doing will be thrilled with the Sound of your Voice and those who may mock you and/or complain about the Sound you are making while spinging, really don't care or matter anyway.

– The END JUSTIFIES THE MEANS – and the 'END' is a great, healthy, beautifully tuned Instrument. Do not let yourself be intimidated. Stand your ground and sping, sping, sping!

✩ ✩ ✩

It is now time to choose a piece of music.

Begin by allowing the Air to rise simultaneously (mouth and nose). Keeping the melody and tempo in mind, begin spinging it exactly as though you were singing it but without the actual melody, just with the Vowels. Lead the Air into the absolute highest place. That should put you right into the top of your Giro. You will hear the Voice very, very high and buzzing inside your head. When that happens, you know you are in the right space.

Do not sing, rather sping into the maximum depth of the space behind your eyes, guiding the Vowel Sound upward and backward, toward the tips f your ears – listening internally all the while, lifting your Vowel Sound on the Air, turning them toward the Third Eye and propelling them with the Intention of the Word.

Imagine the Sound moving inside your head, one by one, higher and higher. **Please remember that pitch has nothing to do with position**.

The height of the Air does not determine the pitch because all Sounds are high and all Sounds are made in the same position. What ultimately determines the pitch, is your thinking and your speaking. Always keep that in mind.

Make each Giro wider than it needs to be. Concentrate on the Movement of the Portal Bones and the Soft Palate moving higher and higher - as far back toward the Bone of Life as you possibly can. See this Movement in your mind's eye and it will become a part of your vocal reality. Please remember that the only way into the sping is through simultaneous Air between nose and mouth and eventually … well, that's for a bit later.

The nose Air will bring you to the top of the Giro every time. But caution: Do not involve the Throat in any way under any circumstance!! You must not feel any pulling or tension in the Throat ever. It is imperative that the Larynx remain in down position and the Throat remain totally open, with the Tongue relaxed and low in its bed. Begin spinging gently and increase in volume as you become more confident and more familiar. The Soft Palate must be in high position; and the facial muscles must be totally relaxed, as should be the mouth, the Tongue, etc.

You are moving the Sound and Vowels in The Chamber behind your eyes (in the Giro) and with your thoughts and the Intention of the Word ONLY. Never allow the Diaphragm to relax. It is forever pumping the Air up gently in support of the Soft Palate.

After doing this a number of times, the melody will almost naturally come into the sping, because essentially, that is what you are doing— you are speak-singing. I ask you to please remember that even in spinging, like in singing, Vowel Sound move up and back only and follow each other, one Sound turning over the top of the other, because the word itself is liberating each and every Sound, so another one can form without effort.

The Voice becomes larger and bigger/louder and goes higher and higher, until you feel at ease with the piece you are spinging.

Now, begin vocalizing the whole piece in "ee." Simply sing the melody in "ee" and remain entirely in 'spinging position'. You will notice how easily even the hardest notes will come to you. After you have done that, attach the words and sing the piece. Believe me I have done this with my students thousands of times. Pieces that initially seemed impossible became easy and sat in the Voice like a glove. **Spinging is an essential way of putting a new piece of music into the Voice.** Don't worry about what you Sound like while spinging. Know that with every sping you are building the position and the size of your Voice.

You will also become aware that your speaking Voice will change in the process. It will be higher and will have more resonance to it. It is not that the characteristic timbre of your Voice will change, or that from a Bass you will suddenly become a Tenor; you will however notice a wonderful height and ring to the Voice that you never had before. The more you sping, the more the Voice will sit in its rightful place. The wider you sping toward the back, the larger your Voice will get; and the more depth you will achieve. It is a most powerful and wonderful tool. Use it to put your repertoire into the Voice. You will be truly amazed by the results.

The concept of spinging is incredibly valuable because you can totally get in touch with what "high position" really is. After a while, this will become natural and very necessary for you. You will automatically go into spinging position when you begin singing and that will give you the height and ring of the Voice that so many singers today lack. It will give you evenness in the Voice, a beautiful vocal line and an easy and natural flow.

There are those who simply do not like to sping . . . who feel that the Sound it makes is offensive ... they can't get into it and basically do not believe that it will do all it is cracked up to do. I have had students that have refused to sping-they thought it silly and unnecessary. Well, I certainly cannot and will not make people do what they do not want to do or consider beneath them; but from the long experience I have had and from the successes of those who have "spung" religiously—I strongly recommend that you give spinging a real chance to guide and build your Voice. This is work, this takes perseverance and this takes real desire to do it right.

Greatness cannot be achieved in a day and few have the "power" to become great because they lack discipline, faith, belief and the total commitment to what needs to be done, each and every day, each and every time. There are no short cuts. The difference between one singer and another is how serious she/he is and how much effort she/he is willing to expend in order to achieve their heart's desire. Single-mindedness and the actual doing of the work will yield extraordinary results.

This is my definition of greatness:

Doing the same thing excellently well, each and every time, all the time!!

Sping and dare to be extraordinary!

(In the Chapter "Putting Music into the Voice" we will apply all of what we have learned here)

Notes

The Art of Humming & Its Importance

We have talked about quite a number of things that I am quite sure are new to you. That is what this is all about – opening you up to the Voice and all its possibilities.

"What," you may ask, "could be new about humming? I know how to hum." Well, I am quite sure you do, but perhaps I can add something special and new to your humming experience.

Close your mouth almost completely. Leave open just enough space for the Air to enter in a relaxed manner. Then allow simultaneous Air from the mouth and the nose to enter The Chamber behind your eyeballs. At the top of the Air, all the way in the back where you feel coolness, release the first Sound, turn it and hum at the Lips. Do not forget that even in humming, just like in spinging and singing, Lag Time is essential. Do this a number of times, and you will find that the Voice automatically goes into the right place and easily makes mini-Giros without any effort whatsoever. You are floating Sound into the head.

Think of the Sound entirely behind your eyes and turn the hum around the Giro in the spheres of your eyes. Intend the word. Even here, the Intention of the Word moves the tension of the Air and Vowel Sound upward and backward. Vowels, which combine with Sound as I mentioned before, are made on the up-swing of the Air at the tips of your ears. The combined Vowel Sound and consonant constitutes the spoken word and meet (diction/consonants) in the front at the Lips, on the outside, not the inside of the mouth.

PLEASE do not forget that even in humming, the same principles apply as in speaking, singing, and spinging. *Always keep the point of the word at the mouth/Lips; otherwise, the Sound will fall.*

The more you hum in that way, the higher the Voice will go and the deeper toward the Bone of Life you will move. That is precisely what we want to achieve. If it is wrong, you will feel the involvement of the Throat, crackling, tension, or tightness. You will feel the Soft Palate dropping and the Larynx will rise. The Tongue will also come up in the back thus closing your Throat. This clutching of the Air inside the Throat will make it necessary to push the Air forward and virtually strangle the Voice inside the Throat.

When it is right, you will feel a heady sensation, perfect vibrations and clear, beautiful Sound.

Now, open your mouth slightly. Take your simultaneous Air, using your mouth and nose in the same position as when you were humming. Make the Vowel Sound, turn it and speak the Vowel. That is the perfect way of "positioning" the Voice. Humming just produces a smaller, deeper, headier Sound. Everything that we are structuring here is designed for one purpose only: to put all Sound and Vowels high and keep them there. All that we have done, from the very beginning of our journey until now, works together in harmony.

The further back toward the tips of the ears you hum, the easier the height and depth will become. The more you concentrate on reaching the Bone of Life and pulling your Sound up and back, the greater ease you will achieve. Hum often; it will help you familiarize yourself with the internal chamber, and you will ease into it without any difficulty... instinctively.

If you have trouble finding the position, allow nose Air to fully rise into canals 5 and 6, and close your nose immediately with your thumb and index finger. Hold it closed and 'place' the Vowel above the bridge of the nose, behind the eyes. The Air will then move backward and upward, pick up the Sounds on the up-swing of the Air and the turn of the Voice is accomplished. Keeping the nose closed in such a way shows you exactly where the Sounds are rotating and whether you are 1. Pushing the Sounds into the nose or 2. Into the mask...

Both of these options are absolute 'no-no's.

Remember that we are training the Brain to recognize the natural position of the Voice so that you can be as free as possible to concentrate on the music, the words, the interpretation, etc. Let the Brain, your thinking and your "intention" (which, of course, is no more than your thinking) do their thing.

Only the Brain knows exactly ***where*** every Sound, every Vowel, every word is located and by guiding the Air into the correct place and thinking the correct "knowledge", the Brain will direct you to the right place and produce the exact Sound and word combination you are thinking of. Your job is to get out of the way and let 'nature' take over. If you hear a nasal Sound, know that you are pushing Air forward into the nose, if the Sound and Vowels get stuck in the mouth, well, you know that it is wrong for sure and why. Stop, re-think and begin the whole process again.

✲ ✲ ✲

We are on a journey to find the natural Voice and in everything, we have discussed so far, we are essentially looking to achieve an alignment of conscious and sub-conscious knowledge.

Let me explain that a bit more clearly.

The sub-conscious mind clearly knows and has always known all this information. The conscious is cognizant of what it has been doing and what it has learned up to now (past knowledge) and what it considers necessary knowledge for processing information.

At this point, we are introducing new material, some totally opposed to previous knowledge, and the mind rebels and wants to go back to what is its comfort zone. When the conscious mind comprehends what the sub-conscious mind knows (i.e., all the information we are now programming), the alignment I am speaking of here will have been achieved.

Once this is done, the physical and mental balances are in line and the Voice will stay in place. This is not an easy feat to achieve. This takes time, effort, and a great deal of patience… **and it is not forever and constantly changing**.

The mind is a very fickle friend. If you do not continuously re-fortify this information, the old "thinking" will creep in again and take over. You are always and forever starting at square one. Progress will be seen in the very beginning and then the curve of major changes will taper off – you will only remain there if you continue to do the right thing.

If however you do not sping your new repertoire into the Voice, or if you sing things which you have done in a certain way in the past, in other words, if you have not "re-programmed" your thinking, you will invariably lose your gains and in a very short time return to your bad habits. Caution please!

A note of vigilance here: The conscious mind always wants to go back to what is familiar. The old ways will always creep in, doubts will haunt you—especially when you are not yet secure and when things are not yet clear—especially if you try to sing without having put the "pieces" into the Voice properly. All the **old memories** of how things were done before will surface. You might find yourself stuck, exasperated and strung out . . . relax . . . take a bath . . . read the Chapters again and then try. Remember, old habits die slowly. Your Brain has had to deal with the other stuff for quite a while, so give it the space it needs to digest the new information and transform your thinking.

This is all natural and human behavior. Give the Giro a chance to find the depth you need in the Voice. The more space you open, the more you will be able to move into that depth, and then you will have greater power of the Voice, and greater projection of the Voice.

You must cultivate the movements, the thinking, and the approach. Rome was not built in a day and empires that rise too quickly fall just as fast. So learn from your mistakes, communicate with your Instrument, and give it all it the time it needs to develop properly. Do not rush. Don't think, "Oh I know it, now I can sing anything I want." Wrong! **Every single piece of music must be "put" into the Voice, into the sping, into the sing....again: There are NO shortcuts, NONE.**

When you hum, make sure that you feel the Air Movement only inside the spheres (orbits) of your eyeballs, not lower. Vowel Sound must move in open space only and you must feel a buzz inside your head.

Please make certain that there is no involvement of the Throat while you are humming. Keep the Soft Palate up and steady, the Portal Bones pulled back, the Throat open, the Larynx down and float, float, float the Sound upwards and backwards, round and round as far back and as high up as you can go. Then you will understand singing, spinging, and speaking - all being made in the same place and all effortless. Be serious about this. If you find it silly, well, that is your business and certainly your prerogative. Give this a chance and you will see a remarkable difference.

Talk to your Voice and instruct it aloud so you can hear it, literally speak to it. This will solidify your own understanding and knowledge. In that way, you hear your own progression of thoughts and re-organize your thinking and *mental language patterns*. Watch how fabulous the response of the Voice will be to your (the right) instructions . . . it does precisely what you tell it to do . . . so make sure you know the rules and communicate properly.

Notes

The Jaw

Think about this, or better yet, do it.

Pull the Jaw down and feel what happens. There is tension on the chin and on the muscles of the Throat. Everything we are talking about here has to do with being as natural and as at ease as possible, about remaining stress free. Most of all we are concerned about keeping the Sound up and in place. If you are pulling down on the Jaw, you are pulling on the height of the Soft Palate and achieving exactly the opposite of that for which we're striving.

When you are speaking, how much of the Jaw are you using? Practically none! **The natural drop of the Jaw is all you need**, so what sense could there be in ripping the mouth wide open when you're singing?

I know this goes against what most others may say, or perhaps what you see many singers doing—but think about this: the Voice begins on the top and ends on the top. Keeping the Voice in line on the top is what we are trying to achieve. Completely opening the mouth would directly influence the smooth Movement of the Sound and the Air on the top and pull it out of line.

Another thing to consider: the larger the opening, the more Air escapes, the less you have to work with and the more dangerously involved the Throat becomes. Obviously, that is not what we want. On the contrary, we want to preserve as much Air as is possible in order to move the Giro. So, the smaller the mouth in final emission, the more Air is conserved and the more precise your diction.

Of course there are times when you need to open wider, allow the body to tell you how wide— let the Air tell you how wide, do not decide that just because you need more volume, the Jaw needs to open wider. The size of the Voice does not depend on the opening of the mouth, but on the opening inside the cranium [head]. It depends on the size of the Giro, on the pull of the muscles behind your eye balls and the depth of the Air – not the opening of the Jaw!

The Jaw, just like your facial muscles should be totally relaxed so it can move as is necessary. This necessity is determined by the brain, by the need of the Voice, not by you directly. The decision is mental, not physical. Like everything we are doing is a natural reaction to the needs of the instrument, so is this. There should be no pressure of any kind anywhere (other than the natural pressure needed from the Diaphragm, of course). The Italians call this total facial relaxation "faccia stupida,"- a dumb face; there is no muscular tension - total relaxation produces beautifully even Sound; no pulling on the mouth, just speak.

The more you do this, the easier the Air moves inside the Giro. Remember, please: Sound and Vowels must always move together and must move only on the top. The Air from the mouth moves from the top (Soft Palate) to the top into the Giro. Any muscular Movement on the bottom (Throat, Larynx, or Tongue) will affect the flow of the Air and, therefore, the Sound of your Voice. In order to have a beautifully homogenized Sound, allow the Air to move freely and interfere as little as possible. **Think** correctly as much as possible.

Concentrate on your 'speech' behind your eyeballs and the formulation of the Vowel Sound behind the eyes, inside The Chamber, where the Voice lives.

The more you accomplish this, the less you will feel the need to pull on the Jaw. Think of actually speaking into your head and out of your head - conversing into and with your Brain without really being concerned about anything else. **Since your intention is to speak, and your Brain knows the Movement of the mouth, the Lips and the Tongue and will perform this task without you really having to do anything other than think the word and the Sound combination.** Your mouth will speak your thoughts perfectly.

Do not worry about what comes out – your intention, which is your actual decision to speak/sing, will guide the Vowel Sound to the appropriate place on the Lips (at the Front Teeth where diction is made)… and since really, only the Brain knows HOW to speak and sing and combine Sound and precisely where to make this combination, YOU are only the guide of the Air, the Speaker of Sound and the interpreter of music….not the Creator!!!

Let's talk about the actual word for a moment.

Pronunciation, articulation (diction/consonants) and intention are imperative to the word. As I have already explained, you cannot pull on the Jaw to articulate and pronounce properly; just the opposite is true. If you keep the mouth in a normal position, as in speaking, the Tongue, Lips, and teeth will have a much easier time producing what you want. Also consider this, better yet, feel it: when you pull on the

Jaw, your whole facial physiology tenses, and that is definitely contrary to anything we are looking to achieve.

So please remember not to strain or pull on the Jaw. The word is natural, easy, loose and entirely without strain, yet at the same time, it is intentioned and powerful. You are singing in speaking position no more, no less.

Keeping the Jaw pressure free will also allow you to keep the Soft Palate from falling. If you pull down on the Jaw, you are losing Air; and since by moving the Jaw down, you are also pulling the Soft Palate down, you have to work so much harder to keep high position. The less you pull on the Jaw, the more height on the Soft Palate, which, of course, is supporting the Giro and consequently the Movement of Sound.

Keep the speaking position of the mouth at all times. That is very easily done when you remember, to make the Vowel Sound behind your eyeballs, on the natural up-swing of the Air and allow them to spiral over the Brain, reverberate in open space, exit through the Third Eye and meet the word somewhere outside, in front of your Lips. ***Want projection***?? Well, that is the way to get it powerfully, easily, and correctly every time.

Keeping these thoughts in mind, what good can possibly come from opening the mouth wide, pulling the Jaw down and pushing forward? None! You are only making your job more difficult and working against yourself. In order to keep everything round inside, you must maintain the Jaw in its natural position. When I recap everything at the end of the book, I'll talk about that again; but in the meantime, just remember that you need no more action for singing than is required in speaking. It's as simple as that.

Notes

Visualization

From my explanations of the previous topics, I am certain that by now you understand many of these new concepts. Paramount to this process is visualization.

We mentioned it earlier, but now I want you to really concentrate on it. In working with my students, I have found that the more they are able to come in contact with their "inner-selves," the more spiritually they are attached, the easier they comprehend the concepts I have explained.

I spoke about the Third Eye and opening it. Believe me, once you discover how to make use of it, the Third Eye will be of immeasurable help to you. By focusing the entire Voice into the Third Eye, you ensure that your thought processes will always be upward; and since the position of the Voice is up, that is just the place where you need to be. With a little practice you develop the ability to see the entire Movement happening. You will cut out all the extraneous ideas about the Voice and put only the things we have talked about here into your mind. You will see how easily your Brain will adapt to this very basic way of perceiving the Voice.

I could give you all kinds of medical and metaphysical terminologies, but that is not the purpose here. I want everyone to speak better and sing beautifully and I believe that everyone can. Although a great deal depends on the actual Instrument you were given, there is no reason for speaking or singing incorrectly. Guttural Sounds are not necessary, and with a little effort and a shift in your thinking, we'll change all that.

This entire concept was developed with great care –Let me rephrase this:

I am the vessel that has been chosen to impart this to you. I do not want you to be confused in any way. I actually can take no personal credit for it - this knowledge is a gift to me.

I want this to be easy, I want your thinking to guide you into a reflexive mode. Oh, I know you are going to be frustrated at times. That is quite normal. I promise you that if you persevere and do what we are discussing here; within a short period of time, (I would say four-to-six months) you will have almost everything under control and will feel fantastic, vocally and emotionally. Trust yourself, your own system and your own motivation; you will be happier with your Voice than ever before. Just do not give up and think that you are not progressing fast enough. It takes a baby a year to walk, two years to talk and three to be potty trained. It took you all your life to get to a point vocally you know is not good for you and where you are not achieving the desired results. Please take the time to experience and explore, and you will see the rewards in the beautiful impostation of your Instrument.

Envision the Voice entering and exiting through your Third Eye. Do not ever think of it as beginning at the mouth. If you do, you are already too low and too close to the Throat. Keep your mind set on height, and you will have it. Think about it constantly. The more you do, the more intimate you will become with your Instrument—and that is precisely what is needed.

You must know the Voice in order to use it properly and not to damage it in any way. So please, take the time and make the effort to open yourself up and use the power of the Third Eye. You will be surprised at how much it will help you tune your Instrument and accomplish what you want—not only with the Voice, but in your life.

Listen to your instincts. Listen to the inner Voices in your body. Hear the Sound, listen to the Sound, and hear the word and Sound combinations; develop that inner listening/hearing which is so necessary. It will not steer you wrong. It has to feel right. If you experience *any type of discomfort*, chances are you're on the wrong track. Let your body guide you. As I said before, you already know all of this; it came along with the gift and the original blueprint. Allow it to flow from you. Do NOT interfere.

Easier said than done - we are taught to always be in control. In some phases of our lives that works and is right; here it is the "out of control physically and in control mentally" that will give you the vocal freedom you desire. But that takes knowledge and practice – always.

Remember that you cannot make the Voice. All you can do is being its guide – a guide has to know where to go and what is he hoping to accomplish. Set your goal and do it right. Follow what I have taught you, and the Voice will not fail you. Just give it the time it needs. PATIENCE, PATIENCE, PATIENCE!

Let me spend a moment giving you some of my thoughts on the Brain as it applies to our work here.

The more you allow the Brain to take over what you are doing, the better. The more integrated you are in right and left Brain activity, the easier it will be for you.

Creative or logical? Most of you probably think of people as being one or the other. Well, in singing, speaking, and communicating, we have to be both — especially in Voice production. In singing, we must allow the Brain to take over. It's difficult for most of us, since we have been trained to manipulate the Voice from early childhood. Because of this training, most of us became even greater experts at making the Voice'.

Now I am telling you to let go completely; to stop controlling; to learn to trust the natural instincts of the Brain; to be a guide, but not to manipulate. The more you let go, the better it will get. But you must know what your job is:

Allow Air to move correctly…

Speak with intention and perfect pronunciation…

Support properly…

Think about speaking. Imagine having to find every word somewhere in the Brain. Where would you begin looking? You have no idea where to find any particular thought or word…. neither do I. We can only be the guides who lead the thoughts and allow the Brain to take over from there—just like it does in speaking – instantaneously and instinctively.

If you think it the right way, you can speak it. Well, if you hear the Sound, you can sing it. When you are in the right position (behind your eyes, high up and back), the Brain produces all the Sound inside the Giro; and you do no more than hear the Sound in your mind, speak, and support.

This is the ideal position of the Voice; and this is what you should strive for, whether in your speaking or in your singing. The Brain will compute Sound instantly once it knows the information and understands it. Re-read these Chapters many times to fully comprehend and believe. When you do, the Brain accepts this information and it will become an instant response; thus, you are free to do what you need to. The Brain knows the way so well. It recognizes the place from the original blueprint (Birth-Knowledge) and responds instantly. The Voice feels so much at home in this territory.

My students are always amazed at how when they let go, they feel nothing. **_"The Voice simply goes away"_**…what remains, and the only thing that remains is a continual vibration somewhere in the back of your head, all around, almost outside the head. I call those vibrations **lawn-mower engines**.

That can be very perplexing. After all, we "must" be in control, or so we have always thought.

Well, here the control lies in knowing what you are doing. Don't worry; in reality, you're still in charge – all the way. Your knowledge is guiding you, which is ultimate control! You are simply *allowing* the Brain to take over what it does best. Let go and trust the natural wonder of creation. Besides, you have plenty of other things to think about!

✫ ✫ ✫

Phrenology is an ancient science, dating back as far as the Atlantean era that predicts human behavior through the precise calculation of various skull measurements. Here is how I found out about this.

Just a few days before actually finishing the first edition in 1999, I took some days off to concentrate on editing changes and went to see friends in Daytona Beach, Florida. Their home was filled with collections of strange and beautiful things. In my room, I noticed a bust with outlines on the skull. I picked it up, and upon closer examination, was simply amazed at what I found.

I immediately realized from the drawings that there was a correlation between my work with the Voice and Phrenology.

While studying the drawings, I realized that where **we** are placing language and Vowel Sound (eyes) is the precise place Phrenology places verbal memory and verbal expression. Then I went to the back of the head, into the Bone of Life area (the focal point of the entire Movement of mouth Air to the back) and found that place is associated with the love of parents, of children and of animals; in other words, the most profound of human emotions.

Then I moved to the Third Eye, the place where we begin and end the Voice and the drawing caption reads, "individuality" - mental and physical." Of course, this makes total sense in our work: the mental work done by the Brain and the physical Air Movement combine to create the individuality of the Voice—speaking, singing, and communicating as a whole.

Then I searched the top of the head, and the precise spot where we are centering the Voice is interpreted as "Spirituality, hope, faith, and wonder." The area of the temple is described as, "tune and modulation" and is exactly where we are placing the Movement of the Voice inside the Giro.

Can you imagine how profound this experience was for me? I wrote these lines to include them in the book and to make you aware of this 'science'.

There is much information available on the Internet, at, for example, www. phrenology.com. There are also books on the subject; but I believe that for our purposes, the information I've just shared with you confirms that the path we are taking is the correct one.

Phrenology is thought by some to be quackery- perhaps, but perhaps not. You decide for yourself. As far as I am concerned, for what we need, the "shoe fits."

After my first book was published in 1999, I met Dr**. Lewis Arrandt** in Miami. He specializes in Neuro- Cranial Reconstruction, a chiropractic procedure which actually moves the cranium internally. He explained that Neuro- Cranial Reconstruction (NCR) expands the same place we are working in - inside the Giro. Suffice it to say, that I personally have undergone numerous treatments to date and many of my students, who have submitted themselves to this procedure, have had extraordinary progress and results in understanding and increasing the actual space of the Giro. The 'connection' on a physical and mental level that NCR establishes is mind boggling. A great deal of time is saved with this procedure in accomplishing our goals – but this, for certain, is not for everyone.

With the way I have instructed you on how to move Air we are accomplishing the exact same thing: actually opening space and moving the cranium to accommodate the Air needed to move Sound. With NCR it is faster- it happens almost instantly when the joints are moved. What then is incumbent upon you is to actually be able to connect to it.

I highly recommend NCR treatments for singers, especially students taught by me or who are working with our technique. Others, who are not familiar with this work, would reap absolutely no 'vocal' rewards, though physical benefits of NCR are limitless. Once an NCR specialist explains the procedure, you will understand how absolutely in tune with our work this methodology is and how it totally compliments *Giro-Vocal Motion Technique*, which is what we are doing here.

There are, to date, only a few doctors in certain states and in the world performing this type of procedure. Check out NCR on the Internet and find a specialist in your area. If you want to discuss this please contact me via e-mail at **musicvisions@aol.com** and I will be happy to tell you about the results we have achieved.

Notes

The Diaphragm:
Truths and Myths

<u>Truth:</u> The Diaphragm is the motor/support of the Voice

<u>Myth:</u> The Diaphragm begins and makes the Voice

The Diaphragm is the motor, the support system of the Sound, the Soft Palate AND THE OPEN THROAT. Using the Diaphragm is really not complicated, but it is of the utmost importance when it ultimately comes to using the Voice correctly.

Think of a beautiful car without a motor, or a gas tank without gas. That is the relationship of the Diaphragm to the Air. The Air is the fuel that makes the motor run, and a full tank gives you the freedom to take a long drive without worrying. Fill it up to the brim and go. The more you have, the less you need to pay attention to the mileage—right? Take this thought and transfer it to the Voice.

We know how vital Air is to the Voice/Sound and that every note needs its own Air on which to float. If you have no Air, you have a problem. It is up to you to provide the Air for the support of the Soft Palate, and thus the support of the Vowel Sound and the Giro, by making sure that the Diaphragm is 'full 'and that the Air is distributed properly. I always tell my students that the Diaphragm is the only support system to high Air and to the Giro, but is not **"the" system**."

I would say that 9 out of 10 people come to me and in the first hour, when I am trying to ascertain their knowledge, will tell me that the Voice starts in the "stomach"…alias Diaphragm.

If they use the word Diaphragm, they have no idea how it works and how it moves or what its real function is. The Diaphragm is a support system for: ***high Air, the Soft Palate, the Giro, and the Open Throat***. It's (the diaphragms) Air is also responsible for the little Movement of the Tongue, the Lips, and Front Teeth in making the final consonant and putting the whole word together. That is all. It is a major job indeed, but it certainly does not have anything to do with the *creation* of the Voice/Sound or ultimately its size. The Diaphragm has all to do with the *support* of the Sound.

If you take Air into the Throat and then use the Diaphragm to support the Voice, you will still need to push forward and the Air will be stuck inside your Throat. If, however, you use high, simultaneous Air to get above the Soft Palate (The Hole, the Bone of Life, the Giro) and start on the top (Third Eye), the Air from the Diaphragm will support the desired height of Sound.

The Diaphragm, as I have mentioned before, should grow in size and power as the Giro and the" Voice" develop. If the Diaphragm does not grow, its support will not be sufficient and the Sound will not be supported properly or develop the depth needed. I cannot emphasize enough how important the use of Diaphragm is.

Please, from the outset of your work, do not slack off on exercising the pelvic muscles that are needed to support the Diaphragm. Coordinating the Movement is not easy, and takes concentration as well as physical effort, but you must achieve the balance needed in order to maintain the height of the Soft Palate and, therefore, the total opening of the Throat. Use the Diaphragm in three instances:

1. On the upswing of the first note, pull in slightly (absolutely essential).

2. On the high/low note, pull in slightly (absolutely essential).

3. On the last note, the Diaphragm is completely pulled in, there is no more Movement, but total stillness in the Throat, and on the Soft Palate, until the last Sound is completely finished (absolutely essential).

Why?

Explanation: If you do not have enough Air for the first note, the Soft Palate will not go into maximum position, and your start will be low. For the high note, or the highest note (and the lowest one, for that matter), the Soft Palate has to move further up and back to create more space. Low notes need as much Diaphragm support as high notes; please keep that in mind at all times. The Soft Palate must remain lifted for both low notes and for high ones. For all intents and purposes, the Soft Palate must remain stationary, non-moving.

The Air will supply the necessary power to do that. On the last note the Diaphragm must be used because high Air is running out, or so you think, and because you think so, you will become anxious and pull forward…NO! Use your support system.

We cannot ever allow the Soft Palate to drop because the Sound would wind up low, crashing into the Throat. On these three occasions, you should make a concentrated effort to pull on your pelvic muscles in order to lift the Air. These are only the guidelines. Use the Diaphragm in these three instances but preferably at all times, continually. It is best and safest to use the Diaphragm with every Sound, so at the end you'll have plenty to finish Vowel Sound on the Air and not in the Throat. Controlling the Diaphragm's power is a challenge to which you must pay close attention.

The more muscular reflexes you develop, the better. The Diaphragm is a tremendously necessary asset to your Voice. It is your Air storage tank. You can count on it to help you out. It is like a life jacket for the Voice. Remember to always pull in on the Diaphragm gently but consistently. If you pull too hard, the palate will shoot up too high, and you will be sharp; if you don't pull hard enough, you will be flat.

Another observation which might be very helpful: If you pull in on the Diaphragm too powerfully, the Air comes up too fast and causes the Throat to close and the Larynx to rise; the Tongue also pushes up, and thus, closes the Throat. If you are pulling too hard, the Larynx will mistakenly get a wrong impulse. So be careful. Learn how to control diaphragmatic power to your advantage.

The Air from the Diaphragm must be led to the back of the Throat, pass the Larynx unnoticed and go straight up to the Soft Palate in order to do the job there. If you move (push) the Air to the front of the Throat, the Larynx and the Tongue will come up, the Throat will close and will prevent the Air from hitting (lifting) the Soft Palate. The Air will be stuck inside the Throat and cause havoc there.

All Air therefore must always be allowed to move up to the back of the Soft Palate, to The Hole and be allowed to pass the Throat undisturbed. Your aim is to get the Air to move as close to the Bone of Life as you can possibly get. Program that into your Brain, internally view that, and it will be achieved.

If you only count on the Diaphragm for Air, you will have the tendency *NOT* to use simultaneous breath and that is a big mistake. You will have no choice but to lead the Air into the Throat. Please be very aware of the difference - always make sure that the Soft Palate is as stationary as can be, no dropping, fluttering, etc. *Everything that happens there is audible in the 'Voice'.*

The first step is attaining high Air, and the next step is maintaining it. That is the job of the Diaphragm. Keep your Diaphragm working/active at all times. Do not let it drop. If you let go of it, the Air in the Air column will also drop; and that makes the Soft Palate and the Sound drop, which in turn causes the Larynx to rise. The Larynx will want to help you out in making the note, but will ultimately close the Throat instead.

The Diaphragm helps the Sound begin and end on top of the Giro in the Third Eye and supports it in that position. The last note is completely suspended on Air, and the Air is closed off on the top in the Third Eye. This is what it looks like: (See drawing, Last note).

For the last Sound/note, the Diaphragm is pulled in tightly all the way, and held there, still, without any Movement. The Air column is holding the Giro and Soft Palate in the up position. *The Air column and the Giro, therefore, support the last note.* The Air (Vowel Sound) is then terminated on the Air, right on the top, at the Third Eye.

Please remember that the Voice begins and ends in the Third Eye—not by lifting the Tongue and not by closing the Throat; simply by shutting off the Air on the top, just like closing a faucet. If this is not done properly, you will hear an ugly, choppy Sound at the end of the phrase. Most singers have it because they sing with the Throat and it's difficult to keep the Air steady when you are pushing. But YOU know better!

Think of it this way: the note is on top of the Soft Palate in the Giro. The Sound remains suspended on top, the Throat remains open and the Larynx and Tongue are down. High Air and Vowel Sound from the Giro turn toward the Intention of the Word and thus carry the last Sound to the Front Teeth where it mingles with the diction of the word at the upper lip and ends. No chopping, no fallen notes—just a note suspended on Air, floating. Now you can see how important this motor is and how much depends on your being able to master its use.

Exercise is very important in developing the pelvic muscles. Here is one that you should begin with immediately. Lie on the floor, legs stretched out. Slowly lift both legs together, all the way up. At the same time allow Air to enter simultaneously they way we now know. Your Diaphragm will extend. Hold it there. Then slowly move the legs down and allow the breath to float out gently. Do not tighten the Throat while you breathe in or out. The only things that are tight are the muscles that support the Diaphragm. Do about 25 of these every day and watch how much power this will give you in just a few weeks. As with all exercises, the beginning will be a little painful; but it will be worth it in the end.

As those muscles get stronger and stronger, you will be able to control them at will. Your Brain will accept this information gladly and use this support system with pleasure- so much so that it becomes instinctive. After a while, you will not even think about it anymore. Because this is such a crucial aspect for the support of your Voice, spend some time cultivating this Movement.

Students will forget about the Diaphragm, no matter how many times they are told. If, from the beginning, you do not work these muscles, you will get to a point when the Voice has grown significantly inside the Giro, but will not be able to stay up, because there is no support. This can ruin everything. So please, pay very close attention to the entire system. It all has to function together. It is like a domino game. If one Sound falls, all fall and in our case, that spells the involvement of the Throat and that must at all costs be avoided.

Some important considerations:

Since you have no idea where Sound are, but the Brain does, allow the Brain to place them. You just enter properly and the rest will be done without your interference.

The words must be spoken in order for the Sound to move properly. The Intention of the Word pulls the tension of the Air, Vowel and Sound upward and backward and keeps the balance between the Sound and the word. Allow the Sound to form on the Air, in the Giro, pulled by the muscles behind the eyeballs. Your thinking propels this action, not your doing. Get out of your own way, <u>allow</u>!

Keep the Vowel Sound rotating only in the spheres of in your eyeballs and speak your consonants as forward as you can . . . at the Lips . . . on the outside of your mouth, not anywhere on the inside. If you concentrate on the MESSAGES you are giving your system, based upon the knowledge you have gathered, you will find that most everything will fall into place automatically, without a great deal of action and effort.

Thinking is more worthwhile than doing. Knowledge goes a long way in redefining where the Voice will come from. Your responsibility is *support* of Sound— not its creation.

After everything I have just told you about the Diaphragm I must also mention something else which I have said before, but you might have forgotten or think is obsolete after reading this Chapter. There are singers who do not use the Diaphragm as a major support system and are not worried about diaphragmatic support at all. Here is the reason – When the Voice is absolutely in the right place inside the Giro, support is natural, instant. When the Sound/Vowels are floating on and over the top, the Diaphragm support is totally there and the body is in the perfect mode. No particular 'learning' is needed, the system does it automatically.

Most singers do NOT fit this category and have to work at it, hence the Chapter. But if you are one of the lucky ones who naturally are in the right place, know how to support the system, don't worry about it and allow the body to simply do its thing.

Notes

Troubleshooting

You need to be hypercritical with yourself now. Always work with a good recording device. Keep all of your recordings and **do not** erase them. They will serve you later when you need to check something specific. Listen and re-listen to your Voice, and if you hear the slightest imperfection, do it again. Before you try again, though, you must know why the Sound were not good, why the Voice cracked, why it went sharp or flat and/or why you ran out of Air. You need to listen, really listen, to your Voice. Every Sound counts. Every feeling is important – analyze!

Greatness cannot be achieved by letting "you" get away with anything. To be the best, you must demand the most of yourself. Most people do not want that. Most people will "cut themselves slack." Well, one note out of place means the rest is out of place as well - No easy way out. If you **feel** it, anything, and I mean **anything**, IT IS WRONG. It takes a lot to be vigilant all the time, but again, the rewards you will gain in the end will justify the means.

Now I want to help you along in shifting your thought patterns by sharing some of the most common trouble spots I have encountered with my students.

The Voice is too low or not on pitch:

This happens all the time, and the reason for it is very basic. You are not starting the Voice on the top of the Giro, all the way in the back. If you start low, you cannot achieve maximum height. If the Soft Palate is not pulled to its highest position from the beginning, it will be very difficult to move it up.

High, simultaneous breath plus the 'support' from the Diaphragm, will allow you to start the first Sound in the correct place every time, and thus, continue the Voice in proper position. Remember to start in the Giro and follow the line upward and backward. Keep the Sound there; always high and always on the top. All Sounds move upwards and backwards; so the lowest Sound is actually in the highest position and the furthest back because the Air moves only in one way and the Sounds follows it; the highest Sounds of course are also in the same place. The turn of the Voice only occurs because you have decided to speak; if you do not have the Intention of Speaking, the words and Sound will simply stay inside your head and mingle with a million other Sound and words that will never be heard. They will then be locked inside of you until you decide to share them (speaking).

The Voice cracks:

Obviously this is not permissible. Here are some reasons why it happens: The elevation of the Larynx and the closing of the Throat cut off the Air. The Tongue is not flat, but instead high and raised in the back, thus cutting off the Airflow. The Soft Palate falls because it is not supported properly. The Sound is not high enough in position; because of improper Air flow and the Vowel/Sound tumbles into the Throat and cracks. The 'Voice' is pushed into a place where it does not belong—namely, the Throat.

The Sounds are flat or sharp:

Easy! You're not high enough in the Giro; and if the Soft Palate is not in correct position, the Sound will not be correct. Too high is sharp, too low is flat. Remember that you cannot make the Sound- you can only mentally guide them into the right place. The Brain knows where the Sound you are trying to make needs to position. It is difficult to accept not being in control, but unfortunately that is it. Allow your hearing/internal listening to notify the Brain, and let the Brain do its job. Use proper support of the Diaphragm. Be instinctive. Why do you have to control something that is already in a perfect place to start with? Let it happen. Assist by doing what is asked of you. Use your Air properly, support properly, and speak at the Front Teeth, with the guidance of the Lips and the Tongue that is already enough to think about. Leave the "making" to the expert—the Brain.

Potato Sound:

By now you know exactly how to get rid of that. Get the Sound and the Vowels out of the Throat. Start the Sound on the top of the Giro with the help of the muscles behind your eyeballs. Always begin above the Soft Palate. When you get the potato Sound, the words are being produced in the back and in the mouth - on the bottom. Vowel Sounds then are also formed in the mouth and that of course is the beginning of the end. Remember that the word must be made in the front (diction/consonants) and come together at the Lips. The Sound and the Vowel must remain rotating on the top, inside the Giro. All Sound must be allowed to travel up and back while the words (diction/consonants) stay in the front.

Keep The Chamber open at all times and always think of Vowel Sound, moving behind your eyes.

Think of actually speaking the words behind your eyes – **Connect with the Sound and the words inside the Brain and follow their desired Movement. –**

the Movement of Vowel Sound is always upward and backward following the Air in toward the tips of the ears, toward the back of the head, toward the Bone of Life. The combination of Vowel/Sound and Consonant=word and is always at the upper lip/Front Teeth. Do not physically interfere (push from the Throat) in the process that is natural.

Speak. Speak. Speak. I cannot emphasize this enough. When you place the word too far back in the mouth, you collide with the Sound, and your Voice will become thick and Throaty. Remember that it is the word, which pulls the Sound over the top of the Giro and brings it to the front. Keep the Voice up at all times and the potato will go away.

The Voice is uneven:

This is more difficult to fix because it takes serious self-critiquing and determination on your part to achieve an even, homogenized Sound throughout the entire Voice. Most singers simply are in love with their own Sound. Emotion and passion take over. It is very difficult to remain objective about ones Instrument, but please try. If you can be objective about your own Voice, you will find that you will achieve a great deal more. If you allow your passion to take over, you'll never be truly honest with yourself - and that is a mistake.

Notice, by the way, that **I never speak about registers, changing registers, chest Voice, middle Voice, head Voice**. This way of categorizing the Voice is used by those who do not have the slightest idea of what a vocal line is and how it must and can be developed. I cannot tell you the nonsense I have heard from students who come which has been taught to them by other teachers.

The Voice is ONE, from high to low. There should be no change, no break. NO PASSAGIO! All notes should be in one position (on top of the Soft Palate, in the Giro) and should flow from there. There is no need for different Voices or changes in position. Colors are achieved inside the Giro . . . pianissimo, forte, etc., all in the same place, in the Giro, **achieved only by the 'Movement' of the Air AND THE CORRECT THOUGHT PROCESS, WHICH CREATES THE CORRECT PHYSICAL PROCESS.**

Resonance of Sound can be found in every cavity of the body, but the only space in which the Voice is totally comfortable and at home, is on top of the Soft Palate and inside the Giro - actually in the empty Chamber and spheres behind your eyes.

The more you allow Sound the freedom to move inside the head, the more resonating and "vibratious" the Voice will become. If you feel as though the Sounds are beyond your head - outside your head - then you are correct. The feeling is liberating and absolutely beyond description. At first, it may frighten you because you are seemingly out of control, in unfamiliar territory; but ultimately you will know that you have 'mastered' the understanding of the Voice.

One of my students quite a while ago, was a very prominent eye surgeon. In our first lesson, we talked about what actually can be found behind the eyes. In his explanation to me, he referred to the spheres as orbits. Well, I promptly advised him to place the Sound behind the orbits and rotate the Air around the spheres. In five minutes, he understood the concept of the Giro, and thus, found the true position of the Voice instantly.

Not having to worry about different places to put the Voice, makes it easy on you and on the Voice. What I am saying is that the Voice must be homogenized, that Sound can only be even when they are in one position and when each note has its own Air on which to float. The top, The Chamber, must always be open, it never closes. The Air needs a passage – a way for the Sound and Vowel in order to be able to carry it up and back and to turn it over. If you close the top, or put pressure on it, you crush the Sound. Only minuscule Movement of the Lips makes the Vowel/consonant formation - no more effort than actual speaking. Only rarely will you need to open the mouth wide - a bit wider perhaps, yes; but only in moderation when the body actually does it on its own.

Let us not forget the Intention of the Word. Never pushing the word toward the front, but intending it in the front. Pushing is physical; intention is mental. **If you think it, you can achieve it.** So make your Brain work for you. Work smart, not hard! Also, remember that the Air from the Diaphragm must be pulled in evenly. You must learn how to do that. If you pull sporadically, you will be able to hear it in the Voice. Every Movement, be it in the Throat or in the Diaphragm, is audible in the final Sound. So forget the Throat and learn to move the Diaphragm effortlessly. It's a tall order, but you can do it. Persevere, and it will become second nature in no time.

Nasal Sound:

An absolutely terrible habit unfortunately present in many singers. It completely takes the ring out of the Voice.

It happens when the Tongue is too high up in the back and closes off the passage of Air to The Hole, preventing the Soft Palate from rising properly. The little bit of Air that does come up is pushed against the roof of your mouth instead of being able to move backward into The Hole. Instead of keeping the mask open and allowing it to fill with Air, creating powerful resonances throughout the open Chambers in the whole head, the Air gets pushed into the nose and creates nasal Sound.

You can feel that easily by taking a high, simultaneous breath and then closing your nose with your fingers. Feel the Movement of the Air. Begin your first Sound where you feel the cool spot on top of the Soft Palate and simply stay there to continue all the other Sound. Spinging that way is also excellent practice. The Sound will simply flow from you. Keeping your nose closed (with your fingers only—in all other cases the nose and nasal passages must remain totally open, as we discussed) will automatically lead you into the right place.

Repeat this many times, and you will get used to guiding the Air directly into the top, allowing it to rise inside the Giro. Keep the Air as far back as you can (in the area of the Bone of Life). Nasal Sounds are a vocal defect. Please keep that in mind.

If you feel the Sound getting nasal, think immediately of the flaps opening. This is a sure way of moving the Air up and supporting the position. In all things, if you feel that you do not have any Air in the Diaphragm, and you feel as if you cannot finish the phrase without taking Air, just think of opening the bridge (5&6). The thought of this Movement alone, provokes its happening and you will be once again above the nose, inside the high position of the Giro. Remember, there is always Air on the top; the universe provides constant support.

Notes

An Overview:
The Whole Thing in a Nutshell

10 Easy Steps:

1. Take a simultaneous breath using the nose and the mouth. Start at the Front Teeth. Allow the Air to move back past the Hard Palate, the uvula and into the Soft Palate, into The Hole, and finally into the Bone of Life. Feel the pulling back sensation of the entire mouth area.

2. Allow the high Air to pull the Portal Bones up and back to lift the Soft Palate and open The Hole to create bottom of the Giro, thus opening the 'back door' of the Voice. Use the Bone of Life as a springboard - guide (mentally) the breath upward and backward at all times. All Sounds are formed on the top of the Soft Palate inside the various heights of the Giro and all words are formed at the Front Teeth, using the Lips, the Front Teeth and the Tongue. High Air from the mouth opens the Throat, drops the Tongue and the Larynx and moves down the column of Air into the Diaphragm, extending it. Keep the Tongue flat and relaxed at all times, slightly touching the roots of your bottom teeth. Use it exactly as you would in speaking, no other effort is necessary.

3. With the Diaphragm now extended, the pelvic muscles immediately lock up and slowly pull the Air back up, through the Open Throat, the dropped Larynx and the lowered Tongue. Make sure that the Air from the Diaphragm is even, as any unevenness will cause the Voice to be out of line. On the last note, remember to always cut the Air on the top of the Giro. Never drop the Diaphragm before you finish the phrase. If you do, the Soft Palate will fall, the Larynx will rise and the whole base we have built will collapse.

4. Always lead the Air to the back. The further away you are from the Larynx, the better; and the further back the Air stays, the better. All Sounds move upward and backward; there is no down position. The lowest Sound is the furthest back and the highest up. Never push the Air forward. Never! Move the Air as far back into the Bone of Life as you can and use the back of the Throat as a springboard to reach the top of the Giro in the Third Eye. The further back you pull the Throat, the larger the opening, the easier for the Diaphragm to support the Soft Palate.

5. **Simultaneous Air** from the nose and the mouth forms the top part of the Giro, opens The Chamber and begins turning the Sounds over the top of the brain in the empty space toward the Third Eye. All Vowel Sounds stay/move/are formed etc. behind your eyes at all times. No Vowel Sound is ever made/constructed/spoken etc. below the Soft Palate /Portal Bones. You must remain above and inside the Giro at all times. The Vowels must remain **out** of the mouth cavity. Vowel Sounds **cannot**, under any circumstances be 'produced' by the mouth. Please remember that Vowel Sounds have two functions: 1. To always move with the Sound/Air upwards and backwards in a spiral like motion, one Sound hooked on to the other, one rising therefore above the other (legato) 2.Vowel Sounds must be spoken with the consonants at the Lips and the Front Teeth to form the spoken Sound and final word.The Voice begins there on top of the Air and ends there. You then deliberately cut off the Air at the end of the phrase on the last note. Think of the space behind your eyes as actually making the word Sound, and then each Sound moving further to the top and into the back of your head. Actually begin speaking inside the spheres of your eyes and creating the word there. **Speak behind your eyes and formulate the words (diction/consonants) at the Lips.**

Little action is required of the mouth; behind your eyes is where the major work is done (Vowel Sounds are created on the up-swing of the Air). If you remember to keep the smile in your eyes at all times, and if you think of wanting to really communicate with someone through your eyes, then you will achieve the proper positioning naturally. Sounds always move over the top; nothing from the bottom, not ever—not the word, not the Sound. Everything comes out of the top and then is picked up by the mouth at the Front Teeth only. **Remember that it is the word that moves (turns) the Sound**. The more frontal the position of the word, the more freedom of Movement you will have in the Giro.

6. The front opens the back and the top. Never close the back and never close the top! Keep the space you have created with the nose Air behind your eyes open at all times. If you feel you need to "cover Sound," (which actually happens by itself when the Voice is properly moving inside the Giro), do so by pulling the Giro very wide in the back, turning it as high as possible and closing the Vowels with the Movement of the Lips. That kind of Sound will remain on the top and will be brilliant, never sounding guttural.

7. Observe Lag Time (the amount of time it takes the Air from the nose to form the entire Giro and all the Sound in it - a mille-second). The Giro turns 360 degrees from the back where it forms the Sound over the top, and thus, moves the Sound toward the Third Eye on a forward angle toward the Lips. This causes the mingling of Sound and word in perfect harmony. **Lag Time** is the single most important Movement in

keeping the Voice on top at all times. Lag Time separates Sound from words. Without it, word and Sound will start in the back, in the mouth. You will either fall into the Throat or have the potato Sound. The angle of Third Eye and the Lips is vital. Stand in front of a mirror and guide the Sound from the back (top of the Giro) to the Third Eye with your hand over the top of the head. You will note the angle necessary to have Sound and word meet about two (2) inches outside your head, is just at the level of the Front Teeth, or more precisely, two (2) inches or so outside from the tip of your nose. That is the actual coming together of word and Sound.

8. Use the Diaphragm as a support system, not the system for producing Sound. Use it on the first note, the highest/lowest note and the last note—and at all times in between. Learn to measure the Air you expend so you will have enough to complete the phrase - that is what "putting something into the Voice" really means. To position the Sound, to position the word and to determine how much Air it will take to create the line of the phrase is very important. Pull the Diaphragm on the last note because if you do not have enough Air, that note will drop into the Throat, make a choppy Sound and pull the Sound out of line. Make sure that once the pull and the last note are established that there is no more Movement anywhere in the system and allow the Sound to float on the Air until you decide to end it with the Intention of the Word.

9. **Never ever sing a piece of music "right off the bat"**. First, learn the music and the words so you can sing it internally without fail. Then sping it, "ee" it in melody, and then, only when you are comfortable with the Giros placement and the Sound, attach the words to it. Sping high and sping wide; and sping deep. The wider, deeper, and higher you sping, the more depth and height you will acquire; hence, the larger the Sound.

Make sure you do not ever touch the Throat while spinging. Vocalize much, **always in spinging position.** Re-read the Chapter on spinging many times; it's tremendously important.

10. The Diaphragm must grow along with the Voice. Exercise the pelvic muscles regularly so when you need them, they will be ready for you. The Voice will grow in its natural position, but if the Diaphragm will not grow along with it, the Voice will fall. Do not rely on the Diaphragm instead of right breath. The breath is essential in the right position, while the Diaphragm is ONLY USED FOR SUPPORT. **There are singers who do not use the Diaphragm very much because their positioning is so high and deep inside the Giro that they are able to do anything they want and the Diaphragm just follows along naturally.**

Most of us mortals need the support the Diaphragm provides, so keep doing your exercises—it's very well worth the effort.

Notes

The Spoon, The Egg, Nose Clips & Ear Plugs

Please read this Chapter with the utmost seriousness and attention and read it many times until you have internalized all the concepts. There is so much necessary information that will put things into perspective for you.

At this time, I wish to introduce you to your new friends: the Spoon, the Egg, the Nose Clip and the Ear Plugs. They will help you move the Air into the right place and will make sure to keep it there. All my students receive a marble/onyx Egg as a gift, when they begin their studies. I have found that the Egg must be of a natural material, not plastic. Nature reconnects you with Birth-Knowledge, man-made material do not. If you absolutely cannot find a marble Egg, you have no choice, but please do not give up looking to find one.

The Spoon also must be metal and not plastic. I have found that if it is not, it too does not work properly. You can find Ear Plugs and a Nose Clip in a drug store.

Get yourself a demitasse or espresso Spoon. It is just the right size. To begin with, place it on top of your Tongue, as far back as is comfortable – bowl down. Now press down gently, just enough so you can feel the Spoon on top of your Tongue and so that you can feel what happens. Now take a simultaneous breath. I bet this is the first time that you have felt Open Throat. The Larynx automatically drops and the Air moves through the Air column into the Diaphragm. Can you believe how much Air is going down there without your actual intervention? It is a natural phenomenon. That is what you have to get used to, so use the Spoon all the time to feel your Open Throat.

For those of you who have a real problem keeping the Soft Palate up, or for those that have a tendency to speak below the Portal Bones (teeth clinchers, TMJ sufferers, etc.,), this method will make absolutely sure that you have no other place to go—except the right one.

Now, the second position of the Spoon is on top. Place it directly into the middle of your Hard Palate (roof of your mouth, bowl up) You will notice that the tip of the Spoon will hit exactly where the Hard Palate forms a ridge to make way for the Soft Palate. Guide the Air to follow the curve of the Spoon directly onto your Soft Palate.

Then gently move the Spoon into the up direction and follow with the Air. That will teach you the Movement of the Soft Palate and help you find The Hole every time. This, too, will soon become second nature. The little Spoon is your big helper. Use it all the time, gently and without force of any kind. It will become invaluable. Carry it with you always and use it especially before a performance.

The third position of the Spoon is really the decisive one. Take the Spoon with the bowl downside up. While looking in a mirror, put the Spoon so far back that it touches the uvula. This will give you a sensation at the end of the Throat. Be careful. The round, smooth part of the Spoon is lying on top of your Tongue, right? Now take in a simultaneous breath, the Throat opens, the Tongue and Larynx drops. You really have no choice—the bottom is useless! You cannot move. You must start above the Spoon, above the Soft Palate, behind your eyes, inside the Giro… and that is exactly where you need to be.

At first you will gag, that is to be expected; but don't be upset or discouraged by this. Once, twice, three times—every time you do it, it gets easier. After a while, you will automatically start in the right place—on top of the Giro, behind your eyes, in the Third Eye. Be patient, please - like the old saying goes, "If at first you don't succeed, try, and try again." The means justifies the end. It may Sound corny, but it is true. It may very well be that positions one and two are enough for you, but if you still find that your Larynx is coming up, that you're not opening your Throat or that your Tongue is still too high in the back, use the third position.

This is the most difficult way, designed for the true-blue Throat singer. Be hard on yourself; I promise that it will be worth it. I cannot emphasize enough that the Spoon is a real helper.

I do not want you to depress the Tongue or hurt yourself in any way. Remember to be gentle. This exercise is simply designed to make you feel the sensations of the Air more powerfully and make sure that you guide the Air into the correct position. Some of you may think that the Spoon is superfluous and not necessary, that you can do it on your own. Well, perhaps you can, perhaps using your fingers to lift the Soft Palate and then to depress the Tongue might work, but after many tries, my very strong suggestion is to work with the Spoon (a metal one only; if you use plastic, there is no transfer of energy). The effect is quite different and will cause you to make the important and necessary changes in the height of the Soft Palate, as well as the dropping of the Tongue, which will cause the necessary opening of the Throat. Learning this will make a major difference in your Voice.

Now let's talk about the **EGG** . . . yes, the Egg.

It is the perfect and absolute solution for finally eliminating the most serious of problems: closed Throat, the lifting of the Larynx and the rising of the Tongue.

I have found this to be the most serious of all problems students face. In some cases, the Spoon did not alleviate the problem because: 1) the student did not like using the Spoon and, 2) the Spoon still allows the opportunity to skirt the issue of keeping the entire mouth cavity open.

Hard-boil a small, medium, or large Egg depending upon the size of your mouth. Once it has cooled, place it into your mouth, the thick part of the Egg to the back... If you must remove the shell, fine. It is, however, better and more effective if you leave it on. By making sure the shell is not cracked, you will learn the discipline of not closing your Throat.

If you recall right in the beginning we briefly spoke about Caruso and the EGG... in a moment I will analyze it all for you and add some other things which will make the Egg completely clear to you.

The Egg must be big enough to fill most of the space in your mouth but still feel comfortable. Now allow a breath through the nose (the way we learned) and place the Sound and Vowel all the way at the tips of your ears. Turn it (up-swing, Lag Time), and bring it back to the front (intention). Actually try to form the Vowel Sound behind your eyes, and you will see that it's entirely possible to achieve that.

The higher into the Giro you set the Vowel, the better and clearer it will Sound. The Voice automatically goes into the right place, because you cannot move the Tongue, the Soft Palate or the Larynx for that matter. The Throat remains completely open, the Soft Palate is up and that is what we want to accomplish. This may Sound drastic, but believe me it works like a charm and makes a huge difference in your approach to high position. Keeping your facial muscles very relaxed, lightly close your Lips around the Egg. Leave the mouth open just a split, enough for the Air to enter. Move the Air through the nose into spinging position, to the top, at five and six, behind your eyes, in the Giro, inside The Chamber. You will soon discover how simple this is. The results are stunning.

I use the Egg with all of my students, bar none. Because of the position of the Egg, so far into the back of the mouth, they begin to understand the pulling back and opening of the Throat, naturally without tension. Then we take the Egg out of the mouth and recreate the space of the Egg's presence the way you need it.

Remember, always make sure that the back is open and the Lips are round and soft for perfect pronunciation. The Voice improves tremendously in depth and volume. The Jaw must be in a natural drop, no more than that, the facial muscles must be completely relaxed. The mouth is soft, as in speaking, no more. Now the Air from the Diaphragm is able to travel up to the Soft Palate and move fully into the spaces without being obstructed by anything. The Larynx and the Tongue are relaxed and the vocal mechanism is able to do what it needs to and does it naturally.

This is truly "Open Throat," the way you need it. Nothing else will do!! There must be total quiet on the bottom, so the top can do its thing. The Brain will take care of all the necessary actions, once it knows what has to be accomplished. Once you understand this kind of thinking, you will see that speaking and singing become one. You now have the freedom to express yourself as you always desired.

This is hard, hard work. Do not underestimate or expect that this will happen because you are reading this book. This takes a total commitment and understanding and as I have said so many times, **one Chapter at a time ... master it and only then go to the next one.**

Using the Egg and the Spoon creates and brings back the **Sound** and **muscle memory** of when you were born and the Instrument was perfect. Remember please, we are reconnecting to the original blue print (Birth-Knowledge). There is an energy connection between natural material of the Egg and the skin (Soft Palate) that is amazing. As with everything we talk about, care is advised. Please pay attention: do not swallow the Egg (obviously). Keep it steady; set it down on the back molars, resting there. If at first you don't succeed, try, try, again. The benefits are certainly worth the effort.

Now to the Ear Plugs and Nose Clip.

Your rightful question at this point would be: Why use a Nose Clip? Am I not supposed to keep my nostrils flared and my nose open so Air is allowed to move up and "five and six" can open?

A perfect question and quite right to be asked.

Have you ever held your nose and tried to speak without Sounding like you are under water? Have you ever felt that when you close your nose and you try to sing or speak, you Sound terribly nasal? Have you ever tried to sing or speak above your nose and found that if you do that, there is no nasal Sound at all, no pressure in the mask, that Sound are just sort of floating inside your head and clear as a bell?

By taking the Air through the eyeballs - actually guiding the Air through the <u>pupils</u>, straight back to be exact, you will be inside the perfect space. The pupils have to be identified as a hole, a vessel that can receive and by pulling the muscles behind your eyeballs backward and by leaving the mouth slightly opened etc., you will be able to enter the Giro without any problem. You will then realize, once and for all, that the 'bottom' (Throat) is totally superfluous in the creation and size of Sound.

The system we have set up is <u>exclusive</u> – the top only...supported by a totally Open Throat, dropped Tongue and dropped Larynx. Only in that way can the entire system work without touching the Instrument and last you a lifetime. The Throat is obviously necessary for the housing and passive playing of the Instrument by the brain, but the <u>sounding</u> of the Instrument is reserved for the Giro.

By now you know, that the Air in **FINAL POSITION** is taken (allowed to flow) **though the eyes, specifically through the PUPILS, attached to the muscles behind your eyeballs.** The Air is thus moved (mentally) to the tips of your ears where it rises (inside the largest space) and creates you Vowel Sound (Lag Time).

You also must know, that only a **minuscule** amount of Air is necessary to achieve this Movement *and that basically you are not taking in Air at all*, **but you are simply attaching yourself to that, which already exists in the right place** (because you now know how)... namely ... **the Air in the cranium**.

In other words, you are simultaneously connecting the three openings - Mouth, Nose and Eyes in the <u>highest place</u>. Thus we ultimately have simultaneous Air flowing without any 'physical' effort. Everything comes together there and only there.

Form the Vowel on top of the bridge as usual and watch what happens. You are not in the nose nor in the mouth anymore, you are above it all and deep in the back behind the spheres of your eyeballs ... Sound are beautiful and clean and float without interference. The most important thing is, of course, to keep the Air and Vowel Sound in line, always moving on the Air, upward and backward. Allow Air and Sounds to move in their own space. The Nose Clip, by keeping the nose closed in all the right places, will make you aware that if you change, if you drop, if you move, the Sound will immediately become nasal and get caught in the mask, pushing forward, getting stuck in the mask. If that happens, just begin again and you will see how little Air is really necessary, how much Air is actually available in the right place, and how free the Voice Sound, when there is no Movement on the bottom.

The minute you move the Jaw, the Tongue or the Larynx, the Vowel Sound will fall out of line, the words will make themselves in the mouth and alas, you will have to use the Throat . . . again.

The Nose Clip is of enormous help . . . it is not the most comfortable thing, but believe me it is quite important. You will have a tough time NOT knowing right from wrong when the Nose Clip is on. You can fool yourself with many things, but this one is foolproof. Your body and the Sound will tell you immediately what is right and what is wrong so please, get over the hump of thinking it is weird and just give it a chance. The results will prove beyond any doubt, what is right and what feels wrong.

Now to the Ear Plugs: This is the most difficult thing of all to accept, because this action closes off your external hearing. The reason the Ear Plugs are so incredibly important is because they finally connect you with your internal hearing/listening. Understand this is the basis for the correct internal Movement of Sound and Vowel. **As long as you are "listening on the outside" (ear level), you will manipulate with the Jaw, the mouth, the Tongue, the Soft Palate and the Sound in the Throat. You will want to achieve the "Sound" you know and are used to hearing.**

As long as you do that, your Sound will be just below the tips of your ears, right below the Soft Palate. This is dangerous territory because you are already in the mouth and very close to the Throat. At the level of the Soft Palate, the Vowel Sound will be low and the chances of them falling into the mouth are better than fifty/fifty—no good! Please understand, that you **DO NOT KNOW YOUR VOICE** . . . not the real one anyway, all you know is the manufactured one you have used in the past.

Let's analyze this concept further: The Brain knows how to move every cell in our bodies . . . ONLY the Brain KNOWS. The Brain is the Master Computer of the entire body and is totally in control of all of its movements and functions. As much as we try to control it, we cannot; and as expert as we think we are in understanding it, we only have but a minuscule understanding of how it functions.

The Brain has the thought: Only it knows where the Sound is; only it knows where the word is positioned. It knows the combination of where it is all made and how to move it, so it comes out perfectly.

The Brain is the mover and shaker of our entire system and we do not need to interfere with it, because **IT KNOWS EXACTLY WHAT IS NEEDED**. When we understand that our thoughts, our knowing, allow the Brain to do the whole job, then we also can easily understand why we should get out of the way.

That is certainly the most difficult thing for us humans to do, no question about it. Our job is to re-program the correct information and then trust the Brain to interpret that information in the right way. Believe that you now HAVE the knowledge that will get you the results. Please allow me to go a bit further with this:

Where do you think from? Your thoughts, your ideas come from where?

Of course all the answers are obvious. The Brain knows how to translate your thoughts, knows how to put thoughts into words, knows how to move the Sound and the word and knows how to articulate . . . knows how the mouth/Lips/Tongue move . . . the Brain knows how the vocal cords move, the Brain knows how the Larynx moves, the Brain knows the language you speak, the words you use, the intonations you desire, whether you want to speak or sing, it's all one conversation . . . it's all in the BRAIN.

Do you feel out of control in this conversation?? I bet you do. It takes a while to "get," that you are not in "control."

Well, that's not exactly so, because YOUR knowledge (conscious and sub/unconscious) is in control - **but without physically controlling**. Because of what you know and because of the fact that you know it, the Brain is able to identify it and make it happen for you. **Remember that I am not teaching anything that you do not already know. I am just taking you back to finding what you have forgotten.**

Example: Do you speak Urdu? No? . . . OK . . . your Brain cannot give you the language because it does not know it. If you learned how to speak Urdu, your Brain would know it and you would speak it. The Brain is a sponge, it can be taught anything and depending on how much, what and how you teach it, it will respond.

All we have been doing in the past Chapters is putting new knowledge into the Brain in order for it to be able to identify with Birth-Knowledge again. All we have done is taken "new/old" concepts and reintroduced them to the Brain, for the Brain then to be able to formulate ideas and produce them. The Brain stores this information and when it needs to, it uses it.

Why do I always tell my students: "Even if you know technique, you cannot take a new piece of music and sing it immediately; you must take it and put it into the

Voice". Every tone must be taught to the Brain . . . every note, every word and Sound combination must be familiar to the Brain for it to be there when you want and need it—the same way, every time. If you learn to listen internally and allow the Sound to GUIDE YOU, instead of your guiding it, things will be very easy for you. If you can abandon your knowledge and your thoughts, the Brain will do the rest.

The more out of control you are, the better . . . the more connected you are to your "head," the better . . . the more non-physical you are in your approach, the better . . . the more connected you are to internal listening and hearing, the better .

The more "mental/internal" your approach, the better—the more faith and trust you have in your Instrument, the more you OWN your capabilities, the better. **YOUR THINKING MUST BE IN COMMAND!**

So, the earplugs connect you to your internal hearing, taking out/away the outside "noise" and making you turn in, rather than manipulating on the outside. Think of being a ventriloquist and speak/sing/sping to the inside. If it goes in right, it comes out perfect. Your connection is always **IN** and the earplugs will guide you there.

Here we are . . . the Egg is in your mouth, the Nose Clip Is closing the nose, and the Ear Plugs are closing up your external hearing. The bottom is completely disabled. You MUST ENTER THROUGH THE TOP. You cannot hear on the outside, you cannot manipulate the mouth, you must allow the Sound to travel through the Giro and exit on the top . . . the bottom is closed, cut off, immobile . . . out of commission . . . you must give up to the "higher power" of the Brain. The Brain is your total connection to all your knowledge . . . past, present and future. By attaching yourself to its awesome force, you are connecting the Sound to its SOURCE and allowing the entire system to function naturally, as it was intended. By taking the manipulation of Sound in the Throat out of the way, you are allowing the system to function at maximum efficiency and giving yourself the opportunity to spiritually and physically connect on a completely different level than what you have been used to in the past.

Giving up your personal control of the Throat and concentrating into the real thoughts of your speaking and singing, will give you results beyond your wildest imagination. You will NOT KNOW THIS VOICE AT ALL. It is different from anything you have ever heard, but it will be your REAL Voice. **Record yourself** and familiarize yourself with the new Sound. **Identify that these Sounds are what you have always heard inside of you, but could never "create." Know that this is the real Sound of your Instrument, not the manufactured and manipulated Sound of the Throat. . . ALLOW THAT SOUND TO GROW!**

In the beginning, you may think it small, because what you hear inside will Sound small, muffled, different . . . but what actually comes out will be large and grow larger yet—just as you intend it. The intention of what you want it to Sound like, will make it happen . . . the intention of how big you want it to be, will make it bigger . . . the intention of the colors you wish the Sound to have, will be precisely the colors that will be produced. You have to **THINK AND SPEAK** . . . and out of your thinking and speaking, will come exactly what you desire. The Brain is here to fulfill your desires. Teach it what you want it to know, and it will please you with the results. Give yourself a break. Allow yourself to think the right way (what we have learned); whether it is singing or speaking you want — it's all the same. The Sound you desire, what you envision, will emerge and will be perfect.

Just one more word on this subject: After you have finished and understood all this, you will see that everything is tied together from a spiritual point of view and you will see that the physiological and the spiritual will again go hand in hand.

As human beings, a great many of us judge only what is visible . . . that which we can grasp, hold on to . . . the "real" stuff. Well, here I am asking you to go beyond your limits. Accept another way to achieve what you normally would have created with your Throat. Open yourself up to the possibilities of an Instrument with NO LIMITS, and watch what happens. Your Voice will go places you never thought it could; you will find that the limits you stipulated for the Instrument are way less than what it can actually give you - without strain, force, abuse, or pain. So use the Ear Plugs, the Nose Clip, and the Egg as much as possible. Sping that way . . . you will enter a new and incredibly exciting world.

Notes

The Secret of the Egg: Revealed

Caruso knew it, used it and discovered it in the singing technique of the great Cantors of his time!

At the beginning of this book, I shared the article "Caruso: The Mouth that could Cradle an Egg." If you do not remember it, please go back and read it again. The few words that are written, seemingly as no more than a comment, hold the great secret of Caruso's Voice and the Vocal Arts.

Caruso, for those who do not know, is considered and probably will be always the greatest Voice and singer in our known modern classical vocal history.

It is not up to me here at this time to give you all the reasons why. There are hundreds of recordings, articles, and books written about Caruso dedicated to his life, his Voice, his recordings, etc.

Here I want to focus on things that the world has either forgotten or does not know. Perhaps no one has put it together in the way I perceive it - perhaps someone has, but it is inconvenient, perhaps too easy, certainly it does not make money. Nevertheless, I will identify these secrets for you and show you the genius of this Artist and the **real truth about singing and the Voice.**

Popular acceptance by institutions or other Voice teachers would be fantastic and make my work that much more public and powerful, but I cannot remain in the background until they come around.

What is important to me is that you have the possibility of understanding and grasping it and that you have the opportunity of benefiting from this knowledge today!

I have been teaching these concepts for many, many years. Those who have refused their forums to me, perhaps now will change their minds, perhaps not. That too does not matter. It is my responsibility to reveal the secrets of the Voice to those who want to know, to those who care and to those who want to better themselves.

The Real Truth lies in the untold story, which I, specifically here in my book, wish to analyze and share with you.

All the comments which I am about to shares were written in the book: *"Enrico Caruso – My Father and my Family" by Enrico Caruso, Jr. & Andrew Farkas*.

For the sake of clarity, I will add page numbers and quotation marks so you can easily find the information, should you choose to do so. Everything that does not have quotation marks will be my personal analysis, commentaries and impressions.

Caruso used to go to Jewish religious services. His personal secretary, Emil Ledner, used to take him to synagogues in Hamburg, Paris, Budapest, Frankfurt, and Vienna, etc., where Caruso listened attentively. Ledner remembers: (pg. 337)

"He (Caruso) would prick up his ears at every solo by the principal cantor. Then he would drive home and practice half an hour the effortless attack and modulation of tone which seemed so precious to him." **Caruso explained**: 'I have discovered that the Jewish Cantors employ a peculiar art and method of singing in their delivery. They are unexcelled in the art of covering their Voice, picking up a new key, in treatment of ritual chant, and overcoming vocal difficulties that lie in **THE WORDS, RATHER THAN IN THE MUSIC**. For this reason I visit the Jewish synagogue whenever I have the opportunity and the time.'"

It is clear to me that Caruso understood the Intention of the Word and the tension of Vowel Sound connection. He further surmised that when a "real" cantor sings the words of the ritual chant, his **BEING** is transported to another place where the Voice is completely free and has no boundaries. *That place, he discovered, was attainable with the Egg, as mentioned by his wife, Dorothy.*

The Throat belongs to the "earthly" part of the body, but the Giro, the turn, belongs to a place that is non-controllable physically, but in which lays the potential for total mental control once the appropriate knowledge is re-programmed. I believe that this knowledge has always been there, is part of the original blueprint, got lost somewhere after the age of three and is now made available for re-introduction.

If you understand how to move inside of the Giro, you will be in total control without the physical need of manipulating anything.

Caruso was not a particularly brilliant man, but he was a consummate student and Artist. He took his Voice immensely seriously, worked diligently on his Instrument, and knew that he was the "case of a man who must, cost what it may, be continually at the pitch of his reputation…." (p.339)

He was aware of the fact that the music is produced in one place and the word in another. His Voice grew naturally and he was able to sing all repertoires in his own Voice. He colored the Voice at will, effortlessly and without the obvious change in registers which today is the norm. He had absolute line in his Sound and was able to sustain notes which today no one can even dream of.

The reason he closed his mouth around the Egg, as Dorothy points out, was because he allowed the Sound to be "pulled forward by the word."

Only in that way, can the Sound fly and be controlled by the Air and Vowel Sound, instead of the Throat. He kept his speaking in place: at the Lips, with the minute help of the teeth and the Tongue. He disciplined himself with the help of the Egg (raw), because he understood that the limitless potential of Sound - there should be no "switches" on high or low Sound, and the entire vocal structure should remain completely in one line.

He heard those qualities in Voices of the prominent cantors of that time, because this is the way they sang…ethereally and vocally correct. (In the Chapter "Hashem, The Voice and You", I will tell you exactly where this comes from.) He further understood that Sound had to move backwards on the Air inside the Giro. If that were not the case, the Sound and Vowel would collide in the mouth and create a potato Sound. He certainly must have conceptualized that the Egg does not tolerate the pushing forward of Air– the Egg would then fall out because the Tongue would rise in the back, drop the height of the Soft Palate, which, in turn, immediately closes the Throat.

Since Open Throat is the key to the lift of the Voice, it's height and depth, it was abundantly clear to Caruso that Sound and Vowel could not be made in the mouth but had to be separated (consonants at the Lips and Vowels in the Giro) - which would give each a place of total freedom.

Only if the Sound and the Vowel coupled inside this open space (Giro), could the word be perfectly dictioned …his pronunciation was impeccable.

He worked his Instrument intelligently, he thought about it and did not accept mediocrity. His Voice was his life.

In my own mind for years I have had one important question?

How come no one knows this???

Well, the answers lie in the words of Enrico Caruso, Jr.'s account:
(Page 337)

"Father knew what worked for him and what did not. What evolved as his own method of singing became second nature to him, a process that was all but instinctive, like speech to an ordinary person. He was no longer conscious of how he did it and could not communicate his technique to others. He once tried to teach a young man and was unsuccessful. After a few months of fruitless efforts, his accompanist Fucito said to him:

"Commendatore, you are a Singer, not a teacher. Stick to singing."

When I read these lines, I cried. Everything I have ever said about singers not being teachers and not being able to communicate their own vocal production to their students was vindicated right here. I do not think it necessary to repeat what I said before, but I have no intention of ever changing my mind about that. Singers are Singers, not Teachers.

The Voice is incredibly "deep." The power of the Voice is awesome. The Spirituality of what is the true vocal connection goes way beyond the individual Voice - it is the secret of life itself.

As you go on in this book, you will learn some truths that I published many years ago, way before I ever wrote this book. Later on, when I tell you where my information comes from, perhaps it will connect the dots.

Just one more comment about Caruso demonstrates that even after his body was wracked with pain for months, after Operations and the loss of most of his physical powers, he sang, better than ever. This, to me, demonstrates beyond any shadow of a doubt, that he was physically almost detached from the Voice and was able to reach the heights of his Voice just days before his death.

When I tell my students that on the day he/or she does not feel well, the Voice will be at its best, they look at me weirdly. I ask them to come to a lesson specifically on those days when they have a sore Throat, a cold, etc. On such a day, when they think the Voice is not there and we prove that it **is** and that nothing has to be canceled just because of some seemingly physical disability in the "Throat", the real truth of the Voice and where it ultimately comes from is revealed to them. That is the day a real singer is born.

On July 25th, 1921, shortly before Caruso's death, a boy came to see Caruso for an audition. In Dorothy Caruso's words:

"I heard the boy's Voice singing the first bars of "M'appari, Caruso's famous aria from (the Opera) Martha. He stopped, there was a pause and all at once the music began again. What a lovely Voice- and then I leaped to my feet and rushed up the stairs. There was only one Voice that could sing "M'appari' like that! I flung open the doors of the studio and there, beside the piano, stood Caruso, his arms outstretched a divine light of happiness on his face as the last note of the song died away. When he saw me he shouted, "Doro, Doro, did you hear? I can sing, I can sing as well as ever, I can sing! Oh, my G-d, I can sing!" (317)

Of course he could. **His body was absolutely out of control**. He did not need his Diaphragm and he did not need his ribs and lungs (contrary to the silly remarks and assumptions by his doctors)....nothing in his body worked anymore. But one thing in all his sufferings no one could take away –his thinking, his mind, his knowledge, the pure essence of 'WHO' he was a person and a singer – his innate ability to form the most beautiful Sound by allowing the Voice the freedom to truly express what only it KNOWS.

What he 'knew' and what created his mastery we are exploring here and now.

Notes

THE CHEST VOICE: THE OUT-AND-OUT DISTRUCTION OF GREAT SINGING

I am adding this discussion to the book at this time because with every student, somewhere down the line, this conversation surfaces and I am sure, if it comes into my studio, it similarly exists in the world of singing.

To my way of thinking, the concept of "chest Voice" is one of the major causes to which I attribute the destruction of extraordinary singing in any genre. As I mentioned before, great singing is dependent on flawless technique and an Instrument that is willing and workable. Most of all, great singing depends on the ability of the singer to follow a logical thinking process: in our case, the process that I have put forth from the very beginning – NO THROAT!

Anyone wishing to use "chest Voice" had better stop here. Please do not waste your time going any further. Forget everything you have read up until now because the use of "chest Voice" simply does not follow a logical progression of this work.

A few questions to start to put things into perspective:

Which part of the vocal Instrument is in the chest? If you answer the lungs, wrong…

Is the chest not attached to the Throat?

Have we not from the beginning established that the Throat and the use of it, is completely out of the question?

How much real Air can you get into the chest that will eventually help you "push out" Sound?

Does chest Air arrive in/at the Giro? If so, how?

When you create/make "chest Voice", how do you bring it out? The Jaw, the mouth? Lifting of the Tongue, dropping the Soft Palate? etc., etc., etc.

I am sure you follow my line of thinking.

Now for the answers - let me be very specific:

For me, there is absolutely no compromise on this conversation.

When the Giro is in use, and I hope that by now you understand how to use it, the production of Sound, any Sound, high or low, is inside the Giro, inside the turn of the Voice. The Giro has, like any circle (360 degrees), a top, middle and a bottom (contrary to the people who talk about registers - a head-Voice, middle- and a chest Voice).

As we know, the top of the Giro is the top of the skull, the middle is around canals 5 and 6, at the bridge of the nose, and the bottom of the Giro, is sitting almost on top the Soft Palate, right above the **Bone of Life** (Atlas).

Since the Air, which creates Vowel Sounds, moves upward and backward, and since we all know those Sounds move on Air, all Sounds are moving only in one direction, upward and backward. The fact that each Sound moves over the top of the head, through the Third Eye toward the Lips and thus liberates the Air to form the next Sound is due to the Intention of the Word and the slight Movement of Lips, with the help of the teeth and the Tongue.

The positioning for speaking and for singing is the same, always.

The Brain, and only the Brain, knows exactly where each Sound is, where it has to be placed, and where inside the Giro it fits. Knowing the music and word combination will allow the Sound to be "positioned" into the proper space inside the Giro without your "personal physical" intervention. Sound Movement is primarily mental, as is just about anything that goes on in the body when you come down to it. Without the Master Computer, there is no functioning of "anything."

It is of the utmost importance that you trust your technical knowledge, because if you do not, you will invariably have the great need to move low Sound from the bottom of the Giro below the Soft Palate, which then does not remain steady and does not stay up. The Throat then immediately must push forward, thus taxing the Instrument needlessly. The Sound "created" in the mouth, the Throat or any place other than the Giro, is different in vibration and color and seems foreign to the rest of the Voice.

The smooth line is gone, the flow is gone, the ease of the Giro is gone…very possibly the next line will begin where the last ended – in the Throat.

The Air which opens the Throat and moves into the Diaphragm (simultaneous intake of Air in the final position through the pupils), fills the entire Air column and creates support, *not Sound Movement.*

The fact that the lungs are attached to that "Air column" is really of no consequence to us. They (the lungs) have a job to do, but nothing that is of great importance to us here or anything that we can really control physically. Contraction of the lungs to get Air to move Sound is hardly possible, even though most teachers will tell you to expand the chest, the back, the ribs etc. The old adage "a great set of lungs" does not hold true…it never has. For lack of proper explanation and supposed "logical thinking," this concept, as well as others was created. That is not to say that the lungs do not have a part in the 'breathing apparatus (I am not that silly), but that their work is passive, whereas the work of the Giro is active.

Lungs do not provide positioning, the Giro does.

The Throat does not provide ease and perfect liberation of the Instrument, the Giro does.

The Throat does not allow the Sound to circulate with roundness and flow, the Giro does…

The Jaw pulls on the Throat muscles and constricts the easy flow of Air, the Giro does not…

The Giro gives you endless possibility and potential for height, depth, coloration and width of Sound; the Throat will ultimately give up. The vocal cords cannot take the constant onslaught of Air; a wobble, soreness, and lack of Air are the results. Usually the height of the Sound goes first, then perhaps the bottom - maybe the other way around, depending on the Instrument- - but slowly and inevitable, the rest of the Sound/Voice/production/ease/beauty, etc., fall by the wayside.

We have learned that our SOURCE for everything we need concerning Sound is in the Giro and the Giro is in the head, not in the Throat. If you count on the chest Air for Movement of Sound, you must, and I repeat, you <u>must</u> push forward in order to get the Sound to come out through the Throat and the mouth and that means that you are pressing/pushing against the Instrument and using the muscles of the Throat, taxing the Instrument.

Instead of allowing the apparatus to be free and relaxed to produce the Sound you desire effortlessly, you are actually maneuvering, modulating manipulating, controlling, and influencing the Instrument negatively to do what you want, not what your thoughts (music, Sound, etc.,) are directing it to do naturally. If this occurs, everything I have tried to teach you is thrown out the window.

You might as well go right back to taking your breath into the mouth down the Throat, making your Vowel Sound in the mouth and pushing the Air through the cords to create Sound. Fine with me, it is your Instrument, the only one you will ever have, your choice.

The mouth is a resonator, the chest is as well and so is every single cavity in our bodies. When you sing correctly, everything in your body vibrates the Sound. *I once read somewhere that a doctor took a stethoscope while Caruso was singing and no matter where on his body he placed it, he heard vibrating Sound.*

There is no question that the entire physical structure is involved in vocal production, the question is only to what degree.

The Throat, without a doubt, has an incredible job to do since it houses the Instrument; and the lungs and the Air column are all part of the great support system needed by the Soft Palate and the Giro to keep the Voice (Vowel Sound) up. The great singers of the past worked the Instrument naturally and, upon being questioned if they used chest Voice, a resounding NO was the answer. Others, who considered themselves more "profound in knowledge," searched for explanations and figured that if the Sound was low and deep it "must come from the chest and must be produced there." Thus, unfortunately, was this verbiage coined, which confused and still confuses the serious student – a pity, but true.

Of course, classical singers, who have always been adored as the vocal elite, have influenced the rest of the world and certain concepts, right or wrong, were therefore accepted, established, and perpetrated. Others have refused vehemently the mere thought that they defaulted and used the chest; many others have tried to explain what they do in terms that "mere mortals" can understand, yet very few have been able to translate what they accomplish into laymen's language. The media and the critics, doctors and "experts" have added their two cents and thus have managed to make everyone believe that the 'chest' is it.

Having said this, I am here to take the myth of "chest" out of the Voice and put low notes/high notes, all notes and Voices into an easy to understand and natural place, so that that, which always existed, but has been hidden under

layers of ... (please fill in the blanks --), will become available once again and give you the joy and satisfaction you deserve, without destroying the Instrument.

This book, in all its aspects, would never be written if I subscribed to those concepts. I have proven a thousand times over that Sound, especially low and deep ones, do not need the chest under any circumstances. They are easily and beautifully executed by allowing the Air and Vowel Sound the natural pull back and up inside the Giro.

The answer to this genuine problem is that it takes real work, work in understanding and thinking, and work in being able to produce physically what the mind perceives. That takes time and effort and a lot of willpower, character to stand against the pack and ultimately trust in what we are doing. Attaching to the SOURCE AIR, moving inside that space and allowing the mind to create its perceptions of Sound and Vowel and word combinations without molesting the Instrument, is not an easy feat, but very well worth the effort.

There are few singers today who are willing to put in what it takes and there are fewer teachers who know how to teach this - hence the lack of **true greatness.**

Here I challenge any singer, any teacher: Come and learn the way the Giro works and you will never have a need for creating and designing chest Sound again.

Don't believe me? Give me a Voice that is open, will learn and listen - I will change your mind forever.

Notes

Putting a Piece of Music into the Voice

You will hear me say it, endlessly. Just because you know a piece of music, doesn't mean that it is put into the Voice; that the Voice knows exactly where it is and what it has to do to get it right. We are right back into the conversation of "what you put in, you get out". In other words: if you have programmed the computer (Brain) correctly, you can expect the results to be virtually the same every time. If you have not done so correctly, or not at all, the easy parts will be OK, but the rest of the piece will come from a too familiar old place . . . the Throat.

The power, which you give to your past memory or the way you used to do it, will take over . . . the rest, is history . . . unless you reprogram, thoughtfully and diligently. Please remember: Each piece of music, no matter how well you "know it," must 'be put' into the new position. It has to be learned there, has to move there . . . not only part of it . . . but all of it. **There are no shortcuts here . . . none!**

This is discipline, which is rarely observed these days. Learn the music, learn the words, sping it with the Vowels only, then with Vowels and melody - make sure everything is in place and does not fall into the mouth . . . then, only then, add the melody. Now, you need do no more than SPEAK WHAT YOU HEAR . . . not sing what you hear, but SPEAK WHAT YOU HEAR. The Intention of the Word makes the combination. If you recall, we said, that singing and speaking are exactly the same thing (well in our way of thinking anyway) and that we are using the same exact Instrument for both.

The Brain, knows the music, knows the words, and knows the combinations and only the Brain knows how to put it all together. It takes the knowledge, computes it and then you speak it. The Brain does not care if a note is high in pitch or low . . . to the Brain, it is all the same. Simple enough—but this simplicity is only possible, if you have the information we have worked on throughout the book very clearly in your head. If one piece of the puzzle is missing, the whole house of cards falls apart.

It is imperative that the information become instinctive, that you don't have to think about anything when you are on stage . . . that the piece is so in the Voice, that you can be free to be the Artist who interprets the material, not constructs it. The Brain is the Master Computer. Everything begins and ends there. All your learning is now stored in memory banks - just like everything you knew, before your read this book. Your Brain has the power to recall information it knows in a fraction of a second and bring it forth . . . sometimes so fast, that you have virtually no idea where it comes from . . . and that is what we are looking for.

When you know something so well, that it just "escapes," without thinking or doing for that matter, you "own it." Sometimes we forget consciously, but that does not mean, that the information is gone . . . it is just put away. Birth-Knowledge . . . In our process, we are only restoring the memory banks to include seemingly forgotten information.

Too much emphasis has been placed by so many, on the "construction" of the Voice inside the Instrument (Throat). From the onset, we know that you cannot play an Instrument to its potential, inside a box . . . end of argument. So if the Brain knows where it (the information) is played, where the combinations of Sound and the words are for speaking, then why would that not hold true for singing as well. The Instrument is the same. The thought process is the same, the knowledge is the same (assuming of course, you know your material inside and out) the Lips formulate the words in the same way—or at least they should - why should there be a significant change in position? Obviously, there is not.

If you now understand, that in speaking as well as in singing, the Vowel Sound are formed on the Air, behind the eye balls, "inside" the Brain - are turned by the Air in the Giro and then, because of the Intention of the Word, become the spoken word - then singing, which is just more of same, should follow the same thinking and effect the same results. In singing, as in speaking, the Instrument will produce what the Brain tells it . . . so make it an internal conversation, not an external one. *What is going in right will come out perfect.*

We have very little control of what goes on in our bodies anyway. If we try to do anything, it usually spells trouble. *We* cannot make our blood run, our heart pump, renew our cells etc. We are, in all things, completely dependent upon the knowledge of the Brain, the workings of the body. So, give up control of the physical manipulation of the Instrument and allow, that which KNOWS, to use your information (repertoire music etc.), to move and guide the Instrument in the proper way. You give up the rest of your body, so why not your Voice.

Who & What Are You?

Well, by now you know something about the Voice, so let us talk about you - you the singer, the communicator, the person. You are different, you know, very different from others. It is true that a singer is born, not made. The same holds true with the Voice: you either have it or you do not (I mean the kind of Instrument required to be a singer). A person who is a singer is primarily that - a singer.

I have met many "would-be" singers who were talented, but in the end, it did not work out for them - not because of the Instrument, but because of who they were as people and how they viewed themselves and the world around them. You cannot be an architect and a singer, or a restaurateur and a singer. It simply does not work. At one point or another, you will have to make a life decision: It is either/or. You can sing and own a restaurant, you can be a great amateur, but you will never be a real, honest-to-goodness singer! There are a million things you can do in your life at which you can excel while doing them simultaneously — singing is not one of them.

Singing is different. Your soul, your passion and your spirit are undeniably connected to your Voice. Being a singer is as much of an *attitude* as it is a vocation. If you are a real singer, you will do anything to get to sing. You will sell pencils in the street (I have met such persons), you will be a waiter or you will go to night school and hold a day job just to pay for your lessons. Whatever it takes, you will do it. The Voice moves you. It holds you, captivates you, inspires and depresses you. In other words, the Voice rules you.

BRWARE! There are those who will take advantage of that passion of yours. One of my students shares her story here…read it…its horrific…run for your life!!!

I have heard much, known too many who have been used and abused and left holding debts and destroyed Instruments…those who have been threatened and manipulated by their teachers (great ones at that). I have been witness in my own personal life to the destruction of a potentially great career because of the abuse of a teachers power over her student…I have encountered deliberate sabotage, unbelievably cruel behavior and manipulation and I have heard potentially great Voices ruined –

Believe me; I have seen and heard it all during the years I spent 'in the businesses' of music/concerts, CD productions/television and film etc. in the States, Italy, Hungary, and Ukraine. What I experienced personally and through others, I hated then and I hate it now!

There are some singers walking around the world who have come to me with their hearts in their pockets and their Voices in a sling. I taught them before they went on stage, at two in the morning if necessary, gave my heart and my soul and when they were through with me, when they took everything I had, 'Bye' – Who needs you anymore –It's all mine –Who are you anyway?...

WHAT GOES AROUND COMES AROUND! MAYBE NOT TODAY, MAYBE NOT TOMORROW, but ultimately justice is done. It's all part of the deal, I spoke about it before. For everyone that has done that to me in my career, there are a hundreds whose love, respect and complete loyalty I have earned. Thank G-d.

You please be careful and be Aware!

Since the Voice is **also** *connected to the heart, you just cannot be totally ruthless,* cold, and insensitive, and, at the same time, be a great singer – there has to be some redeeming quality in you. Yes, I know when the business takes over it is hard to retain one's equilibrium, but ultimately, I want to think and believe that a true musical soul will overcome the pressures of the "evil inclination" and remain spiritually intact. An individual's Instrument defines a singer's sensitivity, by what it demands of him, by how it needs to be cared for, and how it responds to every emotion. Vocalists are singled out from all other Artist - they are divinely inspired. When the Voice is truly in the right place, the real Artist is swept away into another sphere and the Instrument plays without him/her in a realm of total "Oneness".

I know this is a lot to swallow, but I'll explain. I have been involved in all phases of the music business, from teaching, to management, to CD production, to directing, and producing. I have met hundreds of singers and taught so many more. I have been professionally involved with, and befriended countless. The outside world plays cruel tricks on the Artistic personality. One person has to please so many people in order to make a career. Everyone wants a piece of you when you achieve some status.

It's the way things are. Sometimes you might see yourself only as a "slab of meat" in the eyes of those who are looking to exploit your talents. Remember, as you think, so you are. You, and only you, are in control of how others see you. If you allow yourself to be taken advantage of, do what others want and do not go by your own feelings and sentiments, you have only yourself to blame. No one can make you do anything. You always have the last word.

Basically, deep down inside (forgetting the outside influences), the heart of an Artist is pure. A great singer only feels "good" when his Voice responds, and if he has a bad day, 'all the Tea in China' isn't going to make him feel better about himself. If the Voice does not respond, the singer feels let down, depressed, feels herself unworthy, frustrated. You know what I mean; and there is no cure for that, other than regaining the 'complete use' of the Instrument. That is the heart, the passion—this incredible connection between the psyche the spirit, and the Voice.

✫ ✫ ✫

When I hear a Voice, I melt inside. I turn to mush. I want to caress it and love it. I want to bring out its greatest potential, make it the best it can possibly be. I feel its power and beauty inside of me. I think and dream about it. I imagine how it would Sound singing "this" or "that" repertoire. I also know, that should a Voice come along which is naturally in perfect position, to leave it there, not to touch it technically at all, just be its guide and put music into the existing position –nurture and grow it, nothing else.

I am quite sure that most Voices are ruined because teachers MUST put THEIR mark on the Voice of their students and do not allow for the individual perfection of the Instruments (ego, ego, ego).

Example: For a while, I personally sat in on **Carlo Bergonzi's** lessons with an extraordinary young Tenor in New York who had incredible vocal qualities and fantastic height in the Voice … (Carlo Bergonzi was a very famous Opera Singer from Busetto, Italy, who runs the International Verdi Competition there). During that time, in 1981, I suffered in the Studio of a very well known Voice Teacher on 57th Street in New York and witnessed vocal destruction taking place and I could do nothing - no one would listen to me then. I do have very detailed notes and drawings of that time period and what I learned there, has lead and guided me all my life. I understood clearly that the abuse of power of the 'Greats' is devastating.

Later on in Italy, I realized that every Tenor who came out of his (Bergonzi's) Master Classes and Workshops had a definite signature on his Voice: Carlo Bergonzi's. [I obviously have lots to say about him and his competition, his Voice and professional practices etc. … but I will refrain at this time from doing so].

Before I went to live in Italy in 1982, I secured a position as a journalist, reporting for the prestigious **Opera News Magazine** about European Opera competitions. [At the competition in Enna, I met Giuseppe Di Stefano and Fedora Barbieri, Joan Sutherland and Richard Bonynge etc., and that was how my first directing job of Opera – at the arena in Augusta, Sicilia came about].

If anyone ever interviews me on the subject, I think that somewhere I still have the Article which I wrote as an expose' in 1982 regarding the Busetto Competition. When I sent it to New York for publication, it was flatly refused and I was told by Tony Russo, then with EMI Management, that the contents were 'politically incorrect' and that it could not be published]. I was fired and of course that started the other piece of personal history, which has brought me to this point. My autobiography **"Surviving the Survivors"** which is on the drawing board as the next big project, will tell the whole story in great detail.

When I lived in Italy, I met many teachers and vocal coaches whom I worked with, (even accompanists at the Conservatory in Milano) who sang repertoire and vocalized to and with their students. They all, bar none, demonstrated the work and the music/lyrics/interpretations with the help of their own Voices.

Unequivocally, and without a doubt, Singers who need to teach, should stick to only teaching, not ever sing to their students. Accompanists and coaches should learn how to do exactly that, teach and coach etc. repertoire, but never teach or touch the Voice. I have heard Instruments lose their height, color, and beauty because a student tried to emulate his teacher.

It took twenty years of hard work and a great deal of pain along with it, for me to carve out my own space in which to share my opinions and my outrage.

✲ ✲ ✲

These are powerful emotions for someone who does not sing.

The Voice stimulates me to listen with all my heart and soul. I can well imagine how all encompassing it must be for the person in whose body this Voice is actually housed. How can a vessel containing such beauty be anything but good? The Voice is ideal, ethereal, G-d-like. It is beyond human comprehension and will not be denied.

If you are a born singer, the Voice insists on being heard. Eventually, you must give in. I have had some students who are way past the age of sixty, but their Voices returned to be young and unscathed. The 'old' Instrument gave way to the 'new' and in this process, they too were renewed. I have taught them because I understood their need and their passion. In most cases, their lives took on new meaning—they felt rejuvenated and full of life. Their accomplishment was valuable in how it affected their outlook on the future, and I derived great satisfaction in facilitating such major life breakthroughs for them.

If you are having trouble with the Voice, (after applying our work), I believe there is something wrong with the connection to your heart. Something is "off" about the way you view the Voice and your life. For instance, if you consider the Voice your own personal property, if you think it will perform for you no matter what you do to it and no matter how you live your life—well, think again. In the beginning, I spoke about the Voice as being a gift, and so it is. The One who gave it can also take it away.

In order for you to establish the spiritual connection which I am talking about, you must dedicate the Voice anew every day. You must have a deep understanding within every fiber of your being that you are the Voice, and the Voice is you. You must realize that you are a chosen vessel to disseminate beauty and love through your Voice. You are inseparably connected to each other and, without a doubt, influence each other. If your heart leaps with joy, your Voice will be soaring. If you are unhappy and negative about something in your life, you will not be able to raise the Voice. Have you ever experienced that? I thought so. Consider this thought before you sing and understand that your emotions and feelings play a major role in the way you will express yourself vocally.

There are times in everyone's life in which you have to separate yourself from your Voice. By that, I mean that your life as a basic human and your life as a singer cannot always be connected. For example, if you had a fight with your boyfriend and have to sing that evening, you'd better forget the fight, completely disconnect and just be the singer. Only then will the Voice serve you. Easier said than done, but that is what it takes. People may think you are a miserable, self-serving person that you will walk over dead bodies to get where you are going. Oh, the reputations of singers—I know them all too well; and most of what you hear has an element of truth to it—but that is show business! When it comes to the Instrument, you are its slave. It controls your actions and feelings and never allows you to forget who is boss. You must learn to live your life according to the needs of the Voice. And your Instrument is demanding; you can't deny its needs. If you do, sooner or later, it will fail you. So please, be aware.

I explained this to one of my students. She partied, drank, carried on until some un-G-dly hour of the morning, and then came to her lesson. Need I say more? The Voice needs rest. It needs to be kept sheltered and warm, nurtured. It is within you, so what you do, to or for yourself, is going to be reflected in your Instrument. Please remember that before the next time you stay out until all hours and have to sing the next day. Think of the Voice before you make decisions on how to spend your time. A side note here: when you sing the way you were taught throughout these pages, usually you will be able to sing, no matter what.

If you have a sore Throat, a cold or even laryngitis, you can still sing. If however you have Pharyngitis (the two flaps in the back just below your Soft Palate will be inflamed and full of mucosa), you will be stopped in your tracks. Here we stop! Thank G-d, it happens very rarely. Through almost everything else, once you master the technique we are working on here, you will sing beautifully if your "head" is in that space. So do not be afraid to sing when you have a bad cold. If you work through it and apply our work, you will have a major breakthrough in your thinking and understanding technique. Be careful, never strain, sping quietly first and then increase as you feel more comfortable and confident.

By the way, in my conversation about taking care of the Voice, I am by no means looking to cloister you, or to make you into a vocal hermit. I am, however, cautioning you that if you do not take care of the Instrument and treat it with kindness, tenderness and a great deal of love, it will quickly un-tune itself and not serve you in the way you expect.

Think of the violin again . . . sitting in its case for months, stuck in some damp corner. Just imagine its condition when it is finally picked up again… and this is a man-made Instrument. A few new strings and a careful tuning, and it will be as good as new. The Voice is not like that—for obvious reasons. Everything you do, it does; everywhere you go, it goes; how you treat yourself has a direct bearing on your Voice. So cherish your gift and consider it.

Your emotions are a barometer for your Voice. I wish I had a dollar for every time a student came to me for a lesson uptight about something that had happened during his day. It is quite a task to get the Voice into place when you are in such a state. Everything that happens in your life is reflected in the Voice. When you are happy, the Voice is up; when you are depressed or strung out, the Voice is down. Obviously, if you are going to sing professionally, that cannot and must never be a factor. You must separate yourself totally from the rest of your life. When you sing, it is the Voice and only the Voice you think about. It is tough to do this in the face of the hectic and highly charged lifestyles we lead, but without a doubt, it is necessary.

Anyone who shares your life must be aware of this, respect it, commit to it and understand it. If not, they do not belong in your life. Perhaps until today (prior to reading this book), you may have given "the Voice"- the actual Instrument and its workings- only a fleeting thought. Well, from this moment on, this must change. You have to accept the responsibility for your Voice- technically, emotionally, physically, psychologically, and spiritually. Before you read this book, you thought of the Voice in a certain way, in one place; now you will begin to perceive the Voice in quite another way.

The road has been paved for you; all you have to do is follow. I pray you do - because unless you do, my mission in life will not be accomplished – at least not with you, and you are very important to me, every one of you. This book is your guideline to follow and is devoted entirely to you, the singer. Nothing else matters to me. So spend your time wisely, search inside yourselves and find the way. I have given you the tools, but the rest is up to you. I will repeat it again: Have patience; allow the Instrument to grow at its own pace. Do not push and do not go backward—trust and go forward.

Notes

The Career

This is not a book about how to make a career. I leave that in the hands of the management. My interest in the subject is purely directed at the Voice. I know you can sing, and I know you think you are ready for the "big time." But consider a few things before you throw yourself at the mercy of national and international competitions and/or management. There must be preparation - not only vocally and musically, but psychologically and spiritually, as well. You will be pitting yourself against some strong competition, and you must be ready. Your whole being must be geared up for the events to come, and I'd like to give you some pointers that I've found helpful in preparing students and that I've observed while talking to many a singer at competitions.

Choose your repertoire wisely.

If you trust your teacher, consult with him/her regarding the repertoire you should prepare. Do not overstep your vocal boundaries. Stay within repertoire that may be a bit easier than what you think you can handle so what you are singing is exactly right for you and effortless. What is the point in showing off what you can do when the risk is so great? If you take on more than you can handle, it will only add extra pressure - and you surely do not need that. Prepare your pieces with great care. Technically and musically, everything must be perfect. Never, ever present yourself anywhere, at any time, with music that has not been put into the Voice properly, no matter how much others encourage you to do so. Ultimately, no one cares about your Instrument – they care about their needs. I could tell you stories of things that happened in my life with singers that would definitely hold you back from climbing that ego ladder. To do this, I need to write another book. Please trust me, when I tell you: Never ever allow anyone to coerce you into singing repertoire that is not geared toward your Voice or that is not correctly studied and worked on. One such oversight may well determine your entire career.

The audience and management have a very long memory for bad performances and a very short one for good ones. You are always in the hot seat!

Think about sleepwalking. That is how you have to feel when you sing. When the music is in the Voice and you are totally secure of what you are doing, you can step in front of anyone, at any time and be vocally prepared.

Put the Music into the Voice.

Take your time to learn the music and the lyrics. Every note has to be thoroughly 'known' before you can be put into the Voice. Once you have mastered that, you know exactly how to do this: sping, "ee," and then add the words to the music. You cannot just pick up a piece of music and sing it. No one who is really serious about singing can. The Brain must be re-trained to give the body the right impulses, and that takes time. Not once, or even twice—but maybe twenty times or more. When you begin a piece of music, you're like a baby: first a helpless infant, totally dependent; then you learn to turn, to sit, to crawl, to stand, and finally to walk—then you're off.

There are NO Shortcuts in this, none. The same work has to be done with every piece – day in and day out. Once it is in the Voice, you can access it almost instantly, but know that the work is endless. The body changes constantly and you need to change with it – the Voice changes with the body and all these differences will be audible in the Voice. The constancy of your vocal workouts, just like those in the gym, is paramount. An athlete would never skip training – think of yourself as a runner getting ready for the Olympics – No Shortcuts!

When you begin any piece of music (unless you are a genius), there will be spots that seem out of reach. Patience, fortitude, love, and lots of hard work will enable you to make headway every time you sing. The notes will place easier; the Air will begin to flow more freely; the Giro will know exactly when to turn, when to cover (the natural cover is inside the Giro); the Brain will know how much Diaphragm you need to sustain a phrase, where to take a breath, and what the coloration of certain passages should be. The understanding and awareness of it all comes with thoughtful practice, patience, and trust in the Instrument and its functions. Give your Voice a chance. Do not push it into doing what you want. Follow its course, not yours. Work with it, not against it. Ultimately, you want the Voice to win. Let it make a winner out of you. Respect the fact that the Voice needs time to settle into a piece of music. You will see that sooner than you expect, the result you are seeking will be achieved. Close your eyes often and hear the music inside your Third Eye.

Visualize the Movement of the system before you actually begin.

Speak the music as though you were singing it. Sping, sping, sping. Your phraseology in speech is the same as in your singing. Always remember that. There is no difference. Place the speaking Voice into the Soft Palate and on top of the Giro. When you are spinging, measure the breath you need for the phrase. When you sing it, you will notice that it is exactly the same. Guide the breath always upward and "follow the yellow brick road" up, back, then toward the tips of your ears and the Bone of Life. You will see how powerfully you develop and what a profound relationship you will begin to have with your Voice. Remember that great wine is never sold before its time - so let your Voice ripen; and then offer it.

Be in control of your emotions

Nerves are a big factor. If you were not nervous, something would be wrong. Everyone is and should be; however, a person is overly nervous when he is not sure of himself. I f you have done your work and you have prepared, there should be no reason for you to be shivering before you sing. Nerves put you in touch with your vulnerability, and that is quite necessary. However, use this to your advantage; feel it, experience it and make it into a positive, rather than negative thing. That is adrenaline, and you need it before you step on stage.

Dedicate the Voice and ask for help

If you do not ask, you will not receive. Believe in your spiritual nature; allow it to lead you and trust it. Think of "giving" to those who listen to you. Think of enriching their lives with the beauty of your Voice and know that with such great spiritual power behind you, you will not fail. You will be calm and composed, leaving your fate to the will of heaven. If the universe supports your efforts, you will be secure and in control.

Notes

Colleagues & Friends

In every part of show business, you get the gossip, pettiness, and all of the other mean and rotten things you can think of, that's just the way it is'... Scratch that thought. Forget it immediately. That kind of negative thinking is for others, not for you. You can see all and hear all—but do not react. Be proactive, but do not be blind. Know what there is out there, be aware. Think of your Voice, your role, the music, the conductor, the band, the staging—anything—but do not let yourself be sucked into intrigues. This is not what you want or need. Keep your opinions about other singers to yourself. Do your job. Be pleasant, cordial, professional, centered. Know who you are and be sure of your own worth; but do not be a snob. No matter how big you may become, remember that you meet the same people on the way down as you did on the way up – the only difference is that they will be cruel to you on the way down while they were …lickers on the way up. Not nice, but very true.

Try to create only good feelings between yourself and others. Concentrate on being quiet and centered inside and out. Only then will you have complete control of the Voice. Be friendly with everyone, but make friends with few. To be more precise, only make friends with the people whom you have "tested" many times and who have proven their loyalty and sincerity to you under different circumstances in your career. Compliment sincerely, or be silent. Smile, but do not be false. Try to find the good in everyone and in every situation – hard, but ultimately good for you. Do not be aggressive. Be tolerant and assertive when necessary, but always stay within your bounds. Do not make waves. In the end, it will not benefit you in many ways.

Being called a "diva" today is not 'always' a compliment. Capriciousness and temper tantrums went out a long time ago even if scandals make headlines and sell newspapers – rise above. Look for harmony. Only in that way can you find yourself on the winning side. Do not be a "woos" either. Show character and know who you are; always stand your grounds. Put the Voice first. **Think before you speak; the ramifications of your words create your future.** Respect others, and you will be respected. Take a stand for yourself and for your Voice, and you will see that others will begin appreciating you. It is important to look good, but do not sell your soul for it. Be an individual, but in all things, be circumspect, diplomatic, and tolerant.

There is a great deal to be said for what we just discussed. In my years with many different professionals in the business, I have seen it all. I have also been witness to many a promising career ruined by all the superficial nonsense. So please, heed my advice and take care of your ego. That is really what it all boils down to, the ego. A healthy ego is good to have and is necessary in order to be able to step out onto the stage and give your best, but don't let "it" get the best of you. You achieve more with honey than with vinegar - an old cliché but important to remember when you are trying to enter the rat race of show business.

Notes

Speaking &Communicating

(Doesn't apply to you? Well, look again.)

I have mentioned a number of times that speaking and singing is the same thing. If you learn to "put" your speaking Voice in the same place as your singing Voice, you will have an easy time of it. Imagine if all day long you spoke in the Throat, as most of you do. You grate the Voice and then all of a sudden, when you start singing, you expect the Voice to perform for you from another place altogether. It does not work. The system works equally in both cases, and you should begin visualizing your speaking Voice in your singing Voice position and vice versa. The more you are able to do that, the easier it will be for you.

I want to talk about communicating for a moment. Most of us do not think about it much, but as human beings and of course as Artists, we need to spend time talking about this. Communication is such an important part of our lives. The way we communicate, dictates how we are being understood. Much is at stake. If there is a breakdown in communication, be it in interpersonal relationships or in the professional world, it is usually due to some form of verbal misunderstanding. Whether we are speaking to a large group, expressing our emotions, or just engaging in a normal conversation, our communication depends on our intonation, pronunciation, diction, and the way we modulate our Voices. Our Voice reflects every emotion. Have you ever talked to someone over the phone and immediately, after the first hello, you knew that something was up? Of course-it has happened to all of us many times. Our tone reflects our mood, and our words have an enormous impact on the people around us. With our speaking, we create our world; and it is in our speaking, that we open all the possibilities in our lives.

In my years of teaching, I have developed a methodology of speaking with my students. I think I mentioned before that I am very demanding as a teacher. I give a great deal of love, but do not pamper. I demand the utmost, because I believe that is what it takes to be able to use the Voice properly. A relationship must be built with affection, caring, and mutual respect, combined with a great sense of professionalism. I can teach a friend of mine, but while I am teaching, I am the teacher, not the friend—and there is a major difference.

Even if a lesson is not going so great, and we are struggling, at the end of every lesson I compliment my student. This is not to falsely make anyone feel good, but to acknowledge his/her effort. Sometimes, the student will be surprised by that he/she had the feeling that there was no progress etc. or that the lesson was not" successful." I explain that every lesson, no matter how difficult, **holds a key to future success.** In doing it wrong, there is learning and an element of gain. Even if you do not think you got anything now, the Brain has absorbed the material. The Brain will then compute, digest, store and process. More than likely later, when you least expect it, the Brain will make it (the knowledge) available to you. Encouragement, acknowledgment, and praise are the cornerstones of learning and necessary in developing communication with anyone, especially a teacher with a student.

My students will tell you that I can really be tough, but at the same time, they will say that I give my all to that one note that ends up making the whole lesson worthwhile. The little things count, the extras. Always be ready to step beyond yourself and "go for the gusto." I do so in my teaching, in my life, and in my dealings with others. I do not leave a stone unturned to help, as long as I see that the student is trying his very best. If I perceive a student not to be giving his all and feel that all of my effort is in vain, or if I feel that his heart and soul are not in the work, I let him or her go—with explanation of course, but I cut the cord.

Finally, it is all about humanity and if I wanted to really get into this subject, I would have to write yet another book. However, please consider humanity in all you do and allow that to be your yardstick in communicating with others. Sometimes, things seem very black and white, but nothing ever is. Give the benefit of the doubt to everyone and think with your heart, not only with your mind. Most of all, be patient; please be patient. Patience is a great virtue, and the Voice needs you to be patient and give it time to develop naturally. Always talk to your trusted teacher/friend. Communicate; if you have something to say, say it. If you need an explanation, ask for one. Think about the system often and do not be afraid to address your fears. It is all part of learning, and a good teacher will understand and be open and honest with you. Communication on every level is so important. Most of us go through life and have no idea with whom we are dealing. We have friends, lovers, and siblings and colleagues whom we really do not know. Make an effort to give of yourself to others. Be open. I am not saying to tell everyone your life story, but in your dealings with family and acquaintances, be able to say what you mean and mean what you say.

There is no point in playing games. Oh, I know - we all do it from time to time. It is expected. However, try to limit this habit as much as possible. Remember that with your word, you create your world. Honesty is not about hurting someone. It is about sharing with them how you feel and listening when they share with you. There are always two sides to every story. Always put the shoe on the other foot and see if it fits. You may think that you are right, but if you examine a bit more closely, you might see that the other party has a valid point, as well. Talk about it, and you will see that honesty and sincerity go a long way.

Did you ever hear the expression "the tone makes the music?" Well, that is the key. You can say almost anything to anyone as long as you say it in a way that they can understand. If a person feels your sincerity and genuine caring, he will not be angry with you when you say something he might not want to hear. Do not criticize, but critique instead; be constructive and kind- that is a completely different thing. Make sure that your points are valid, to yourself and to the person with whom you are communicating. Base your opinions on facts and on your feelings; always be sure that your words hit their mark gently and with compassion. Talk to someone the way you would want him/her to talk to you. More easily said than done, I know. Your ability to listen is imperative.

Your communication skills on stage have everything to do with how the audience perceives you. Pavarotti was a great communicator and so is Domingo. These Artists have learned what makes us spectators 'tick' and they use their Voices, their musicality and personality to the max. A smile, a gesture, the use of a handkerchief, the way you stand, the look in your eye, the way you accept the accolades from the audience, your humility. All these important factors enter into how your future will map out. The generosity in your communication is important. Be large, giving, expansive and open. Do not hold back. Let go of yourself and share yourself.

Pavarotti, Domingo and Carerras are actually products of our hyped-up society. Oh, do not get me wrong. I am not putting down their abilities as singers and personalities, by any means. They are communication masters on and off stage. They have done so much to make Opera more broadly accepted and appreciated. They have sparked the imagination of so many and brought the art to a wide spectrum of our society. They have made it exciting for us, and I applaud them as Artists and as humans. I am just talking about the whole image thing.

Let us take for example, Caruso and Gigli, Pons, Ponselle and Curci, Sutherland, Tebaldi, Pinza, Chaliapin, Di Stefano, Gedda, Tagliavini, Tucker, Warren, Pierce, Bjorling and so many more. Those singers in the classical world were masters of the Voice. Their names were not household words like the Beatles for instance, but in the circles of Opera and music lovers those are GREATS. None of them ever achieved the incredible popularity that the immense publicity wheel of today has conjured up for the Three Tenors.

Alfredo Kraus was one of the greatest Tenors of our time. He never sold out to the media hype. His Voice was his love, and his love for the Instrument ruled his entire career. His later career was as glorious as his early one, because he kept the Voice in the forefront of his dealings with the music. He never sang repertoire that was not indicated for his vocal abilities. He was a consummate Artist and greatly respected for his personal and Artistic integrity. However, he was not a "people's Artist;" he was an "Artist's Artist." It is a pity that the general public did not learn to truly appreciate his mastery, but that is a part of the times in which we live. I believe that Artistry and skill, stage presence, and true vocal excellence in any genre will always be respected, revered, and certainly always coveted. Those singers will live on in our hearts, and when we talk of the Greats of Opera, it is to them that we are referring. Their communication to us bridges the information age, and so their recordings will live and inspire us forever.

No one is perfect. We all know that, but the public wants to see only the best. So give it to them in all ways. The more you give, the more you will receive. I suppose that about sums it up. Open yourself to the possibility of being the best you can be and watch—the universe will support the noblest and highest thought to which you aspire. Never settle for mediocre, go for the gold

I KNOW YOU CAN DO IT — AND I WISH IT FOR YOU.

Notes

Hashem, the Voice & You

The Revealed 'VISION'

Before You Read This Chapter:

Please do not read this next Chapter unless you have read and digested the entire book previously.

Nothing I speak about here will make any sense at all unless you have a firm foundation of the previously outlined knowledge. Everything in this Chapter is based upon the understanding of the work we have until now.

The "Revealed Version," which was the actual name of the third edition, I now call the "Revealed Vision."

What I outline here is my personal understanding of the concepts of Torah, the five books of Moses, the Old Testament, which is the foundation of Judeo-Christian spiritual beliefs.

For me, this way of thinking has combined the technique of Voice, which I have been teaching for so many years, with my spiritual studies. This is how I understand the Voice. This is the way I have ultimately found my answers and this is what keeps the flow of my work fresh and forever innovative.

This is also the reason why my teachings achieve the results they do. It is important for me to share this with you. Whether or not you agree or disagree, believe or do not believe, is of no importance to me and does not influence your ability to grasp these concepts in any way. What I and so many of my students have experienced and the work, which is the consequence of this knowledge, has been amply demonstrated. I am obviously not telling you that in order to "get it" you must believe as I do, what I am prefacing here is in what manner this information came to me and opened the door to my life work – in other words, I am sharing.

I do not intend to convert" anyone – I just want to help those who are looking for truth in Voice, find it!

Many years ago, when I began this journey, I had no idea where it was going to lead me. Certainly, I had never thought that my professional life would evolve in the same way as my personal life structure, my belief system, and my ethical and moral values. To me, the Voice has always represented the essence of my own communication, but until a few years ago, it did not take on the deep Spirituality, which I now fully understand is necessary in order to become ONE with the Voice, to use it to its fullest potential, to understand its depth and to realize it's astounding power.

When I wrote "The Voice: A Spiritual Approach to Singing, Speaking and Communicating" (1st edition 1999, 2nd edition 2001, 3rd edition-Revealed Version, 2004), I could not possibly have conceived the impact this book would have on the world of "Singing." I never fathomed that so many people would be affected by it - but then, who understands the ways of Hashem (one of the names of G-d) and who knows why He chose any one of us to accomplish our tasks - and to what greater purpose? Let us think for an instant about the incredible potential which lies in the Voice . . . truth is, we mostly take it for granted, pay it no mind, simply use it and sometimes even abuse it, until the moment when we suddenly realize that something is wrong, and that it no longer functions the way it "should."

Like everything else in our bodies, the Voice hangs in a delicate balance. We have learned, since we were very small, to perceive the Instrument inside the Throat. We have no reason to question what is considered by "all" obvious; after all, the vocal cords are in the Throat and everyone knows the Voice box is in the Throat; besides, no one gives us other information to the contrary, so we are satisfied with this knowledge and use it as part of "what we know to be so." Since Ear, Nose and Throat Specialists support this way of thinking, and Speech Pathologists/Therapists base their thinking and professional work on it, therefore IT MUST BE SO.

Please ask yourself simply: can you realistically PLAY an Instrument in a BOX???? The answer is NO. Perhaps it is possible in some way, the cynic would say, but for certain, the potential of the Instrument can never be accessed in the box. The Sound must be set free in order to achieve the Instrument's fullest potential. This is only logical.

Let us go to the beginning, to the Master Computer of all things, and connect with and to the knowledge, that everything in our bodies is controlled by the Brain. Every organ, the flow of blood, every cell, the entirety of our complex nervous system, its functions and interactions, all is carefully orchestrated and regulated by the Brain. It alone guides the whole system; it is in complete control of everything that goes on inside our bodies.

I call the Brain "Hashem's Space," or "G-d's Space," THE SOURCE OF ALL THOUGHT, because it is and will always be a mystery to us - something we desperately wish to explore, control, and fully understand, but cannot. Even with all the research being done today, glimpses are gleaned, but I truly believe controlling the Brain will elude us because we are not meant to ever 'know' it. We will never understand the ways of G-d.

We, as human beings, are curious and try to figure out and label everything. We want to have definitions and answers , but when we come right down to it, the Brain is an enigma, which eludes total definition and remains elusive and out of our control not matter how "advanced" we consider ourselves.

Today so many parts of the body are replaceable - the heart, the kidneys, the liver, limbs- but not the Brain. It is the very place reserved for Hashem's (G-d's) communication with us and it is there (in the Brain only) that we are able to connect the INNER and the OUTER Voice. Only there can we connect to our thoughts and to the reality of our communication.

Like Hashem, the Brain is an intricate part of our humanity and its magnitude and significance is unquestionable. Our understanding of the workings of the Brain is so very limited and, as much as science thinks it has "figured it out," we ultimately have to admit that we have but a minuscule understanding—that the ultimate potential of the Brain is too vast, far beyond human comprehension. The Brain has a life of its own and we are very dependent upon its ability to guide and develop us—from birth to death, it is all-powerful. If the heart stops, we have a chance; if the Brain stops, it is all over.

Every Brain is different, much like every other characteristic in the body- personality, psyche, and sensibilities of the person to whom it "belongs." All these facets have a great effect on the overall performance of each individual Instrument (Voice). The Voice masks and mimics the deep-rooted power of the individual and, in many ways, mirrors his/her life. The Voice tells us much about a person. How they speak, their intonations, if they are humble or aggressive - if they mumble and hide or speak clearly and confidently; if the Voice is subtle or soft, if it projects authority etc. . . . the kind of vibrations it creates within us, how we therefore respond, how we reach out vocally, how we express what we want to say, our diction . . . the Voice provides infinite possibilities, which are at our personal disposal. How we use this potential defines our lives.

Language as a whole is a fascinating kaleidoscope of the persona. The implications of the Voice are endless and its influence astounding. The Voice can cloud or reveal, fashion or devastate . . . create joy or lead us astray, project love or hate . . . the Voice is all-encompassing and stores secrets beyond belief. Think of life without the ability to communicate for just one day and you will appreciate this very special gift and never take it for granted again.

I personally have always had a great connection and deep respect for the Voice, but it was not until after I began my work with the Rabbis and Cantors, that the knowledge of the Voice and the profound spiritual connection to the Voice revealed itself to me. By way of my personal Teshuva (Return) and learning of Chassidus (the Chassidic Teachings of the Lubavitch Movement of Chabad), information and clarity "arrived" and I began to understand, that the original version of the book must make way to the "Revealed Version" which I began formulating and expanding six years ago and which I am actually expounding on now.

Technically, everything that we have outlined in the previous Chapters remains the same. Little has changed on that score, more illuminations perhaps, some terminology adjustments, some definitions added, but by and large, everything is the same.

What has changed, though, is the depth of the spiritual connection, the availability of which has significantly affected my own thinking and teaching over the years, and from which ALL my students have benefited. Because of all this, it is now possible for all students of the Voice, to access the hidden possibilities and connections to the Instrument.

I mentioned before that I teach Orthodox Jewish men who are not allowed to 'hear the singing Voice of a woman'. By now, you know of course, that I personally do not sing a single note in any of my teaching and that everything is achieved through in-depth communication ONLY. All of the work with my students is carried out by means of pure understanding of the internal working origin of the Instrument. The Movement and physical expression of the Sound is my guide and the ability to feel each vibration in every Voice, in each and every student of mine, is the key. I have been gifted with an extraordinary capacity to "feel" and "internally hear" every Sound in my own body. In other words, the Sound you make reproduces itself inside my Brain, provokes responses in my thought processes and guides me into knowing exactly what you are doing. I access the information, Sound by Sound, and guide you into the hidden and secret spaces where your Sound lies. Since I have been "taught" not to have the EGO of my own Voice, I become "Every Voice" and because of that, I am able to take each individual Instrument and tune it according to its individual capacity without interjecting my own "vocal needs" and habits.

Most teachers demonstrate by singing—the student follows—repeats, tries to imitate, emulates . . . I do not. I communicate with the Instrument in its own language, on its own playground. Taking the students into their own bodies and leading them into the sacred spaces, which Hashem has created for the Voice, that is my job. I do not have to literally 'see' the student in front of me, once we have created our own language (which usually takes three personal hours) we can be anywhere in the world and continue our work with extraordinary results on the Internet, anywhere in the world.

When I teach on the Internet, I teach behind a virtual Mechiza (a divider in Orthodox synagogues to separate men and women). I do not "need" to see, I need to hear, to feel, to listen WITH and TO the internal Voice, in order to guide my student into the sacred space, reserved for accessing humanity's most precious gift.

Here is the question which is always asked of me: "Where did you learn this?" My answer is always the same. I have been blessed; Hashem (G-d) has revealed this knowledge to me so I can share it with the world, so I can teach it to anyone who wants to know, and so this book can be written and help those who desire it. As I mentioned in the beginning, I have not been trained by any formal institution and if that is what matters to you, choose one of those teachers who comes out of the folds of a "Vocal Pedagogy" program from a 'reputable' University. If the Voice matters to you beyond all the other extraneous considerations, then continue on the way we have paved here and your vocal success is virtually assured – never guaranteed mind you – that, in the final analysis, depends on you.

My personal road has been arduous. My life and how I arrived at this point after years of personal sacrifice and suffering, is material for movie scripts. The apparent loss of my own Voice due to vocal cord surgery nearly destroyed me emotionally. The realization that I wanted to sing but that I was not 'meant' to do so, took years to comprehend. I was born to teach and give, rather than look for the stage for myself. I was not born a Singer . . . (singers are not made, they are born). Only many years later did I understand that I was a vehicle, a vessel to help others achieve and realize their dreams.

Many things about my own Voice and my own struggles with the Voice did not come clear until a few years ago. I have had to change my own thoughts and views and discard much of what I held on as truth for a long time. All of these realizations, which have dominated my professional career, coupled with my becoming religiously observant, are responsible for these illuminations. Once I came to terms with this incredible task and accepted my "lot", it took years before

I could actually dedicate totally and completely to G-d's work. Once I accepted wholeheartedly, the answers became readily available . . . one by one.

This is not in any way meant to be an autobiography, and it is not. It is simply meant to explain that I did not get the knowledge that I am sharing with you at any university, or through study with individual teachers or pedagogues, who propose singing lessons around the world. Divine Providence (Hashgacha HaPratit) has revealed each piece at various times over the last 35 years. The conversation which we are about to enter, has evolved over the past twelve years (it all began in 1997), almost simultaneously with my final decision to become Shomer Shabbos (Sabbath observant).

I have always taught the same concepts of vocal production, learning myself all the while from my work and my students. Not until recently did they take on the deep spiritual meaning that they have now. Never has it been easier to make all concepts flow together, so every student can understand them almost instinctively. Torah (the Old Testament, the Jewish bible, the five books of Moses) is the key to life and since our lives as human beings revolve around communication, Torah is the key to the Voice.

Hashem SPOKE to the people at Sinai and the people swooned/died/lost consciousness . . . "the Voice" of G-d was so beyond the capacity of human comprehension, beyond the capacity of the human psyche to grasp, that the mind could not fathom it.

King David sang his praises to G-d and through his singing, connected with G-d. Similarly, we, through our recitation, search to do the same. Song is 'G-d's delight', it pleases Him. The Psalms are filled with references to the Voice, to singing, to the Sound of Hashem's Voice and to the joy that it brings to man and G-d alike.

The Levites, the singers of the ancient Temple, the Beis Hamigdash, prayed in captivity:"Let my Tongue cleave to my palate." They understood the awesome power of the Voice and knew how to stop it from "Sounding." They understood that THAT Movement of the palate would silence and destroy the tones of their Voices. Miriam the Prophetess, sang with the women at the Sea of Reeds, through song empowering the people during the crossing, giving confidence and fortitude in a time of great tribulation.

Examples abound endlessly throughout the Torah and throughout human history from the beginning of time. Hashem used the "Voice" to communicate with our ancestors of Blessed Memory. His words filled their consciousness and by acknowledging the "Voice" of Hashem, thoughts, laws, information, demands, edicts, etc., were revealed for us to follow.

Each of us possesses the capacity to listen internally and hear "The Voice," yet few listen, others deny, but no one can convince me, that at one point or another in their lives, the INNER VOICE has not contacted them. The OUTER Voice merely reflects what is going on in the deep recesses of one's mind—the conversations that we perceive in our daily lives are nothing more than the inner workings of our subconscious, which is ultimately attached to our ALL KNOWING. What we hear, and how we interpret what we <u>think</u> we hear, depends, of course, on how "connected" we are and how well we access the communications of the Inner Voice. Listening deep inside, allowing direction and guidance, may to some constitute a sign of weakness, dependence, or being out of control. Perhaps, but it is all a matter of how you USE the information you receive and how adept you are at interpreting what it means.

YOU KNOW EVERYTHING! The secrets of the universe are locked and to be unlocked, in your subconscious. You know TRUTH, ALL OF IT. You have been taught through lifetimes to understand Hashem's language and His Voice and you are aware of that knowledge in the deepest recesses of your soul. Only there do you fully exist! Only there do you fully connect to your true potential which then, in a watered-down version (which we consider palatable for human consumption), projects itself to the outside world.

When we are born, a very special Angel touches us in the spot right under our noses on the upper lip and we forget our knowledge. We then spend a lifetime looking to reconnect to it again. (The spot we are talking about is where the Intention of the Word meets the Sound ... right at the Front Teeth.) Some obviously, have not been touched HARD enough and are able to learn and connect faster than others and, as we go through life, things reveal themselves more easily. Those unhampered minds are privy to information others are not; those are chosen to direct and affect.

You must be open, receptive; you must ASK to deserve to receive and when Hashem deems it so, He opens your Reservoir of past memories and the "Re-Educational Process" begins ... Again.

Nothing is New - Absolutely Nothing! All the cumulative knowledge we possess. It is what I call "Birth-Knowledge." This is the innate knowing of all things-the ability to distinguish between truth and falsehood, the primal cognizance of choice-this is our greatest gift and separates us from all other of Hashem's creations. This is our instinctive capacity to connect to our deepest spiritual yearnings, representing the holiest levels of our beings.

All this is available NOW!! We know everything and we possess the ability as human beings to achieve immense spiritual depth. Every person has a reservoir of lifetimes of knowledge, which becomes more viable through meditation, learning, discipline, and study. By allowing the listening for the information that Hashem imparts to us to happen, to allow this information to enter our conscious minds, the Inner Voice, which tells truth and connects to the outer being, creates our reality on a daily basis. Listening to the internal Voice is the key—identifying its source is paramount; acting upon it depends on each person's individual capabilities, sensibilities, and level of Spirituality.

When I ask my students in their first lesson, where the Voice IS, the answer I invariably receive is, "In the Throat". The Throat (in Kabbalah, the mystical part of the Torah) represents limitations (Meizarim), Egypt (Mizraim) slavery, exile, the inability to move, being stuck, no exit, no light, darkness and restriction. Yet, the key to freedom lies in slavery and the key to the Instrument lies in the Throat. Liberating the Throat and allowing the Instrument the freedom to "PLAY" as it was meant to, represents the challenge of EXILE VS.REDEMPTION, FREEDOM VS.SERVITUDE and BONDAGE. It is only because of the existence of exile (Diaspora) that deliverance is possible.

Everyone knows that the place is known as "The Voice Box." All of us are aware that you cannot play an Instrument in a box. It is therefore necessary to find a place outside the box where the Instrument can be played, can expand, shine, move, glow, reverberate, come into its own glory, find freedom, come alive, develop, and more than anything else, express itself without ever being constricted, enslaved, forced, and tortured as it would be in the confines of the Throat. The Throat is merely the house for the Instrument . . . it is a small space, restricted and full of many other elements that inhibit free Movement. You have a choice . . . a choice between slavery and freedom, restriction and liberation, illumination and obscurity. YOU can make that choice! You can choose NOT to accept all the negativity associated with the Throat; you can choose to give up control and manipulation and ALLOW the "system" to do it all for you. You can control without controlling . . . you are the captain of your own ship . . . but a captain must know HOW to navigate and work with all the related elements in order to maintain a great and safe vessel under all circumstances and conditions.

One of the most difficult things for us humans to do is to give up our Control. We want to feel that we are the "cause" in all things, that our intelligence and abilities are a reflection of our beings and that we are, of course, appropriately appreciated for all of our talents. We need to "create" everything that is happening in our lives. When things occur that seem beyond our control, we feel lost and cannot find our way. We respond with anger, hurt, embarrassment - a myriad of negative emotions. It is only when we do not know where to turn, when desperation becomes our companion and the inability to cope surrounds us, that we then reach out and search for the inner strength, which Hashem has given to each one of us. Then we can only hope and pray that our knowledge and training and letting go of control will again connect us to the greater potential we all possess.

We have been given incredible abilities - potential beyond anything we can fathom. It is our mission, in each lifetime, to connect with this potential, to find the greatest talent which Hashem has bestowed upon us, and bring it to its highest level—for the good of all Humankind - and then give it BACK to Hashem in its purest and most elevated form.

This is what I tell my students when they come to me and want to become singers. This is my conversation with those who are already singers, who cannot live without achieving "the Voice," - who are intent on their desire to share their Voice with others, who are depressed and miserable when their Instrument is not free - those who feel debilitated when they cannot express themselves openly and freely. There are those who hurt physically, because the strain is too much for the Instrument to bear – and then there are those whose psychological/physical/emotional repercussions cause them to lose their Voice altogether.

They come with problems inflicted upon the Voice by "The Outside World' because, at birth in most cases, the Instrument was perfect. Hashem created it to last a lifetime- its purpose to sing, to speak, to communicate. We, unbeknownst to us of course, take it (the Instrument) out of its natural habitat and bring it into exile - into Diaspora, into 'limitations'.

Somewhere around the age of three, we begin receiving information from external sources making us believe that the Voice is in the Throat, and slowly, ever so subtly, the Voice moves out of its "natural space" into the Throat. It does not take very much ... "just the wrong thoughts." We forget Hashem's space. Our peers who, after all "KNOW," tell us that the vocal cords are in the Throat, (and of course, they are). This truth makes sense and so our belief system is again in tune with external information. After all, if you have a sore Throat, you cannot sing or speak. They also tell us that this is where the Voice needs to be manipulated, that this is the place where the "vibrato" is produced, and that the Throat is the mover *and the shaker of the Sound. That is what we know, that is our Truth! And this is precisely the place where we ultimately ruin it.*

The good news is: IT is NOT Ruined, it CAN be Saved - Almost Always.

WE MUST RETURN! Return to the original blueprint, return to Birth-Knowledge, return to listening and return to Hashem's space. How do we find the way back?

Who knows how to regain entrance into the Holy of Holies? Where is the knowledge that unlocks the secret of entering the "Crown" (Keter) and connecting the Voice to its initial potential and power? Where is the space through which Birth-Knowledge 'entered' and through which it will return to the universe?

Again, the answer lies in Torah.

The Voice is divided, separated into two worlds: The world above and the world below. It is the illumination of the world above that allows the world below to function perfectly, to find its way, to find completion. It is in the space that no one can touch (the Brain), where no one can enter, that the key to all knowledge is buried. It is the place where thought reigns, where ideas are formed, where all knowledge is stored, where physical manipulation is impossible; where we can only abstractly conceive of thought and verbalize to make it real.

We can physically touch most parts of our body, fix them, Operate, replace. But where we are working now, in the world above, little can be done if something (in the Brain) does not function properly. We try to make sense of what really goes on there, but in the event something happens, G-d forbid, chances of recovery are minimal. Risks are great and we know that few survive intact, once the Master Computer is tampered with. Few remain whole once the Brain is invaded; few withstand an onslaught of loss of Brainpower, without sinking into the oblivion of dementia, Alzheimer's or autism. Brain-related illnesses are very difficult and virtually impossible to fix . . . even today with science's advancements. Touching the Holy of Holies (Kodesh Hakodashim), as I call this place, is entering into the realm of the Almighty, invading His power, grasping at His space.

The Brain is reserved for Hashem to enter into conversation with us. This is the space where we hear Him, where He instructs us, where He communicates with us. That place - the Master Computer Control Panel - is grander and more spectacular than any invention of human making (which of course also comes from there). This is the place from where the entire body, mind, spirit, and soul are governed. This is where the "internal knowledge" is stored and so, of course, "THE VOICE."

This is the space from where the Soul speaks -this is where the "Thought of the Voice" is conceived, elaborated, and moved.

Here our thoughts are aware of everything and can achieve and create beyond limitations, way beyond the limitation that we, ourselves create for ourselves. This is place I call 'Ein SOF' – Limitlessness, beyond limitation- this is where everything is possible and our creativity and individual possibilities reign in total and complete freedom. <u>We have only to think and we can achieve</u>. Actually, we have little to do but to trust our innate knowledge and "let" the Instrument be played by that which "KNOWS" how to play it perfectly   ... the Brain!

From earlier conversation, we have ascertained that the Movement of the Throat is very limited, but since we have no idea about how to find another space, we learn to move inside "A Black Hole," which inherently has very limited powers of Movement. The tiny, sensitive, hair-like vocal cords are shoved, pushed, forced, and constricted, while we insist on them giving us what "We" want -even though, deep inside, we know that what we are doing cannot possibly be right.

I cannot tell you how many times a singer has come to me and confessed:" I know there is another way - I know this cannot be right - I always knew that somewhere inside of me there must be something else. But WHAT and WHERE?" This internal knowing, this innate cry for help, is what I call "the Singer's Survival Instinct" or the "Primal Call of the Inner Voice" and I suppose that when that yearning gets strong enough, and only "alternatives" to what is being offered out there can help, that is when somehow they find their way to me.

The stories of how all of my students arrive to study with me are material for sci-fi episodes. They all have something in common: They ARE SENT! No one looks specifically for me in particular because, initially, they do not know for whom to look. They all find me through divine intervention. My book falls off a shelf at Barnes & Noble or Borders, they find it by accident, or they hear someone talking about it on the subway. The stories are incredible, but all are spiritually inspired— and those who come are somehow already primed as to what to expect and how I will teach them.

Once the Instrument has been instructed how to enter Hashem's space, it begins to bloom, resonate, move, flower and create itself. It is freed and has been redeemed from slavery to bask in the sunshine of freedom. Even seemingly destroyed Instruments- old, wobbly and "ugly" ones- begin to shine. Know that Hashem did not create anything ugly or imperfect, or anything that does not have a divine purpose.

People, who think they are tone deaf, are, in most cases, disconnected from their Instrument and the Instrument simply cannot play in the Throat. I have proven, repeatedly, that once the Instrument is reconnected to its proper place and coupled with Birth-Knowledge, the Voice that they hear inside actually comes out. I cannot tell you the joy when that happens. When that happens to a person, the whole world opens up. I ask you, the singer, to remember: WHEN YOUR VOICE COMES TOGETHER, YOUR LIFE COMES TOGETHER.

It therefore may be said that anyone who can speak can also sing (contrary to popular belief). Not every Instrument is a Steinway (the best piano in the world, in my opinion) and not every singer or Instrument has the capacity for greatness; but every Voice certainly can and should be played to its best potential, without infringing upon its health.

When you have the overwhelming desire that you WANT to sing, when the Voice makes itself heard and demands to exit - then you know, no matter how old you are, no matter how tone deaf you think you are, that the inner Voice is communicating and searching for a way to express itself.

We spoke before about the two spaces that constitute the upper and the lower worlds, which needed to be divided in order to function in perfect harmony. Between them, there is a connecting factor, which assumes the awesome power of holding and keeping both worlds in place: That place is the Soft Palate!

The Soft Palate represents the Power of the Steadfastness of Torah, the LAW - The Rock, the ever-present stillness, and the quiet - the one thing between the worlds above and below that separates, yet creates the bond. The worlds are dependent upon each other: one needs the other, yet both function independently, the perfect synergistic relationship; the same interdependence we as Hashem's Creations have with Him.

I am not asking you to accept this concept in order to achieve it, but I am asking you to give it a thought and draw your own intellectual and/or spiritual conclusions from it.

The Soft Palate is the portal, the opening, the <u>One</u> space inside the mouth that can move to the top. This is not to be confused with YOUR moving it (manipulating it in any way), because, as you by now know, you are not, under any circumstances, allowed to manipulate or move anything. What does move the Soft Palate however, micro-millimeters upward and backwards, is the Air and the Movement of Vowel Sound above it (inside Keter, the crown)... moved by the muscles behind your eyeballs and the continual opening of "five and six" (the internal nose openings). Because of this "involuntary Movement" of the Soft Palate, the Throat can now open to a mega space and, of course, the more space there is inside the Throat, the greater the freedom for the Instrument to play.

"AS ABOVE, SO BELOW". Because there is now space on the bottom, inside the mouth and in the Throat, there is also space on the top. Because the bottom is relaxed, the top can open wide; because the Instrument is free to play, the Movement of Sound is also unrestricted and can float. The larger the space inside the mouth, the larger the expansion inside Keter (crown). This allows the Air / Sound/Vowel to completely turn 360 degrees, using the entire circumference of the cranium, thus achieving extraordinary vibrations – vibrations which cannot ever be created with/or by the manipulation of the Throat.

There are those who will disagree with me on this point. The proof lies in the fact that after a few years of this kind of strain the Voice wobbles, becomes hoarse, looses height, looses pitch etc. Even if you could prove to me that you can do it successfully for a while, the price you pay with your Instrument is much too high in the long haul. Everything can be done by manipulation – but why? When there is such an easy, natural AND secure way of playing the Instrument perfectly.

In the Psalms, the Levites, after the destruction of the Second Temple cry: "Let my Tongue cleave to my palate" when asked by the captors to sing the songs of Zion. They understood that if the Tongue cleaves to the palate, the Instrument is closed, strangulated; no Sound of beauty can be uttered. The Soft Palate would, in that case, be down and the Tongue up; the Throat would be closed. The Air would have to be "pushed" out through the Instrument, causing muscular tension and strain and an unnatural force on the cords- - all of which would, of course, result in a Sound crushed Sound. They understood!

✧ ✧ ✧

Some years ago, I was teaching a student with a retractile Tongue (automatically moves back and closes the Throat). No amount of instruction or effort on her part would keep the Tongue down. I remember sitting at the piano and "asking" for help (something I do quite often) and requesting guidance. The thought of the "Egg" arrived in my mind. I immediately understood that an Egg placed into the mouth would keep the Throat open and liberate the Instrument; keep the Soft Palate up, the Tongue and Larynx down. I went to my refrigerator and got an Egg ... Imagine my students' first reaction. Then I tried the hard-boiled version, which was chewed up and eaten by the end of the lesson - now I use an onyx/stone/or marble Egg, which combines the appropriate shape and the necessary weight to do the job right. In my way of thinking, the Egg spiritually connects us once again to Birth-Knowledge.

By creating resistance in "the lower world," the "upper" has the advantage of being freed. By closing off the bad, we connect to and accept the good. You have very little choice; you must begin to move Sound on the top otherwise you gag. Instinctively you recognize the space; move into it and all the Sound begin to create themselves. The Voice searches and remembers its natural habitat almost instantly and begins to feel at home. Sound become audible that you neither know, nor feel and, in most cases, do not even hear or are able to distinguish other than inside your thinking; but that is the entrance, that is the beginning, and that is the most important part of our conversation.

The fact that the Sound "happens" virtually without your manipulating it, is probably the most difficult thing to accept. After all, who wants to give up control? And how can something that is cracked up to be so difficult, be so easy – and how can it all happen without real "physical intervention" on your part?

<u>This is the final position</u>: Entrance through the Eyes, THE WINDOWS OF THE SOUL. What do the eyes have to do with our conversation? Is it so impossible to imagine that the space behind your eyes, which is the opening to the Holy of Holies, is also the secret to the Movement of the Sound?

Eyes breathe, did you know that? They breathe just like every part of our skin. It is not that you need an enormous amount of Air, but you need to know HOW to attach/connect yourself to the Air that already exists inside your cranial cavity. The whole conversation about needing lots of Air to sing (in your lungs, your Throat, in your Diaphragm) is <u>false</u> ... totally! You simply have to know where what you need <u>is</u>, and how to attach yourself to its power.

The space behind your eyeballs is huge. Once you understand how to connect to the muscles behind your eyeballs, how to begin your Vowels at the bridge of the nose, you are actually moving "inside" the Master Computer. Here the only thing you need to know how to do: Think, and allow the right knowledge to do the rest for you!

So, what is actually necessary to create Movement inside? Well, we know that Sound move on Air, we know that Air creates expansion, and we know that Sound has to attach itself to something that will make it move ...

The key to vocal Movement (Sound Movement) is none other than the VOWEL!

Nothing is more important than the Vowel, which connects one Sound with the next (legato). Moving together, Sound and Vowel, inside Keter (crown), creates the combination necessary to achieve the slight upward and backward angle in order to then allow the Vowel Sound to exit through the Third Eye and instantly connect it with the consonants, at the Intention of the Word (at the Lips/upper teeth). Vowel Sound is moved by Air, Air is moved with the muscles behind your eyeballs and the entire construction is based upon your thought of Sound, Vowel, and word combination.

Here is the MANTRA you need to tell yourself over and over, a thousand times:

**CONNECT THE VOWEL SOUND TO THE MUSCLES BEHIND MY EYEBALLS, TO THE THOUGHTS IN THE BACK OF MY HEAD AND STAY THERE! **

This, bar none, is the single most important statement that will put all of what we have discussed together for you. If you think this, put this into your thought process, along with everything we have previously discussed; if you "actually become these thoughts", you will sing, speak, and accomplish what you want. Once this process becomes a part of your" instinctive behavior," you will not ever need to think about it again, it will simply be there. With this thought, the position, the Giro, the entrance, the exit - in short, the entire system- is put into place.

Sound and word combine on the OUTSIDE, NOT on the inside of the mouth, thus leaving the inside of the mouth- the Tongue, the Soft Palate, the Larynx, the Instrument- relaxed and free.

In the prayer, before the recitation of Tehillim (Psalms of King David), Vowels are mentioned specifically. Let us go further. When Hashem gave the Torah (The Five books of Moses) to Moses (Moses, led the children of Israel out of Egypt, etc.,) there were No Vowels written on the tablets. The consonants yes, but NOT until Hashem SPOKE the words THROUGH Moses, were the actual words physically understood and written into law. Thus, the Vowels are the foundation of language, of all understanding and verbal communication. Only because of the Vowel is there 'upper' connection.

Only the correct Movement of Vowel plus Sound creates and opens the space to height, depth, roundness, light, dark etc. Only they (the Vowels) move with the Sound into the deepest recesses of the Kodesh Hakodashim (Holy of Holies) . . .

only they move ON AIR into the head, through and above the Brain into an open space above the Brain where free moment is totally possible; only they find their way to exit Keter (crown) through the Third Eye and only they ultimately reconnect to the universe, back to Hashem.

<u>Only the Vowel is responsible for all internal Movement and connection of Sound</u>. The Vowel must <u>never</u> fall out of its place (space behind the eyeballs . . . it must always remain above, only rise, only seek to be connected, one to the other - Vowels and Sound - a 'couple' moving through space and Air together, seeking and knowing the exit through the Third Eye - always striving upward and backward, deeper and higher, a never-ending spiral, one above the other.

The Vowel Sound Movement is the key to our entire conversation. The importance of the appropriate placement and Movement of the Vowel unravels the secret of the Voice.

Hashem gave the Vowel to the world so we can understand His words. The Vowel moves inside <u>Hashem's Space</u>. We understand the bond between the Voice of Man and the Voice of G-d and know that interference with the Movement of Vowel Sound is as impossible as creating one's own soul's destiny. Our thinking allows the Sound and the word to BE ... our knowledge of where the Sound, the Vowel and the word combine, allows the process of Movement to occur (inside the Brain); and our ability to speak (Lips, teeth, Tongue) brings it, through the thought and desire to speak (Kavanah, intention) together, so we can actually communicate, be heard and understood.

The combination of all these things is beyond human physical control. You cannot touch it, you cannot move it; you have to think/know it and allow it to be created. Once you understand the process and allow the Brain to do it, it will create exactly what you desire. Your thoughts, your knowledge, and that which you have "placed into the Voice," will be interpreted. It now belongs to your spiritual self - it will guide you and allow you the freedom actually to express your Artistry. Obviously, when you speak or sing, you cannot worry about how to do it, how to manipulate it. You are now the messenger (the Scheliach Zibur), the one who has the responsibility to represent the people (specifically Cantors and Rabbis) before G-d. Your Intention (Kavanah) is now your guide and your word and the combination of Sound create the final thrust of the interpretation of the word.

You are free to connect with your Soul!

You are the expression of your Soul!

You speak truth - from the place where your Voice originates and emanates; your words will fly on the wings of angels to do Hashem's bidding in the world. You are the messenger! You are the chosen one! In the scheme of the Voice, the most essential thing is to allow total quiet within. Patience, stillness, letting go! Feeling, rather than doing!

Thinking is more powerful than acting/doing, but without actions, thoughts are not implemented. The internal Movement – thought - not forceful action, defines the external. Everything that is on the inside- Sound/Vowel, word/thought, etc, - demands total introspection, not physical action. However, in order to be heard by and to communicate with and to others, the physical act of speaking is the necessary end result.

Isn't everything in our lives just about the same? If the internal is set up correctly, the external will shine. If it goes in right, the outcome will be perfect. The person of inner beauty and substance will ultimately be perceived as beautiful "inside and out."

The superficial is just that, while the internal ultimately determines your place in OLAM HABA (THE WORLD TO COME). The whole process of the Voice is "simple in its complexity and complex in its simplicity," just like each and every one of us . . . and Hashem as well!

THE VOICE CREATES AND DEMANDS CONNECTION . . . YOU ARE THE LINK TO THE DIVINE!

Notes

Illuminations:
My Special Gifts

Every lesson with my students is recorded - not only so that they have a record of the lesson and can then use the information, but because the recording serves as personal history of their Instrument. It is quite amazing how short a memory the body has. You simply forget, after a few lessons, what you actually sounded like, before you came. Well, it is extremely important for the student to be able to measure his/her own progress and by being able to listen to past recordings and compare them to what is being achieved now, he has a yardstick of his achievements. So, even while you are working by yourself, keep a record of what you Sound like, listen to yourself and make the mental adjustments necessary to create the positive changes necessary.

There is another reason why I record everything - and that has to do with me, and what happens during a lesson - not every time, not with every student - but I never know when I will receive a 'piece of information' for a particular person, which then is revealed and I can use it for all of my other students. In this Chapter, which I call "My Gifts," I would like to share with you the various pieces of information that 'arrived' exactly the way they were given.

In other words, I am teaching, I hear myself saying something. I instinctively know that I have never said this before, never said it in that way never thought about it in those terms before. I replay the recording and immediately write it down so I do not forget it and so I can "learn and use" this information appropriately when necessary with another student. These are chronicles of illuminations, which I have received since the publication of the second edition in 2001.

AT THE RISK OF REPEATING MYSELF:
NONE OF THIS WILL MAKE ANY SENSE UNLESS YOU HAVE READ AND
DIGESTED THE CONCEPTS OF OUR WORK in the previous Chapters.

✫ ✫ ✫

"I am 'scared' of coming to class"
"WHY?"
"You are the mirror . . . "
"Why?"

"Because you mirror me - In you I see myself . . . "
With Rabbi Chay Amar

✲ ✲ ✲

There is no safety, not even in you - because you are not a safe place for yourself – you are always in the way…

The Sound creates itself – it is what the mind hears!!

The Instrument cannot produce it Sound or word) alone . . .

The minute you do not THINK ONLY ABOUT THE MUSIC, THE MUSIC AND THE VOICE GO AWAY . . .

The thought of the music is responsible for placing the Sound . .

Allow your Brain to make the music –

Let the music be your guide!

Allow the Sound to play the Instrument . . .

With Tanya Movtchan (Palma)

✲ ✲ ✲

Your inner perception has to perceive the Sound, not your conscious mentality, otherwise you start physically manipulating.

With Mary Jane Pianezzola

✲ ✲ ✲

Spinging is the place where we "create" projection –

The difference between speaking and singing is 'the thought of the Sound and the Vowel as one entity' - instead of the thought of how to create the size of the Sound and the action it requires to make it.

✲ ✲ ✲

Air compression makes things smaller -

The Air is compressed when the Vowel is not large enough in its Movement on the Air inside Hashem's space.

The 'cranium' does not 'open' and the Vowel Sound will therefore not grow… the full Giro is not available under such circumstances.

The Sound will be strident and much smaller…not homogenized and certainly not round and beautiful.

Perceive the word and Sound as being a combination, which is created and fashioned only in the Brain . . .

So, compression makes things smaller and expression (projection - speaking the Vowel Sound at the Lips) makes the Voice larger.

✲ ✲ ✲

Lag - Time is the link between the conscious and the sub-conscious mind.

✲ ✲ ✲

The line of the Sound expands with relaxation of the cranium, rather than with the tension and force of the Throat.

Be in control of your mind before you can be in control of the Instrument. If you think about the Movement of the Sound, you lose it. If you think about the thought of the Sound, you have it.

✲ ✲ ✲

Speak the Sound out of the Brain through your soul (eyes).

✲ ✲ ✲

You have to speak the Vowel into the Brain for it to come out as a 'Vowel word' . . . Connect with the word internally (legato, on the Air, upward and backward) instead of trying to make it externally.

With Verena Wagner

✲ ✲ ✲

Speaking is the conscious expression of the sub-conscious placement and interpretation of Sound . . . Connect the Voice to your thoughts.

✲ ✲ ✲

You must train your perception to listen … It will hear your thoughts and produce the desired responses.

✵ ✵ ✵

You must allow the melody to move you, instead of your moving the melody…

✵ ✵ ✵

You cannot physically hear your thoughts… You can only hear the expression of your thoughts through the words.

✵ ✵ ✵

The thought of Sound, produces the motion of the Sound.

✵ ✵ ✵

It is the expression of your desire to sing that creates the spoken word.

✵ ✵ ✵

Sound Speak "is the thought arriving before the exit of the actual word—without the thought of the Sound, there is no speaking or hearing of the Sound.

✵ ✵ ✵

The only thing that stands between you and what is perfect, is your own judgment of how imperfect you are.
Play the Air!

✵ ✵ ✵

The only thing that the formulation of the Vowel achieves,
Is Sound connection - The word then creates the formulation of the Vowel, which is the final the form of the spoken word…

✵ ✵ ✵

You do not hear your thoughts, unless you speak them - If you speak them, you no longer hear them - If you speak them, then they are the expression of what you are thinking … When you do not hear your thoughts, but speak them, you are in the right place, for perfect placement . . . Your knowledge is then in control.

✵ ✵ ✵

Use Air flow instead of Air pressure.

✵ ✵ ✵

The only time it is right is when you feel nothing, when the Sound, the Word, and the thought (Brain) are ONE, otherwise they are disconnected, and so are you from the Source.

✵ ✵ ✵

Lipping the Sound (making the combination of Vowel Sound and consonants at the Lips on the outside) allows you to keep the back open (inside the mouth, Soft Palate, and Throat) and therefore completely free up the Tongue.

✵ ✵ ✵

The Soft Palate is the connection between the upper and the lower worlds . . . Torah is the key . . . Torah stands between Man and the World as the rock.
With Shimon Boyer

✵ ✵ ✵

The thought creates the action.

✵ ✵ ✵

Focus equals formation . . .
If you focus on the Intention of the Word, the formation (of Vowel Sound) will be created in the correct place at the Lips, on the outside, with the Vowel Sound and word combination.

✵ ✵ ✵

Simultaneous breath involves both Mouth and the Nose but passively, the ACTIVE 'breath' comes together only behind through the pupils, behind the eyes.

✵ ✵ ✵

Your desire, and what you want to say, is translated only through your speaking (Intention of the Word)
With Smuli Eizenberg

✵ ✵ ✵

The height of the Sound is in direct relationship to the Intention of the Word . . . because the Intention of the Word pulls the tension of the Air and therefore Vowel Sound, upwards and backwards.
With Cantor Murray Yavneh

✧ ✧ ✧

The Vowels position the Sound for the word.

✧ ✧ ✧

The Power lies in the word . . . without speaking, the Sound has no life, and it is stuck and will never get out.

✧ ✧ ✧

The breath is a thought of internal Movement, which shifts Air into the right space to do what we want.

✧ ✧ ✧

The Sound is not you - it is only connected by your thought of the word -the Sound belongs to the inside, the word to the outside -
The inside is G-D, the outside is you . . . The inside belongs to
Spirituality, the outside to reality!

✧ ✧ ✧

Your Knowing creates the right action . . . Action (word) is the outcome of your knowing.

With Cantor Israel Rosen

✧ ✧ ✧

The physicality of what the outcome will be is of what you perceive mentally . . . the possibility of limitlessness exists only in the Brain.
With Jim Parker

✧ ✧ ✧

"Sing on the interest, not the principal".
A quote by Zinka Milanov, which totally explains what, we are doing.

✧ ✧ ✧

The attachment of the word to Keter (crown) is the key to Kavanah
(Intention of the Word).
With Cantor Yaakov Wechter

✧ ✧ ✧

The Sound is moved by the Brain, according to the Brain's
Interpretation of your desire (accessing the subconscious).
With Mark Bleeke

✧ ✧ ✧

Your speaking is the expression of your Artistry . . . Only
because you are free from worries about technique, can you truly express yourself
as an Artist.
With Elin

✧ ✧ ✧

Where you hear it, is where it actually is! Go and stay there, always.

✧ ✧ ✧

We are changing the position of the Voice from being in danger, to being
infinite.

With Chana Motchkin

Notes

Comments from some of my Students

*[This **not** a 'slap on the back' or 'how great I am' Chapter… I could easily publish a whole book with all of the letters and stories which have made up my almost thirty years of sharing my teaching–I wanted something from right NOW. You can go on the blog or to Amazon.com, or just put my name in the browser and continue to hear more. These are real people, with real problems and real words to share. Please read their accounts and perhaps somewhere you find yourself].*

Neria Cohen

www.neriacohen.com

This is my story:
Four years ago I began giving lectures and workshops at Chabad Houses around the USA.

After twelve workshops I strained and lost my Voice and had great trouble speaking. I was hoarse and feeling pain. I visited an ENT (Ear Nose and Throat) Specialist who was unable to help me.

I then went to Miriam Arman for Voice lessons and 200 workshops later I can say that I never lost my Voice again.

I have had challenges with my Voice since I was a teenager and have tried many methods to use my Voice correctly. When I first encountered Miriam's unusual approach something inside me knew that this was an answer for me. It has not been easy as I have been speaking in my Throat for forty years and changing muscle memory is challenging. It has been an interesting journey.

My lessons are like therapy sessions as the Voice reflects ones Malchus (kingship), ones sense of self and confidence as a person. 50 lessons of my perseverance and Miriam's inspiration and patience are finally paying off, as I begin to touch and use my 'real' Voice. I am singing. I look forward to the next stage in this wondrous journey.

✫ ✫ ✫

Andrea Duplechain

[Here is a woman who really wants something and is going after it and NOTHING is stopping her. She used to come into NY from Washington DC twice a month at least... the rest of the time we work on the Internet and the progress is incredible. She had some awful] habits, very heavy southern accent to boot, really terrible mouth and Throat problems, but all this is gone now and what is coming out of her, is a beautiful lyric soprano with dramatic overtones (we will see). A few days before this book was finished she sent me this email, I think you will find it very interesting:

The statement she found by Joan Sutherland (one of the greatest Bel Canto Diva's ever), certainly indicates that she (JS) had an idea in her body of what she was doing and it served her well and for many years. How to teach this is a different story and of course that is what this book is all about.

The original statement actually dates back to a 'Classical Singer 'interview with Joan in 1999, very shortly, or just around the publication of my first book "The Voice" ...

Dear Miriam

"I was perusing Renee Fleming's book, "The Inner Voice", when I stumbled upon Renee asking Joan Sutherland how she managed her extreme high notes. Joan said she aimed them directionally, not just out of the front, but more toward the back of her head as she climbed into the stratosphere...

Now that Sound to me like she was saying she aims upward and backward!!!"

Andrea

I am a woman in her forties and have been studying Voice for many years. I have done a fair amount of singing, but have never gotten past being an "amateur" singer. I struggled with the feeling that something was just not right. I was never internally satisfied with my vocal production. I have had several teachers and all had a different way of teaching. They were mostly former singers who required that I replicate what they were doing. Yet through these former teachers, I was unable to settle into a concrete vocal technique or vocal placement.

Everyone had a different explanation. It was confusing. I was told to sing from the head, sing from the lower abdomen, grunt, and make many other body contortions that I care not to repeat. The end product was a completely contrived vocal production and an annual bout with laryngitis. Each performance found me more and more nervous as I was not sure if I could continue to imitate what I was being taught. I noticed these same problems with other singers. Some had a very irritating nasal Sound, others sang with a protruding jaws, and others struggled while grasping tight of their lower abdomens. I feel in my heart that my teachers have done their best with the knowledge that they have, but I knew there had to be someone who could better explain the art vocal production.

One day, I happened to find myself on Amazon.com and bumped into Dr. Miriam's book "The Voice - A Spiritual Approach to Singing, Speaking and Communicating". I had to meet this author and wanted her to teach me how to sing. I would not stop until I was a regular student of hers. I finally found a technique that I can understand and that allowed me to reproduce lovely Sound each and every time I sing, without the struggling as I once did. Now I know exactly what to do. There is no more contrived singing and no more laryngitis. I have finally found my Voice. Both my speaking and singing Voice is now in a completely different place than before I began to work with Dr. Miriam two years ago.

Although, I still have much, much work to do but I love the way my Voice is progressing and cannot wait to get out there with the big boys (even if I am old enough to be their mother). I wish everyone had the opportunity to work with Dr. Miriam to find their true Voice. There is nothing like it.

[This is one of my most challenging students. He had terrible problems speaking and communicating – the idea of his ever being able to sing in a beautiful vocal line would be preposterous to anyone listening to him when he arrived. It has taken a great deal of work to get him here, but thank G-d, here we are. He does not wish his name revealed. I left his words the way he wrote them…he is not American, some interesting verbal construction, but you will get the gist] ….

I started lessons with Miriam seven years ago. In the first lesson I suddenly found a different Voice, coming from a different place and Sounding higher and strange, in that I have never heard it before. It lacked the basal Sound of before, which was in large part why it sounded strange. It was like hypnotism.

As the years went by, oral manipulation reduced significantly. But the Voice remained in the Throat. On occasion, I would find the Voice higher during lessons, but not to the extent of the first lesson. I would again feel the hypnotic feeling, but this time with a lot of tension in the face and limbs. Many a time, I tried pulling behind the eyes, but did it wrong and sometimes hurt my eyebrow area. It did not connect. Even though Miriam was explaining it repeatedly and showed diagrams, the verbal knowledge did not translate into physical bodily knowledge. It felt like I was trying to put a pipe through a Hole, but couldn't find where the Hole was - and hence I was hitting the wall instead of the Hole.

Every once in a while, something seemed to work, but I couldn't put my finger on it. Things were fleeting, and thus frustrating. Something seemed to go right, only to find that the next day or few days later, I didn't know what or how it happened, and then felt back at square one. When things went right, it felt good, but then the next time, I couldn't bodily (or verbally) remember the same feeling.

Then one day, out of the blue, something happened. The next morning, I suddenly relaxed the entire face much more so than I had ever done before. This was not a conscious decision, but it just happened. Mornings always seem to bring in something new. Perhaps the sleep at night takes away the tensions. I suddenly realized how much tension there was in the middle of the face. It was a realization. When all hope fades and one is ready to give up, it strikes, it reveals. It was right in front of me, or rather in me, but I could not realize it before. And reveal it did. It was not a full revelation, but a big one. I suddenly found that Air was seeping into the eyes. All that I had to do was to relax and wait.

When I sang at that time, the Sound was high up, vibrant, and un-constrained. To repeat it, I had to prepare myself to relax the face, and then after some time, Air seeped in, and then I could sing that brilliant free Sound.

It was the first time ever I had that experience. I don't know if it was the same as on my first lesson, as it was so long ago. Then, for a few weeks, I was able to sing high, and was very excited, and felt that I had finally stumbled upon what Miriam had been teaching all this time. Things went well for a few weeks, but then gradually faded away (déjà vu). I could no longer bodily remember the feeling. Sounds were back in the Throat.

Then a few months later, it happened again, and I was again able to bodily remember the feeling and sing high - The feeling of Sound moving past/through the eyes. The big breakthrough had happened, and I feel elated and grateful. Things are in ascent now. Years of patience, both on my part and Miriam's.

[There is a great deal contained in this account – read it over a few times please. This man is very intelligent, but not very verbal and not very communicative. What he shares here is quite remarkable to me …it is an immense testimonial. Patience though is not the word…unrelenting faith in an elusive vision I had that I would be able to make his wish a reality for him. You should hear him sing Italian Art Songs…no one would ever

believe it if they heard his recorded lessons – he is a dedicated student and we have made incredible personal strides as well. He is a very special gift to me].

☆ ☆ ☆

Y.D.S… Brooklyn, NY.

[This is written by a young cantor. He came when he was 19 knowing that he 'could', that he had 'something'! Between knowing that you can and doing it is a world of work, commitment and standing up to a lot of others who tell you different. You know by now, that I have a very special relationship with cantors as a whole, but this young man who is now reading Torah in one of the most important Synagogues in the world and is beginning his vocal career, is a very special blessing to me].

When I met Miriam I thought I was going to learn how to sing, but before I knew it. I wasn't only becoming aware of my Voice, but started becoming more aware of my inner self. The change that I experienced was an amazing one, one which will be everlasting. I really want to thank Miriam and that is not even enough of a word to use.

Miriam is a special person. She is not only inner connected to herself, but connects herself to others and is really devoted and cares about every student not just at the time she is teaching, but always.

I have never met someone of such a caliber I don't have the words to express how this is the real teacher and student relationship which is also spoken of in Chassidus.

I wish You Miriam health, happiness and long life to be able to have lots of "nachas" (satisfaction) from your students me included.

Thank you for everything.

- Your very dear student

☆ ☆ ☆

Elin

www.elinmusic.com
www.gigmasters.com/Artists/elin
www.myspace.com/elinsings
www.cdbaby.com/cd/elin

[When I read this account, my mind flew back to her first lesson in my beautiful home in Florida. Today it seems a world away and it literally is (The book is being finished in South America)… I remember exactly how shocked I was at the condition of her Voice and realized it's potential. I could not help but insist to give her a lesson right then and there. In truth, I never give up on a student unless I am pushed to the brink of my own strength - sadly it has happened a few times in my career – she is right, it's been an uphill battle, but a great one – she deserves everything and a million times more for standing up to life and never compromising on her ideals. For a teacher the most outstanding thing is a student who is always trying to better himself and understands his/her own shortcomings and defects – but also knows personal strong points. Elin is an Artist – born to sing and one of those who would sell pencils in the street – Onward and upward my dear, I love you much]

Miriam Arman is a miracle. Not just as a human being and in how she has lived her life and in all the things she has accomplished, but by the gift she was sent here to bring to us. Whether it's to a singer in his or her Voice, or to the fortunate ear of a beholder, she is blessing us all with one of the most beautiful things in existence: purity of Sound and vibration.

Miriam is the first and only teacher who was ever able to bring out that Voice in me that I just knew I had, but could never seem to find. And I had to wait twenty years to find her, or rather, for her to find me. But thanks to that chance meeting, my life and my Voice will never again be the same.

Our journey together has now lasted 10 years and counting, but for me they were often tumultuous years where my transformation was difficult and complicated, perhaps partially due to the fact that I was trying to make a living as an Artist in "the big apple" – New York City. Nevertheless, Miriam always opened her arms to me – inviting me back sometimes like a prodigal son – never giving up hope, and always knowing just when to encourage me and when to crack the whip!

I have been a singer now for more than 20 years, and I went through many teachers along the way, but somehow things just never felt quite right. I couldn't figure out why I kept having the vocal problems that I did. I would often get hoarse throughout the course of a performance, and several sections of my register were always difficult to access with a clear tone, or with power. I just knew there had to be something else, some other way to do this, to make it work.

Then – just after I'd moved from Florida to New York – I was back in town for a show and a friend insisted I meet her Voice teacher. For some reason she was adamant about it. In retrospect I understand why… The moment Miriam laid eyes on me it was as if she had always known me. She insisted on giving me a lesson right then and there, before I flew back to NYC that afternoon. So one of her students gave up her lesson for me on the spot. And the rest, as they say, is history.

I cried in that first lesson. So certain was I that I was in the presence of a very wise, knowledgeable and powerful person. The exercises she took me through were unlike anything else I'd ever done and yet in that first lesson, she had me singing things I'd never been able to before. I was sold! For the first time in my life I was truly excited and confident about my future as a singer. I was finally on the right path – and guided!

Then came more difficult times. It was often very hard for me to reconcile the work with my old thought processes and habits. It was tough for me to keep the faith, the hope that I could and would make it as a singer in NYC. And it was always an uphill battle for me to stay disciplined in my work, when Miriam was so far away and we only had a few lessons per year. Nevertheless, I always knew she held the key, the truth, and the way, so I stuck with it. And now 10 years later, the proof is certainly in the pudding: I have performed all over the world at prestigious venues and festivals, I'm a regular at New York City landmarks like the Blue Note and Dizzy's Club *Coca-Cola* (Jazz at Lincoln Center) and I have shared the stage with Artists such as Chaka Khan, George Benson and Nancy Wilson.

Together, we became the 'little engine that could'. We kept at it through the heartaches, the trials & tribulations, the misunderstandings, the challenges, the differing opinions, the life changes, the tears, the sweat, the anger, the pain, the confusion. And Miriam, in her infinite patience, stood by me through it all. Not only was a beautiful career built, but a beautiful friendship and a deep sense of respect and commitment. And, of course, the ongoing relationship I now have with my Instrument: THE VOICE. Thank you, Miriam, for everything.

✧ ✧ ✧

Chana Motchkin

[Singer, songwriter, an extraordinary young woman, mother of three beautiful children and wife of a wonderful man who generously supports her and her dream. At present we are working on a full CD release on which all of her original songs are featured – look for it – the message is as special as she is].

Behind every shadow there is light. Behind every light there is a soul, and within every soul there is a Voice. My Voice was hidden behind the secret shadows of fear and uncertainty.

I didn't understand the mystery of singing and I failed to recognize the power of my soul. I want to thank you for guiding me to a place that binds my mind and my heart. I now can escape to the endless space in my Voice where my Instrument finds liberation.

In the garden of music, every note is a seed that with the mystical strength of the Voice becomes the flowers of melody. You walked with me through the path of truth and helped me find my Voice. My soul, my inner light. Thank you for your wisdom. May you continue to inspire and encourage singers across the world to share their light and understand the complexity and simplicity of the Voice.

Your devoted student and friend

Chana

✼ ✼ ✼

Rachel Panay

http://www.rachelpanay.com

http://www.myspace.com/rachelpanay

http://www.myspace.com/rachelpanayjazz

[Singer, songwriter, femme fatal extraordinaire! She really has stardom written all over her – she is a wonderful person and a real go getter – All of us are always looking for the 'big break – Rachel you will get there – stick to it kid. Every one of my students is special in their own way. Each one has a particular spark which needs to be accessed and with each one, I work differently, but the same. As a teacher I am incredibly grateful for all these gifts.]

When I began working with Miriam in 2002, I had recently graduated from music conservatory. While I had done well in school, my vocal "technique" had not yet been put to the test of real-life, working situations (i.e. loud, late-night club performances, lengthy recording sessions, etc).

I was not prepared for the challenges of back to back performances, nights in a row at a busy and, at that time, smoky, South Beach hotspot. Within a month I was breaking down vocally by the end of the first show, and spent the hour in between shows terrified of the second one!

Then a series of divine "coincidences" lead me to Miriam. At our first lesson, she told me I had no idea of what I was really capable of as a singer and that I had only just scratched the surface of my potential. At that time, my main goal was to merely become functional again! I also had the beginnings of scar tissue on my vocal cords which the doctor warned me would lead to nodules if I did not change the way I spoke and sang. In other words, my hopes and dreams of a career in music were in grave danger.

Thus began the process of reforming my entire understanding of and approach to the Voice. In 2003, only a short year after almost total vocal breakdown and beginning my work with Miriam, I would write and record the song that would gain me national exposure in the Dance music industry, "The Walk of Shame". This breakthrough song became the foundation on which I built a career that has produced five consecutive Top Ten Billboard Club hits. With Miriam's guide to the Voice, I have been booked across America for festival and club performances, and most recently oversees to Europe for a song writing and recording tour that spanned six cities across four countries in under thirty days. From this tour, I have two upcoming releases in Holland and Switzerland, and my sixth U.S. single, "Epic" is currently a runaway club hit.

I credit the work that I have done with Miriam as the single most important factor contributing to my success as a performing and recording Artist. In giving myself over to Miriam's teachings, I experienced full vocal recovery within ONE YEAR and far surpassed anything I had ever done previously as a vocalist. Indeed as Miriam promised, "the Voice that would come out of me was unlike anything you have ever done or imagined possible."

One of the most important realizations in my work with Miriam was to see that while working in the studio, I am able to stay internal in my vocal approach. Whereas when on the stage, I tend to revert back to the external grasping for and reaching for the audience's attention, and my vocal approach becomes very external. Through the breakthrough work that we've done, I now see that in live performance, the more internal I become, the more powerful and magnetic I am because it is the Voice drawing the audience in. I still have to remind myself of this often, especially before a performance, to choose the internal focus rather than the external grasping.

The listener response to my Voice has been overwhelming and one common denominator is how big, clear and seamless my Sound is. Critical acclaim and fan support aside, I now have the joy and freedom in singing that was NEVER consistently mine before Miriam. I am still excited about the journey as I grow in the Voice with each lesson and I am confident of continued and even more wonderful successes with Miriam's teachings.

✧ ✧ ✧

Verena Wagner

http://verenamusic.com

[The Voice of an Angel – listening to her takes you into different spheres…smart, beautiful, intelligent, talented – a winning combination…listen to her on the blog or go to her website, it's a treat.]

Miriam Arman has been the most Instrumental part in the development of my Voice and career as a singer. Her keen ear and thorough understanding of the Instrument has allowed me to transcend self imposed limitations as well as the bad habits of previous wrong coaching. Her expertise and never tiring guidance and support has allowed me to soar and reach for my full potential as a singer. I can't express enough gratitude and love to this extraordinary soul.

✧ ✧ ✧

Riccardo Foresi and Benedetta Conssigniani and…well read on and KNOW!

http://www.myspace.com/riccardoforesi
www.riccardoforesi.net

[… They arrived at my door in New York – there was not a shred of doubt in either of them why they were here and what needed to be done. We have worked through so many things, distances, various promises that were made to Riccardo that were not kept –disappointments, joy, successes, – but through it all, oure work and the Voice kept it all going. Benedetta,what a gorgeous Voice, please don't stop!!!- Riccardo is well on his way to a big recording career with some of the top people in the world…dreams become reality through hard work, endless love and real dedication…The world is a tiny place

– We are always together, always working -wheref there is a will, there is a way – I love you both so much].

As I am doing the last edit, Mr. and Mrs.Riccardo Foresi are the proud parents of Matthew, a beautiful healthy baby boy born of love and music and 'hard labor'. This is how it happened, don't you remember?

(Original text by R&B)

When we decided to move to New York during the summer of 2004, I started looking for teachers in New York so at least we will have someone to go to once there, and after goggling (Vocal Coach in New York) you popped up together with other 1000....If you remember, you had moved to New York not long before....I got emails and links from hundreds of vocal coaches but I wanted to follow my instinct and without even knowing who you were, we came to your door on September. 26. 2004 for a first lesson.

I remember that after 3 or 4 lesson, you asked me something about the book... and I told you " What Book?" only then you discovered the strange connection and you told me, " if you came to my door without even knowing where you were going, God has a special role for you in this world".....
Well you know the rest of the story....

When we started working, we really had no idea of the possibilities of our Instruments. Basing our teaching on myths, after each performance, we needed days to rest because off all the straining of the Voice. Working with you, we were able to understand the movements of Sound, opening new spaces, without using the Throat and keeping it open all the time. Few weeks after we started working, singing became easier, size started to grow and range started to increase. The Voice became rounder and higher and what before seemed to be impossible, became possible.

Everything is possible with trust, dedication, and a constant use of the Egg, the nose clip, the year plugs and spinging each and every word.

We feel so blessed that we were given the opportunity of crossing paths. This journey with you has been incredible, and every minute we spent together was new discovery, and made us realize what a great gift the Voice is and its endless possibilities. We owe everything to your knowledge and dedication

✲ ✲ ✲

[**Misuse of power**, *destructive teaching, sham, deceit, psychological warfare, and misrepresentation etc. – everything which I have talked about in this book and everything that has and is bothering me is contained in this account, which my student Leticia has written; This is a drop in the bucket – certainly no news to me, but it is written for you, to give YOU an idea of what is going on out there. Unfortunately she is one in so many who got seriously hurt and thoroughly taken advantage of… the difference is, she found the strength and fortitude to seek another way and not give up!*

I have not changed, neither added not subtracted a word of what she wrote … I want you to hear and feel the unedited desperation of a person, who with the proper teaching has blossomed into a real Artist who will, with a little bit of luck and the 'elusive brake' make it and go far.

I wish it for her and will do all I can to help her along. Her story will hopefully have a happy ending…as far as I am concerned it is a privilege to work with a person of her personal and artistic integrity and quality].

Leticia M. Reyes

I started with a dream. A dream to perform. A dream to touch people with beauty. I wasn't sure what road I was going to take to get there, but I knew that I had to get there. I've recognized my talent since I was young. Always performing, always somewhere in the arts, I used to sing every free moment as a child. I had always been told I had a beautiful Voice but just needed the right opportunity, the right team, the right training. Only then would I feel confident enough to launch a career or embark on the road to show business.

One day I received an inquiry from a Sound engineer. He worked for an Artist who was also a vocal coach and producer and from seeing my picture; he believed that I had "it". They had a studio in New York and another in a country house in Pennsylvania. In other words, they had a total "in-house" Operation where I would be able to easily develop as an Artist. I met with the engineer first and immediately was impressed with the looks of the studio as well as his intelligence. Apparently he was impressed enough with me to set up a meeting with the producer/Artist/vocal coach.

She was a strong woman. That I could tell. Right off the bat she had a commanding presence and an Air of 'wisdom'. But perhaps most impressive was that I thought she sang really well in a style I most wanted to 'imitate'. I sang for her the best I could. I was already at a disadvantage because I had no discipline where the Voice was concerned and I knew it. I clung on to this woman as my hope, my choice as a guru and mentor. She told me that because she had already taken the long road to achieve her level of 'talent', that she would be able to give me *the shortcuts*. She told me that as long as I listened to her explicitly, she could guide me to avoid all pitfalls and prepare me for stardom. These people were 'serious' and made me feel that if this was my chance to achieve my dreams, then I would put everything and anything I had into achieving it'. And so, I gave them my complete trust in all things.

For the next four and a half years, I sold my soul. I listened to their advice and direction as though it was my bible. I quit my job, changed my diet, exercised more, disciplined myself to never miss a lesson, I stopped going out, disassociated with anyone who doubted my team or my talent, including my family, dated for money, changed my style, and shamefully used people .

We spent two years just on vocal lessons. I was charged $225 for three one hour lessons a week. She decided not to spend time on breathing exercises. She was going to teach me everything at once, which meant that I was going to start singing right away, to incorporate emotion at the same time as technique. In the beginning, she would sit at the piano and play scales and have me sing along to the exercises. Eventually, I was to practice scales at home from a CD of one of her old vocal lessons and come in ready to sing a song. Her instruction taught me that I was to sing from the bottom, meaning the Air comes from flying up the Diaphragm. Somehow, while taking in a deep breath from the Diaphragm, I was supposed to be able to relax my Throat enough to create an Airy Sound. She had me doing leg lifts and told me that singing would create a sensation in my abdomen similar to that. I attempted to tense my abdomen and relax my Throat but the result was minimal.

What made it even worse was that my success was also predicated on my diet and exercise. In order to create a clean vessel with which to sing, I had to convert to raw veganism. Once I educated myself on the benefits, I felt happy to be on the diet because I knew I was doing something good for my body. However, I could never figure out just how it affected my Voice or how I used it.

She became so frustrated with me for not singing 'correctly' that on many occasions I would spend a lesson in front of her in tears, while she scolded me for being "lazy" or for not drinking enough green juice to support my singing. According to her, there was always something I was doing in my life that prevented me from executing correctly, whether it was who I was dating or how much I exercised that week.

After tearing me down, she would reinforce her belief in me and tell me that I had all the potential in the world and remind me that she was there to support me.

The constant back and forth of this was making me miserable. I loathed going to vocal lessons for fear that I wouldn't perform well. I had no real technique to go by. There was nothing that she would say to me that would make me understand how to achieve correct vocal production. In fact, according to her, I was supposed to just memorize the sensation whenever I got it correct. She however, couldn't instruct me as to exactly how to produce said sensation.

I compared this to a complex math equation in which the teacher gives you the problem and the answer, but had no real idea of how to get from one to the other. I felt confused, constantly on edge and unsure, but I kept going because I, along with her, blamed it all on myself. I thought I was dumb, un-motivated or just plain afraid of success.

When **she** thought it time to produce and record me, she asked me to pay her, a first time producer, an exorbitant amount of money for each track. She commanded $10,000 per track. That included production, arranging, vocal development, engineering and final mix down. I was already struggling to pay for vocal lessons so in order for me to come up with the money, I was encouraged to seek it out in anyone who would help. We developed a letter to investors and I started shopping around for $30,000 to get three tracks done. I went through dozens of people. There were many of them who could see right through me, knowing that I was interested in them because I was money hungry.

Lots of people checked out what I was up to, but refrained from investing. I was able to convince my parents to give me my inheritance in order to come up with the money. They took out my father's pension and gave me the money. At the same time, a friend of mine decided to borrow the money from his credit card as an investment in me and another friend of mine took a loan out from his business lender. Instead of finding one person to give me the money, I found three! I told my vocal coach and asked if I should take the money from just one person and she suggested I take the money from all three and use it to purchase more tracks or to do videos. After all, according to our plan, I was soon to make the money back plus tons more!

Working with her was deteriorating me in many ways, and only after enduring substantial psychological damage and considerable financial loss, I wound up sneaking off to have lessons with Dr. Arman. Eventually, I ran out of money, and after seeing considerable difference in my progress and understanding with Dr. Arman, I parted ways with them.

She closed her end of the deal by giving me only two mediocre tracks of mediocre production and telling me that I "wasted" the rest of the money away in vocal lessons and nonsense.

I spent $74,000 and wound up with three things:

1. Destroyed self-confidence,

2. A Voice that un-usable to show-case my talent,

3. Two 'master' tracks on a CD that couldn't come close to being of professional use.

My salvation came thru Dr. Arman.

It was through her patience and incredible insights in being able to teach vocal production, that I was able to clear the fog away and see that what I went through was a sham. She single handedly gave me my Voice back and in only a year in a half, I am producing beautiful Sound with my Instrument which truly has me believing in myself once again. She is an incredible source of support for me and none of her techniques have anything to do with my diet or who I date or what's going on in my life, but are concrete definitions of what I have to do in order to realize my Voice. I am not hoarse, I have no pain, I can reach height that was inaccessible to me previously, and I feel great when I am in a lesson and when I leave my lesson. I am really learning for the first time and able to apply this learning. She teaches clearly and makes astonishing sense. There is only truth and application in her world.

Whether or not I make it onto the world stage with my music, she has already given me my happiness.

This is the first time that I have publicly admitted to the whole story. As a result of this experience, I have spent the last year silently and painfully acknowledging to myself just how grave my situation really was. I would like to send my apologies to all those I hurt along the way and most of all to my family, who, through everything, stuck by me. Thank You!

Notes

LETTERS AND COMMENTS
FROM PEOPLE AROUND THE WORLD

Dear Miriam Jaskierowicz Arman,

Just want to express my appreciation for your wonderful book. It has helped me so much as an Artist, a musician, and a singer. My training was in the Bel Canto method, I studied for 5 years, with a teacher named Edith Veigund, who got me out of my Throat. When I moved from Toronto, it was with regret that I couldn't study with her anymore. Years later, a friend recommended your book. I've been working with it one year, and it has got me so far beyond my Throat, into areas I never dreamed my Voice would go. It no longer gets, "stuck", and goes through my spiritual eye. When reading the book, it is like reading something I've known before, as you say, Birth-Knowledge. So, just want to say thank you for your book, your skills in expressing the ideas that are so good, and your generosity in sharing this knowledge with as many people as possible.

Yours Truly,

Sharon Scott-Baron

✧ ✧ ✧

…After our Kurt Weill Abend, in which I get to sing the very legitimate aria Lonely House, from Street Scene, my friend Eric approached me and said, "Damn, that Egg thing is workin' for you. I wanna do that!"

I did sing well that evening, and found places as I spoke the text that was actually disarming. I went to the tears of vulnerability, and something just dropped away for a couple of seconds. Most of the song I felt I was the same old me, but then, as I noticed I wasn't grabbing and worrying about the frickin' note coming up, a beautiful letting go happened, and it was not the same old me anymore. It was me without the baggage, and without the need for approval. It was - this is MY Voice! And I AM talking, and I AM touching these people, and I AM touching you too!! I AM That I AM thanks be forever, Omein (Amen).

I hope that's not too over the top, but stuff is happening and it is exciting. It's been a long time since I've allowed myself to be excited. Thank you Miriam

So in answer to your question, "how's my Voice?" She/he/It is alive and speaking! As always of course, but now a new song may begin to speak, in spite of me! ...

Mark Bleeke

✻ ✻ ✻

Hello,

I have recently begun to read your book (granted this is you!), and immediately was filled with a sense of joy and a renewed sense of hope that my Voice is not lost, but merely yet to be discovered. I feel grateful for all the work you've done to discover these truths that are already meeting my need for a deeper connection to life through expressing me through song. I was hoping there might be some workshops available in the near future. If so, I would be pleased if you could send me some information on them. Blessings and endless gratitude. Sincerely,
Raven Bradt

✻ ✻ ✻

Dear Mrs. Jaskierowicz Arman

After a long struggle with my Voice and technique, I have found exactly what I was always looking for in your book and your instructions! I always loved the singing of Rosa Ponselle.... I really feel that I have a Voice but I never knew how to use it. I started training with your book gain (after being sick for quite a time when I couldn't practice) and also wanted to ask you, if you maybe will be giving lessons somewhere in Europe. Could I maybe get a full education in your academy in NY in about two years (I have to finish my studies first, or would I be too old then with 28?) That would be so great because nowhere else I can find someone who teaches this technique I was always searching for... Meanwhile I'll give my best to practice with your book and I'm looking forward to receiving all your informations!

Best regards! Céline Tschirren

✻ ✻ ✻

Dear Dr. Arman,

I have nearly finished your book," The Voice..." I had to write. I am so excited about your approach. I am three years into a late call to Bel Canto singing. I am so deeply immersed and making headway. I study at a California Community College with a solid music dept. I have twice experienced singing when I thought I was hearing rather than singing, because I could feel nothing. I have two more years here before I decide what is next. I believe I can be good, and I have musical dreams that play in my mind constantly.

I have experience with training in sports that involve discipline and perseverance. I love to practice in these sports, but in these (karate and golf); I knew what to do at a high level. In singing, I want to have the same quality methodology. That is why I am excited about your approach. It is very knowledge based. I want to learn how to apply myself in the most fruitful manner. I both perceive and am in some ways unclear as to your approach.

Hookupdoc

✲ ✲ ✲

Jose Arturo Rodriguez, Houston, Texas, USA

"The price of the book is nothing to compare with the gold of your words and your knowledge. Thank you so much and thank G-D to have you here... I too am teaching and all my students have your book."

✲ ✲ ✲

Daphna Cohen-Licht, Voice Teacher/Speech Pathologist, Israel

"Miriam Arman came to my life while being on my way to become a professional singer. She gave me the key to the real truth of how to approach the Voice with her unique devotion and love to me and to the very truth. This key is my fortune, my treasure as a singer, as a Voice teacher for classical singers as well as actors and as a Voice and Speech Pathologist every day of my life.

It probably takes a lot: Wisdom, Honesty, Talent and Devotion to reveal the real and simple truth and to be able to pass it onward; and Miriam has got it all!! I am so grateful to have had the chance to meet Miriam and have her come into my life." (Original text)

[Just as an aside to keep the record straight...I have not heard from Daphna in years...have no idea what she is doing...or whom she is studying with...I know she has made several recordings]

✲ ✲ ✲

(Here are some comments of participants in a Master Class which Shirley Kout organized for me in Oakland, California... (You read Shirley's letter to me in the beginning)

Dear Miriam

What a splendid day it was yesterday! I felt in the presence of a Master! What a great teacher and dynamo you are! I am using my Egg and earplugs, just have to put a nose pin. Your class has brought singing to a new and different level. I cannot wait to be so sure of my Voice knowing always where the placement is and to sing with total vocal freedom. What possibilities! I also cannot wait for my lesson with Shirley. You are both (Shirley and Miriam) gems. I thank you both for everything you do. I thank you for the "gift".

Love Monica

✲ ✲ ✲

Dear Shirley,

Thank you again for bringing Dr. Arman to the Bay Area for such a wonderful class!! I truly hope I can learn from her in person again. Also, thank you for the opportunity to be evaluated, what an honor and a pleasure that was.

WOW...you've certainly set me on a fantastic journey. I feel I am just touching the very surface of a lifetime of joy in music. From my heart...I feel very blessed to study with you...you amaze me...

Love,
Sam

✲ ✲ ✲

Hello Shirley:

Thank you for arranging for Dr. Miriam to be there on Saturday. There is a lot of information to digest. Ginny demonstrated a perfect example of what Dr. Miriam was telling us to do on the phone Sunday morning. Truly phenomenal! It made an INSTANT difference in Ginny's Sound. I cannot wait to get my book! Thank you for arranging the workshop and thanks to Adele and those who made all those wonderful preparations.

I am focusing on taking the breath in the manner suggested by Dr. Miriam, and I am finding that it helps me release the worry and unnecessary technical tricks I've been doing.

I hope we can have Dr. Miriam come back and that more people can take advantage of hearing her speak. It is a beautiful person, fun to listen to her and she has the most terrific smile. Next time, do you think she would be willing to give us individual coaching?

After listening to her sensible knowledge, I wonder how I'm going to feel when I hear those well-meaning chorus members make suggestions that actually make singing much more complicated than need be. I hope that Sweet Adelines directors are aware of Dr. Miriam's book. I want you to know that you have already been very successful in helping me find my Voice, and I want to thank you for that (as Dr. Miriam said, I was moved to tears at that coaching session when you were working with me on Colors of the Wind). Thank you so much.

Love, Gloria

✧ ✧ ✧

Miriam,

My head is still reeling from our time together over the weekend. The letters, e-mails, phone calls keep coming in. You were a smashing success. Thank you for giving us the opportunity to learn about you and your methodology.

With that said, I want to personally thank you for being available to do this class under the most difficult personal life circumstances. I do pray that you will garner the strength to deal with what lies ahead for you with your family. May you find peace in release...
I have forwarded some of the e-mails to you - it is always nice to hear from participants.

Chuck was blown away by your class and instruction. He told me this morning you were one of the best teachers/presenters he has had the opportunity to observe. And believe me he has seen a lot. Your energy and presentation skill touched him. He also wanted me to tell you thank you for the Egg and he will use appropriately... I have been busy with the studios teaching and enjoying the new techniques you taught. Every time I re-read the book I find some new gem. Thank you so much for sharing so generously. My students are all doing quite well-with the occasional ill student with a virus-all were able to sing recital...

Shirley

SHIRLEY D. KOUT

VOCAL COACH, MASTER DIRECTOR, CERTIFIED SOUND JUDGE, CERTIFIED INTERNATIONAL FACULTY DIRECTOR, RIVERLIGHTS CHORUS, REGION 12, and MEMBER: PRIDE OF PACIFIC CHORUS

Notes

BOOK REVIEW

The Voice: A Spiritual Approach to Singing, Speaking and Communicating - The Revealed Version

This book is very interesting and unique way of approaching vocal production. The author works primarily with stage performers, Operatic, Broadway stage and hopefuls. She has found a method of teaching where she is not the singing example to the student. As she so simply puts it, "I am a Teacher, not a Singer." She does, however, address the spiritual aspect of the Voice. She states, "I understood from the beginning, that without Spirituality, the real potential of the Voice could not be accessed."

As a reader you will learn how this method came about, what is in her personal culture and background to direct her in this manner. Many of the ideas in her method are familiar and yet, they are a totally different approach than I have ever read before.

Even though she is a Voice teacher and not a choral director, her ideas and tools can be utilized in either setting.

I feel the need to re-read this book because I don't believe that once is enough to best understand this material. There were some real eye-opening moments for me. She has included fantastic drawings of the Voice toward the back of the book which, once you find them, will help you to understand what she's writing about. Even though, at first, they remind you of cartoon character heads, you must look at the details to best take in this pictorial representation of the words in the previous Chapters.

I highly recommend this book for anyone who is looking for new/different ways to help their singers and/or themselves improve. It's probably not what you're used to. How great is that! One more thing-there is also an audio CD titled *THE VOICE: A SPRIRITUAL APPROACH TO SINGING, SPEAKING AND COMMUNICATING: THE FIRST LESSON that includes additional materials on vocal production. This is also quite enlightening but I would recommend reading the book first to understand the concepts she's discussing.*

September 2007 Forward Motion Publication, Sweet Adelines, International.

✲ ✲ ✲

Ms. Arman,

I purchased you book around 2 years ago randomly online. I keep it with me at all times in my book sack while I'm at school and have truly gained so much from it. I am currently a 21 year old junior at Louisiana State University. I am transitioning from Baritone into Tenor, and I discovered my head Voice thanks to your image of the Giro. I noticed that you posted videos of a master class onto you tube; that is wonderful! I hope that more people discover your philosophies on singing, which are after all the most natural...or so I have discovered thus far. Thank you for writing this book...truly.

Best Wishes, Darren

Notes

Sharing my Story

The Voice has always played a powerful part in my life. I sang from early childhood, brought pleasure to my parents, to the listeners…I loved to sing and expression with my Voice elated me, satisfied me and connected me. Even as a very small child, music was a primary focus in my life.

I grew up in post-war Germany. Being Jewish, my life there was very difficult. My parents were concentration camp survivors and, most of the time, there was great sadness around the house. There was no joy, no laughter, no children of my age as friends…I was always very alone and I did not understand why.

I had to find a way beyond all of the sorrow surrounding me, so I turned to music. I remember taking my little radio, which I received as a gift from an American soldier who came to our house, to bed with me, hiding it under the covers and listening to music—not rock-n-roll, either—but operettas, Opera and classical music. The Voices of Marika Roeck, Cornelia, Fritz Wunderlich, Caterina Valente, Rudolf Schock, and Richard Tauber (just to name a few) constituted some of my happiest listening memories. While absorbing these beautiful Voices (and others from all over the world), I would dream of being able to sing.

Well, I don't want to bore you with my trials and tribulations of not being taught properly and singing repertoire that was not for me (basically, all of the no-no's of which I've warned you); but by the time I was nineteen, I already had severe problems, nodules and a few years later, surgery. After the second one, I did not speak for six months and ran around with a pad and pencil. I will never forget my desperation. Vocal cords that have had nodules on them and have undergone Operations will not perform for you unless you know how to re-position the Voice properly. I went to several doctors of course; no one seemed to be able to get my Voice back for me – neither with medicines nor so called vocal exercises.

My students are always impressed at how I have re-constructed my own Voice (my speaking Voice); the truth is that I could never have done this work myself. I turned to G-d for help and piece by piece the 'Voice' was revealed. People were amazed and wanted to know what I was doing, who was helping me etc. etc… But all I could say was that I was working on it all the time and that divine inspiration was guiding me. I was not religious at all then in a traditional sense at least, but as so many times before and after this, when I had no way out of my personal anguish, I turned to G-d for help and He, in His infinite love and patience, guided me.

Once I re-constructed my own Voice, others came for help and I helped them. Over many (40) years of my own work, the puzzle came together piece by piece and every day and every student is still and will always be a revelation and a guide for me. I started teaching, really teaching in 1982, but working to help others pretty much dates back to the beginning of my own woes. I could not sing at all or so I thought – and then I forgot about it; anyway it became a secondary need…speaking was primary.

Years later I realized, that not singing, but being able to 'communicate' the Voice, was my life's work. I honed my speaking skills to become proficient. No one has heard me sing publically or privately …there are some recordings of my own compositions and when I really feel that a student needs to hear me, to show just how awful things can get, I share – but it's very rare.

My students cannot emulate me. They cannot try to copy me; they have to rely on their own Instruments. I cannot influence anyone with the brilliance and Artistry of my Voice—or with the fact that I've had a brilliant singing career myself. I have to communicate with words—giving examples, painting pictures, explaining details, sharing knowledge and using gestures, etc. I rely completely on my hearing and on my depth of understanding of the Instrument. I am able to identify how and where a Sound is made, how and why it is the way it is (cause and effect) and how to perfect it. I give you what I know. I rely on my skill, my aptitude, my intelligence, my feelings, my instincts, my vibrations and emotions. I cannot rely on my Voice. I have to communicate with words, and I have learned to do it in such a way that even a young child can understand the rudiments of the Voice follow my instructions and do it!

Your vocal abilities are as personal as your individuality, and I am only a guide. I am grateful for not being able to sing. I never studied music formally. I have some basic idea from learning to play the piano, but I am self-taught. All of what I have shared with you here has come to me via spiritual knowledge, deep thinking, reflection and learning—from and with my students. I have not read the books of other experts of the Voice; but as I mentioned before, I have worked with some great Maestri—not as an apprentice, but as a Maestro myself, in collaboration.

I do not hold a degree from an accredited 'conservatory', but have taught in some with great success. I realized many years ago that I was not meant to sing, but to teach. After a long and hard road, which took me to many parts of the world and through many personal tragedies, I finally accepted the challenge of giving up all other music businesses, production, television, movies, organization of spectacle, Artist representation etc .and dedicate completely and only to the teaching of Voice and the writing books about it.

With this final acceptance came the necessary, vital and critical information.

All I can only tell you is that I know what I know and have the ability to do what I do because I am chosen to be the vessel that imparts this information to those who wish to know and accept it. Birth-Knowledge is what I call it; the sum total of what I have learned and know from my past lifetimes. I know music that I have never heard before. I say words that seem to come out of nowhere, but the moment I speak them—they hit their mark. I sometimes marvel at what is coming out of me. I do not challenge my knowledge; I simply accept it and share it.

I have taught and teach Voices that any other teacher would have given up on as lost, destroyed or beyond repair. I take them on because I know that I have the capability of reconstructing them in the right place. My scientific colleagues, whom I respect sincerely, may not agree (because they do not bother to find out the truth of this work); but I have proven over and over again that it can be done. I teach with the knowledge of being guided, and with the understanding that my own learning process is constant, and that I will be led to give to each individual student precisely what he or she needs of me. I open myself up to them, and they open themselves up to me and together—we achieve their destiny, whatever that may be.

I do not take any credit for my knowledge. I am simply grateful for it. I know that whoever comes to me and crosses paths with mine has a special spiritual lesson that has to be learned and the Voice is the vehicle. This is not intended to Sound pompous. Believe me, this is not an ego trip; this is simply what my experience has taught me. I have been teaching for more than 30 years. I've refined and honed my own skills so I can adjust to every student. The work is all encompassing – mind, body and soul. There are so many factors involved in helping a Voice emerge. Sometimes we spend our time discussing the problems in a student's life. Why? Because they directly influence the Voice. I have no set 'lesson plan'…we have a set direction which we work for, we have a goal and whatever it takes to get us there, will be done; whatever is necessary for the Voice and its health and well-being is what I do.

I follow my student's progress at his or her own pace, but under more or less normal circumstances, it takes about forty hours of study to put a Voice together well enough to begin with repertoire. To completely finish a Voice in all its nuances and get it ready for the stage (classical) takes between four and six years; Pop takes less. If the Voice is badly damaged, it will take longer; if the student is very instinctive, much less.

For all intense and purpose, the Voice takes a lifetime. The Instrument is never static, just like the mind and the body – it moves, it grows, it changes. It is influenced by a million variables – it moves with life – you never own it – when you think you do, when you think you are its master, you lose it!

A great deal depends upon the Spirituality/will/desire of the student—what he wants to accept, how much of an ego he has and how much he will allow it (his ego) to interfere with his progress. Openness and determination are key factors, dedication a must and patience, trust and faith, the cornerstones.

I am not always successful. In the cases where I am not, I know that spiritual growth is not being achieved; I will send a student away only if I am certain I cannot help. I cannot teach if I do not love *or if I feel that ethically the student is not on a level where he can grow, both as a human being and as a singer. It takes a great deal for me to end a relationship and stop teaching. I have cut the strings a number of times in my career - mainly to protect myself.*

The Voice is an integral part of YOU. It is YOU! Once you discover it, it will overcome you; if you use the proper tools you will be able to achieve what you desire. Your direction for singing must be there. You must know where you are going with the Voice.

I generally do not teach students who are very casual about singing, who really do not have a long-term goal. I want the desire to share the Voice to be powerful enough to motivate. I do not teach students who are looking to be famous only for themselves, those who are only interested in becoming stars for the sake of fame and fortune. My students must want to give of themselves, to offer their Voices to the world and receive from the 'Light' the guidance and the power for the Voice.

Perhaps you think me presumptuous. That's okay. Everyone has his or her own personal value structure, ethics and beliefs and above all, integrity. These are mine. I choose my students not because they are going to be famous (because a great many will never be), but I search for what singing will do for their souls. With this in mind, we go on our journey to discover the Voice. Incredible things happen when you discover the Voice. **Your life changes**; your outlook is broadened. Your personality takes on a whole new glow. Your self-esteem increases. Your confidence is strengthened. The Voice is a tremendous source of power.

One thing is for certain: I will not teach anyone for the sake of money. **When your Voice comes together, your life becomes whole.**

I am, of course, remunerated for my work. In our society, unfortunately, I need to be. I say "unfortunately" because if I could, I would teach for free. I would go anywhere in the world and spread my teaching and give it without thinking about how much it costs to get there, to stay in the hotel and to buy the food, etc. It's my dream, and who knows? Perhaps, one day it will happen. I was able to do this in the Ukraine and in Russia when there was no money. I taught for food and lodging and the pure joy of doing what I do best. This was one of the greatest personal and professional experiences of my life. I shall never forget the Voices that touched me, and the ones that I touched.

During the hour we spend in a lesson together, you own me. I give you all I have; I empty my vessel. When I finish, I am depleted yet elated. What I in turn need from my student to give to me is his or her enthusiasm, love and trust. Without that, there is not the exchange of energy necessary. After I finish with you, I have to give to someone else; so if you only deplete me without giving back to me, I cannot fill up again. What I am talking about is a constant recycling of energy and a renewing of the vessel, a constant search and acceptance of the 'Light' into our teaching relationship.

Some years ago (thirteen to be exact) I was in a music store in Coral Gables, Florida. I had recently returned from Kiev, Ukraine where I lived for 21/2 years and I was searching the shelves for some Arias for one of my students. As I mentioned before, I never read material on singing. I am generally not interested, except for that one time and I would like to share this experience with you.

Anyway, as I was browsing through some musical scores on that day, I noticed something very out of place that definitely did not belong in the musical scores section: a very small book entitled, **_Hints On Singing,_** by Manuel Garcia. I had no idea who he was. I do not know, really, why I picked it up or why I thought it was familiar… why the name stirred something in me.

I opened the booklet, leafed through and read a line that mentioned the Spoon. I got the chills. I read some more. The book is basically questions and answers. I bought the book and quickly read it. I found such incredible similarity in our methods that I felt that perhaps, here was the connection for which I had been looking. I do some things quite differently from him, explain the terms in my own words (most of which you have read). I have refined my own methodology, but some of the real bread and butter basics are the same. Other very important segments are completely different—like some of the terminology that I have coined and now use, etc. But on the whole, it fascinated me, and I wanted to find out if there was some connection somewhere.

Coincidences? I don't think so. I don't believe in them. Birth Knowledge? Yes, only that makes sense to me—a past life connection, without a doubt. I know that everything in my life has brought me to this point. I share my knowledge with you because I have to, because I have no right to keep it to myself. The more you give, the more you get. The more open I am to sharing, the more the 'Light' will provide. So I ask you to partake, but please think about giving it back. Only in that way can you, too, become a vessel that continually fills itself and has a never-ending capacity for giving.

As far as time line is concerned, this occurred about six months after I lost my daughter."ZL". I desperately searched for a way to cope with my loss and desperation and to find my center. I needed to connect to strength and fortitude – I needed an anchor to survive. This was also the time when I moved into the religious life searching to find structure and meaning spiritually. I decided to go into regression therapy and contacted the studio of Brian Weiss but to no avail. However, one of his disciples did some incredible and life changing work with me.

We arrived at one of my lifetimes in Barcelona, Spain which coincides with the lifetime of Manuel Garcia. Manuel Garcia is still considered the greatest Voice teacher that ever lived. He created a dynasty, but very little is written about him. He too lost a beloved daughter. Malibran , a phenomenal vocal talent and consummate Artist. His son Manuel Garcia II wrote the book I read. Manuel Garcia's wife, Joaquina Garcia, and I share the same birth date in this lifetime - July 28.

Over the years I have learned to trust my instincts—the Voices inside of me that know – I have learned to listen.

I am grateful that I was the one chosen to disseminate this information to you. I hope that I have enlightened your life, that I have shared the 'Light' with you, that you will gain the right use of your Voice and confidence, happiness and success through what I have tried to give you.

I invite you, no matter where I am in the world or no matter where you are to contact me and share with me. I will always answer.

GREETINGS AND BLESSINGS

Notes

THE DRAWINGS
AN OVERVIEW

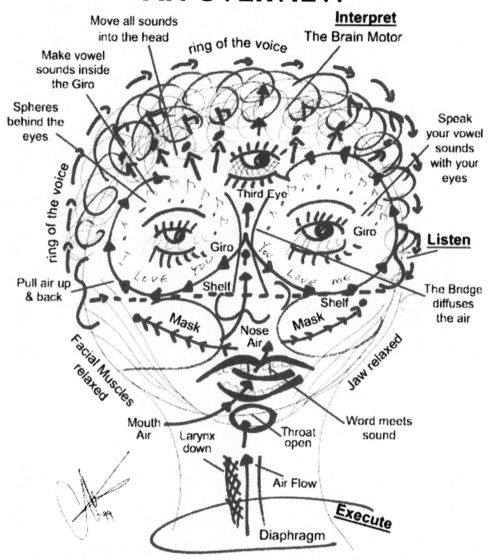

1) Breathe simultaneously through mouth & nose
2) Lead the air up & back past Hard Palate, Uvola into Soft Palate
3) Soft Palate pulls up & back, lifts & stays lifted at all times
4) Pull air from mouth as far back as possible toward Bone of Life, open hole
5) Air from nose opens Chamber & allows the Giro movement

6) All sounds are formed in the back
7) Air remains in the back to make sound & move the Giro
8) Intention of word moves sounds over the top of the Giro toward Third Eye & angles to the lips.
9) Sound & word (diction/ consonants) meet at the front teeth & lips & exit together
10) Allow the brain to be the motor of the voice & let the Third Eye visualize the entire movement

THE VOICE PART I

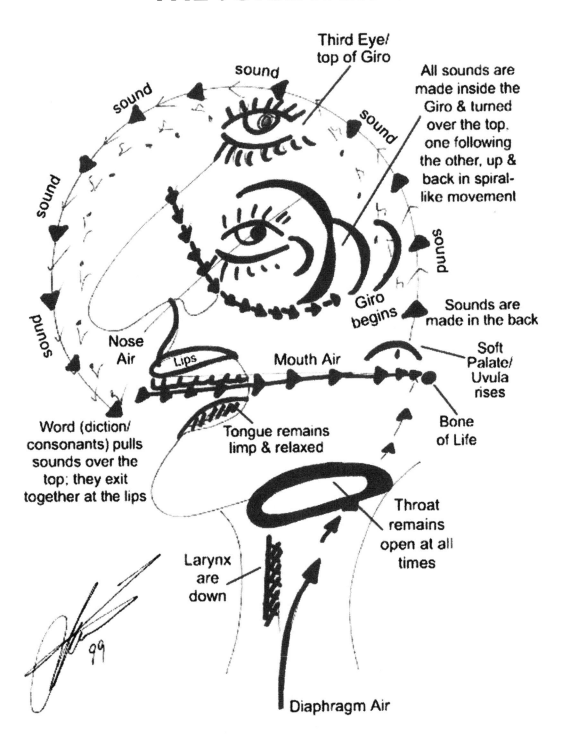

Third Eye/ top of Giro

sound

sound

sound

sound

sound

sound

sound

sound

sound

All sounds are made inside the Giro & turned over the top. one following the other, up & back in spiral-like movement

Giro begins

Sounds are made in the back

Nose Air

Lips

Mouth Air

Soft Palate/ Uvula rises

Word (diction/ consonants) pulls sounds over the top; they exit together at the lips

Tongue remains limp & relaxed

Bone of Life

Throat remains open at all times

Larynx are down

Diaphragm Air

THE VOICE PART 2

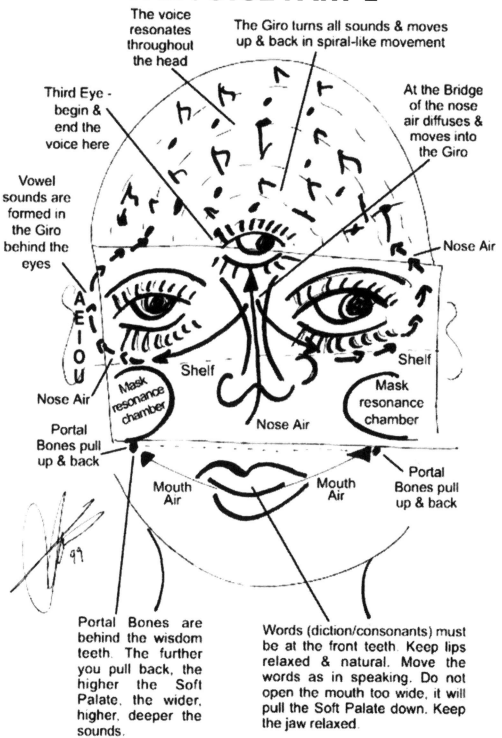

The voice resonates throughout the head

The Giro turns all sounds & moves up & back in spiral-like movement

Third Eye - begin & end the voice here

At the Bridge of the nose air diffuses & moves into the Giro

Vowel sounds are formed in the Giro behind the eyes

Nose Air

A E I O U

Nose Air

Shelf

Shelf

Mask resonance chamber

Mask resonance chamber

Nose Air

Portal Bones pull up & back

Mouth Air

Mouth Air

Portal Bones pull up & back

Portal Bones are behind the wisdom teeth. The further you pull back, the higher the Soft Palate, the wider, higher, deeper the sounds.

Words (diction/consonants) must be at the front teeth. Keep lips relaxed & natural. Move the words as in speaking. Do not open the mouth too wide, it will pull the Soft Palate down. Keep the jaw relaxed.

THE VOICE PART 3

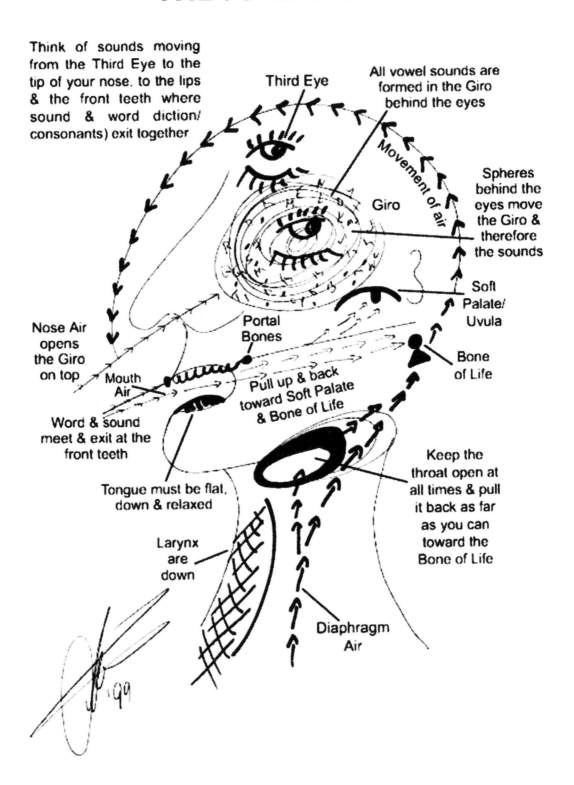

Think of sounds moving from the Third Eye to the tip of your nose, to the lips & the front teeth where sound & word diction/consonants) exit together

Third Eye

All vowel sounds are formed in the Giro behind the eyes

Movement of air

Giro

Spheres behind the eyes move the Giro & therefore the sounds

Soft Palate/ Uvula

Portal Bones

Nose Air opens the Giro on top

Mouth Air

Pull up & back toward Soft Palate & Bone of Life

Bone of Life

Word & sound meet & exit at the front teeth

Keep the throat open at all times & pull it back as far as you can toward the Bone of Life

Tongue must be flat, down & relaxed

Larynx are down

Diaphragm Air

MOVEMENT OF VOWEL SOUND

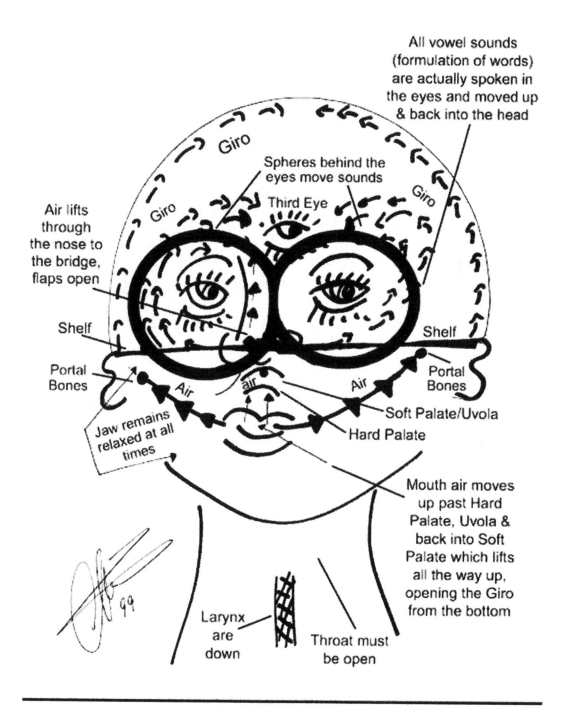

LAG TIME

The second between creation of sound in the back, turning of the Giro & exit of the sound at the lips is **Lagtime - the single most important movement in keeping the voice on the top**

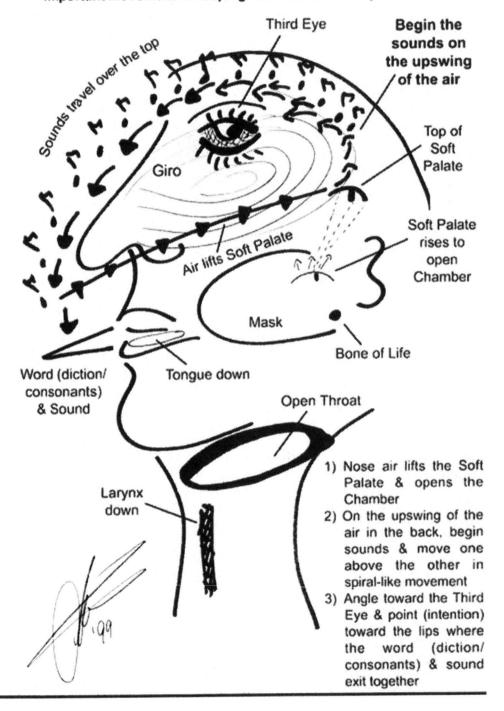

Third Eye

Begin the sounds on the upswing of the air

Sounds travel over the top

Giro

Top of Soft Palate

Air lifts Soft Palate

Soft Palate rises to open Chamber

Mask

Bone of Life

Word (diction/ consonants) & Sound

Tongue down

Open Throat

Larynx down

1) Nose air lifts the Soft Palate & opens the Chamber

2) On the upswing of the air in the back, begin sounds & move one above the other in spiral-like movement

3) Angle toward the Third Eye & point (intention) toward the lips where the word (diction/ consonants) & sound exit together

Air Movement

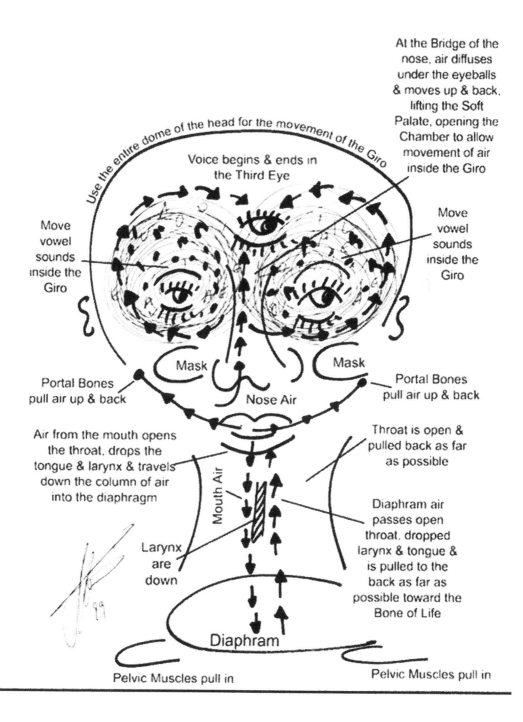

At the Bridge of the nose, air diffuses under the eyeballs & moves up & back, lifting the Soft Palate, opening the Chamber to allow movement of air inside the Giro

Use the entire dome of the head for the movement of the Giro

Voice begins & ends in the Third Eye

Move vowel sounds inside the Giro

Move vowel sounds inside the Giro

Mask

Mask

Portal Bones pull air up & back

Nose Air

Portal Bones pull air up & back

Air from the mouth opens the throat, drops the tongue & larynx & travels down the column of air into the diaphragm

Throat is open & pulled back as far as possible

Mouth Air

Larynx are down

Diaphram air passes open throat, dropped larynx & tongue & is pulled to the back as far as possible toward the Bone of Life

Diaphram

Pelvic Muscles pull in

Pelvic Muscles pull in

Three Sources of Air for the Giro

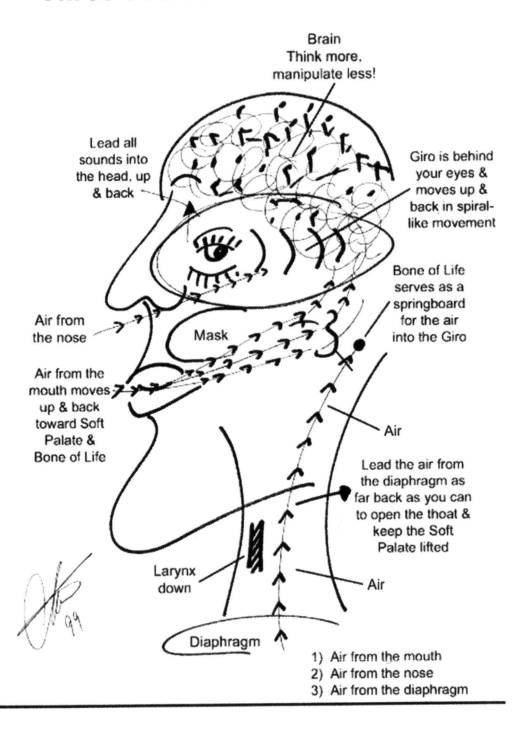

Brain
Think more,
manipulate less!

Lead all
sounds into
the head, up
& back

Giro is behind
your eyes &
moves up &
back in spiral-
like movement

Bone of Life
serves as a
springboard
for the air
into the Giro

Air from
the nose

Mask

Air from the
mouth moves
up & back
toward Soft
Palate &
Bone of Life

Air

Lead the air from
the diaphragm as
far back as you can
to open the thoat &
keep the Soft
Palate lifted

Larynx
down

Air

Diaphragm

1) Air from the mouth
2) Air from the nose
3) Air from the diaphragm

LAST NOTE: FRONT VIEW

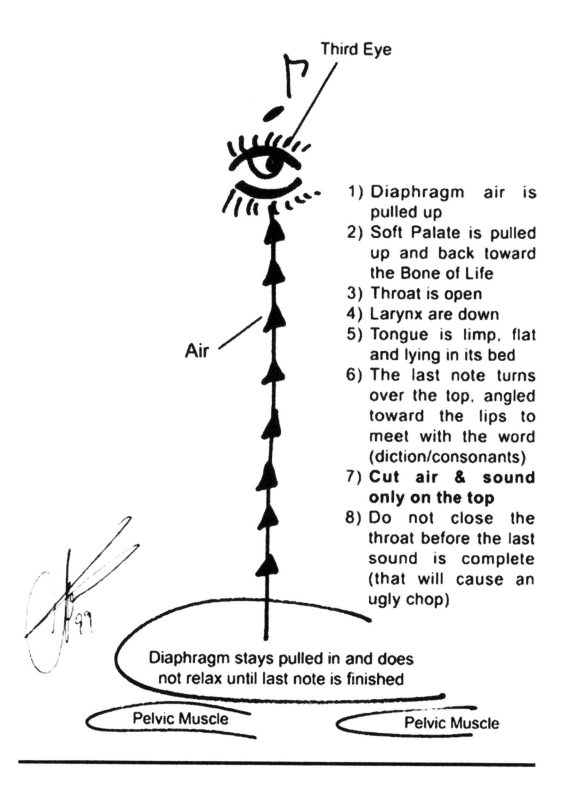

Third Eye

Air

1) Diaphragm air is pulled up
2) Soft Palate is pulled up and back toward the Bone of Life
3) Throat is open
4) Larynx are down
5) Tongue is limp, flat and lying in its bed
6) The last note turns over the top, angled toward the lips to meet with the word (diction/consonants)
7) **Cut air & sound only on the top**
8) Do not close the throat before the last sound is complete (that will cause an ugly chop)

Diaphragm stays pulled in and does not relax until last note is finished

Pelvic Muscle

Pelvic Muscle

LAST NOTE: SIDE VIEW

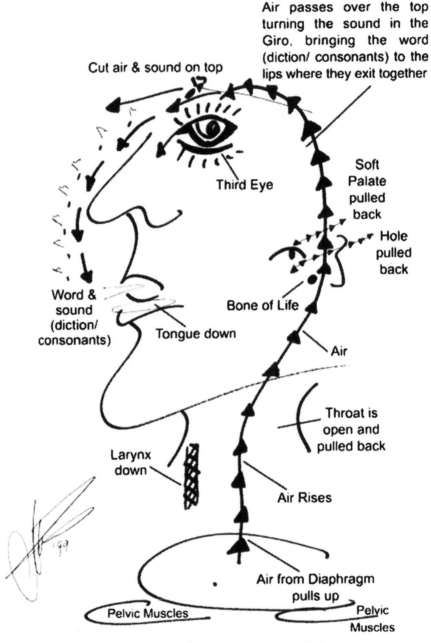

Air passes over the top turning the sound in the Giro, bringing the word (diction/ consonants) to the lips where they exit together

Cut air & sound on top

Third Eye

Soft Palate pulled back

Hole pulled back

Word & sound (diction/ consonants)

Bone of Life

Tongue down

Air

Throat is open and pulled back

Larynx down

Air Rises

Air from Diaphragm pulls up

Pelvic Muscles

Pelvic Muscles

1) Diaphragm is pulled all the way in and held there
2) Soft Palate is in up & back position & remains there
3) Sound must turn over the top, angled toward third eye & front teeth & meet the word (diction/consonants) at the lips
4) Air & sound must be cut on the top, not in the throat

Notes

GLOSSARY OF TERMS

BRAIN IMAGING:

… Brain imaging is almost like visualizing and is done practically in the same way—in the Third Eye.

Basically we project a picture in the Brain of how we visualize the process of the Movement of the Air: the turning of the Giro, the pulling back of the Portal Bones, the lifting of the Soft Palate, the opening of the Throat, the dropping of the Tongue. We image the Movement of the pelvic muscles and the pulling in on the Diaphragm. We project the dropping of the Larynx, the opening of the Throat and the flatness and relaxation of the Tongue.

All this occurs in a split second, before you sing a note. If you want to, you can Brain image at your leisure, at any time, really. It's great to put your head on a soft pillow in a dimly lit room, close your eyes and watch the whole thing in front of your eyes like a movie. Only in this movie—you are the producer, the director, the lead actor, the gofer, the makeup Artist and the scriptwriter. It is your movie, and you are in control. As you design it, so it shall be. If you design it with all the elements we have learned, your Brain imaging will be a powerful component in your total progress; so do it often and be very precise in your projections.

BONE OF LIFE©:

…The most important focal point in the back of the Throat. If you focus the Air from the mouth all the way to the Bone of Life and use that position as a springboard for the Giro, the Voice will be properly balanced in top and bottom vibrations. By pulling toward the Bone of Life, the maximum extension of The Hole is achieved; the Throat is open and allows the Air to come up from the Diaphragm and support the height of the Soft Palate. All of the components in technique pull in the direction of the Bone of Life: the Portal Bones, the Soft Palate, and the Air from the Diaphragm, the Hole, and the Sound in the Giro. In other words, this is a one-way street. Everything moves up and back toward the Bone of Life, the top of the Giro and into the head.

DIAPHRAGM:

…The motor and support system of the Voice. Air is moved (past the Open Throat, dropped Larynx and lowered Tongue) down the column of Air into the Diaphragm. By contracting the pelvic muscles, you pull the Air back up through

Open Throat, dropped Larynx and lowered Tongue to support the Soft Palate in its highest position. Use the Diaphragm a minimum of three times: the first note, the highest/lowest note and the last note—and every note in between.

THE EYES:

…The great movers of the Sound. Behind your eyeballs, the spheres move the Air of the Giro and, therefore, the Sound. You must learn to actually speak your Vowel Sound inside the eyes and make the word in the same place. Only in this way is the line of the Sound secured. If you drop the word, or if you speak the words with your mouth and under the Portal Bones, you will lose the roundness and brightness of the Sound and definitely fall into the Throat.

The eyes are the mirror of your soul, and your soul is in your Voice. So speak with your eyes, and you will always be in position.

The GIRO – GIRO VOCAL MOTION TECHNIQUE©

…The endless loop of the Voice, THE PLACE where the Sound are made; it (the Giro) turns on a continual basis, round and round; each Sound follows over the top of the other, exiting at the Third Eye, angling toward the Front Teeth to exit with the word. The bottom of the Giro is the Soft Palate, and the top is the Third Eye. It is imperative that all Sounds are made inside the Giro. The Giro moves up and back only (never downward toward the Throat, always, upward into the head) and is moved strictly with the Air. The Giro can be big or small, depending on how high or low the note needs to be. The size of the Giro determines the depth of the Voice and the coloration of the Sound. The further you pull up and back, the higher, the larger and the darker the Voice will be.

LAGTIME©:

…The time it takes the Air from the NOSE to enter at the bridge of the nose and diffuse the Air under the eyes (the shelf). The Air has to be pulled all the way toward the back, lifting the Soft Palate to its maximum and creating The Chamber in which the Giro circulates. All the Sounds you will ever need to make are within the Giro. The Sound move to the back and the Intention of the Word (diction) pulls the Sound over the top to the Front Teeth and allows them to exit together. Lag Time separates Sound (in the back) from word/diction (in the front). It keeps the Voice on the top and turning properly inside the Giro. It is the single most important Movement to keep the Voice on the top. There must be a split second time difference between the making and turning of the Sound and the coupling with the word. If there is not that

Lag Time, word and Sound will both start in the back. If that happens, the Soft Palate collapses, the Throat closes and the Voice falls into the Throat. (Please read Chapter 5 many times to re-familiarize yourself with this concept).

PORTAL BONES©:

…These can be found by placing both thumbs at the end of your top teeth, just beyond your wisdom teeth. They are round little bones that you must think of pulling backward and upward, in order to move the Soft Palate into the up and back position. The Portal Bones are also the guideline for the Sound. No Sound should ever be made below that place, and if you are making words below the Portal Bones (which is a no-no); the Voice will fall into the Throat. Visualize the pulling back and up, and you will find that you can move the tissue around the portals along with the Soft Palate.

SPINGING©:

Speaking and singing in the same position. Spinging is achieved by placing the Air all the way on top, behind the eyes and moving the Sound in a circular motion inside the Giro, while pulling further and further back with the muscles of the eyes. (Visualize the Movement of pulling, and the Brain will do this for you.) The higher and the further back you sping, the more flexibility you will develop inside the Movement. The deeper the sping, the larger the Giro; the larger the Giro, the more color in the Voice, hence, the more possibilities for enlarging the Sound. The spheres of your eyes move the Sound and spinging will make sure that you are always in the correct singing position: behind the eyes, moving up and back at all times. Sping a great deal before you begin singing. Please, although it may Sound like a fire engine to you, you must believe me: learning how to sping is invaluable in the growth of the Voice. Use only Sound, at first; then attach Vowels to the Sound and then add the words. After the breath pattern is established, sping the melody and tempo of the piece you want to sing, exactly. Then put melody and "ee" together. After that feels completely comfortable, add the melody plus word. You are teaching the Brain the Movement of each individual note, so pay attention and do it right; otherwise the Brain will learn it incorrectly, and will be very difficult to unlearn.

THIRD EYE:

…The beginning and the end of the Movement of Voice. Here the Giro places the Sound at the end of the turn; from here, the Sound angles toward the word (diction/consonants), which occurs at the Front Teeth and the Lips. The Third Eye helps you visualize the exact place where the Sounds are, and your ability to achieve a total spiritual opening to the Voice depends on it.

VISUALIZING:

The Brain is the great coordinator of our whole being, so the Voice and its production are no exceptions. The more internal conceptualization of the technical aspects of the Voice, the more in control the Brain will be; thus, the more out of control you will be. The less you physically assist the Voice, the better it will be. The more you allow the Voice to find its own natural place, the more familiar you are with the Instrument and the less you seek to manipulate it—the more it will serve you. The work we are doing is internal, not external. No pushing, forcing or pulling on the Jaw; no drastic facial movements. Visualize the Sound, the place, the Giro, the head, and the Bone of Life, the words inside your eyes and the Vowel Sound behind the spheres of your eyes. Feel more than you usually do and breathe life into the Sound. Allow the Voice the freedom to exist in its natural habitat. Be the guide, but not the maker. Trust your Instrument and your singer's instincts and follow what we have already talked about.

Notes

Special Phrases we use in our Work

Take your eyeballs to the gym:

Since the actual Sound is rotated around the orbits (spheres) of your eyes, it is necessary to really get the idea, that pulling the Air upward and backward, is actually done by muscles behind your eyeballs. If you think about that continually, you will never fail. You will always remember that your **eyes are the mirror of your soul** and therefore use them for communication . . . whether that is for singing or for speaking. Learning how to pull backward is the real key to understanding this whole system and if you got nothing else out of this book except, that speaking begins in your eyes and is done with your eyes, you already have learned most of everything there is to know.

Learn how to hear Sound inside your head and go there

When you hear a Sound, you most definitely hear it inside your head. No one has ever told me that they hear the Sound inside the Throat, or in the chest or in the Diaphragm. So it only makes sense to keep the Sound exactly where it is heard and allow the Brain, our Master Computer, to place it exactly where it hears it.

I cannot teach you where each Sound is … No one can. But I do know how to teach you to CONNECT TO the right space so to access the information.

It's all about thought processes and only our Brain knows exactly where and how Sound are moved and what needs to be done to make it (the Sound) perfect. All we can do is 'think' into the same spot each and every time, remember that Sound only travel upward and backward, support the Soft Palate with the Diaphragm, keep the Throat open and then speak, speak, speak.

You are not tone deaf if you are out of pitch, you are simply disconnected from the right place

I cannot tell you how many people have come to me, telling me they are tone deaf, but that somewhere inside, they know they have a Voice. I have studied this for years and have concluded that most people who think they are not even "shower worthy," are really only bad manipulators of the Larynx/Vocal cords/Voice Box or whatever you chose to call it. Once they are placed into the Giro, it's amazing what comes out. Most have lovely Voices and find a very new expression and real happiness. Believe me, it's wonderful to see. Trust your Instrument, it knows better than you do. I cannot tell you how many times I say that in the course of our lessons. If we just believed that the systems, once it is programmed properly with the information at hand, will do exactly what you think.

The whole thing boils down to THINKING AND SPEAKING. If your thoughts are correct, the Brain will perform everything without a great deal of "work" on your part …

The key is to program the Master Computer into a DOT.COM mentality. Once you have set the program, all you have to do is click on the mouse and the same exact web page will come up, every time. Once you put a piece of music into the Voice, the Brain will perform it the same way every time … if you change your mind for some reason, you will have to re-specify to the Brain what you want and change the configuration.

Every type of skill you can think of demands constant practice and endless commitment … Why do we think of the Voice differently and why do we expect from it what is not expected from any other discipline? Take any other profession: stocks, computers, race car driving, acting, mountain climbing, ice skating, skiing, swimming – endless – you know the great ones in any field are always working on it - and tirelessly.

Well, whatever questions you have about: How long does it take to make a Voice and become great?

Here is the definite answer to your question – *Forever!*

Vocalizes for any Voice

Please remember that the middle Voice is the basis for the entire vocal set up

- Work your way chromatically up the scale, in your range. **legato** - turning inside the Giro

- Start with **MEE**

- Continue, adding different vowels to different consonants

Notes

About the Author

Born in post war Germany of concentration camp surviving parents, her family immigrated to America in 1962. Educated both in the USA and Europe, she has lived and taught in many parts of the world: Israel, Italy, Hungary, Switzerland, Ukraine, Poland, Romania, Russia, Slovenia, Mexico and South America, etc.

Her life has been a kaleidoscope of activities: In 1982, she founded Music Culture/Visions International Inc., a company that she led until 2008. During that time, she wrote, directed, hosted and produced various radio and television shows in the States and in Europe. She produced for international recording labels (Olympia, Naxos etc.), taking lost music from Russia and the Ukraine and presenting it to the world at large.

She was Executive Producer and Director of the feature film "Ten Tenors from Ten Countries" dedicated to the life and 100th birthday of Benjamino Gigli filmed in Recanati, Italy. She returned to the United States In 1995.

In 1999, Miriam Jaskierowicz Arman authored the International Best Seller on Vocal Technique: "The Voice; A Spiritual Approach to Singing, Speaking and Communicating". In 2000 the CD, "The First Lesson" CD was released. In 2001/2003, the Second and Third Editions (The Revealed Version) followed.

Her teaching career spans over 28 years and her intimate involvement with vocal technique and vocal reconstruction began 40 years ago. She was the founder of The International Academy of Voice and Stage Inc., a Non-Profit organization, dedicated to the advancement of Bel Canto and Giro Vocal Motion Technique. Her work in the field of Vocal Pedagogy has been featured on ABC World News Now, PBS, Comcast Television, etc.

Her Fine Art career spans over 30 years, with prestigious exhibitions in the galleries and museums in many parts of the world. She has received important grants and worldwide recognition for her innovative works in holographic and three dimensional glass fusions. Miriam spends her time teaching, lecturing and writing.

Her book "**Soul Reflections, A Personal Odyssey in Poetry and Paintings**" and the matching **CD**, with original composed music by cellist **Mme. Johanne Perron**, were released in 2003.

In 2007, "**Coming Home"** outlines her arrival and life in the Lubavitch Community of Crown Heights, New York and features her speeches in the political arena as well as a deep recognition and salutation of her spiritual values.

In 2008 she moved to South America.

Her articles and poetry have been published in many national and international publications and she is listed in the "Who's Who" in International Poetry.

6022306R0

Made in the USA
Lexington, KY
08 July 2010